FLORIDA STATE
UNIVERSITY LIBRARIES

SEP 11 1995

TALLAHASSEE, FLORIDA

Austria, 1938-1988
Anschluss and Fifty Years

Studies in Austrian Literature, Culture, and Thought

Austria, 1938-1988

Anschluss and Fifty Years

Edited and with an Introduction by

William E. Wright

ARIADNE PRESS

Ariadne Press would like to express its appreciation to the Austrian Cultural Institute, New York and the Austrian Federal Ministry for Foreign Affairs, Vienna for their assistance in publishing this book.

Library of Congress Cataloging-in-Publication Data

Austria, 1938-1988: Anschluss and fifty years / edited by William E. Wright.
    p. cm. -- (Studies in Austrian literature, culture, and thought)
    Includes bibliographical references and index.
    ISBN 1-57241-008-6.
    1. Anschluss movement, 1918-1938. 2. Austria--History-- 1918-1938. 3. Austria--History--1945- 4. Austria--Foreign relations--Germany. 5. Germany--Foreign relations--Austria. 6. National socialism. I. Wright, William E. (William Edward), 1926- . II. Series
DB97.A9316   1995
943.6'062--dc20
                        94-41933
                          CIP

Cover design:
Art Director and Designer: George McGinnis

Copyright ©1995
by Ariadne Press
270 Goins Court
Riverside, CA 92507

All rights reserved.
No part of this publication may be reproduced or transmitted in any form or by any means without formal permission.
Printed in the United States of America.
ISBN 1-57241-008-6

Preface

A half-century after the Anschluss of Austria to Germany, the engrossment of the Austrian Republic into the Third Reich in March of 1938, seemed to be a convenient point at which to look back and assess what transpired then and since then. Enough time had elapsed to allow a new, young generation of historians to mature, people who had not been witnesses or participants in the events and were not freighted with the passions of contemporaries to the events. But not so much time had elapsed that there were no more contemporary representatives who had seen, heard, and felt the events, people who could offer descriptions and make judgments from intimacy with the events. Each has much to contribute to any assessment of those most troubled and troubling times. Representatives of both are counted among the authors here presented. Moreover, the authors represent viewpoints of both Austrians, with their sense of immediacy, and those who look upon Austria from outside, with the detachment of the uninvolved.

Academic people, especially in Austria, have been producing, in the last several years, a body of excellent history on the subject of this volume. However, this volume also presents commentary from people whose views grew out of experiences other than those of the academy. When scholars talk to each other, the loaf of our knowledge can be wonderfully enriched, but it needs to be leavened also with the knowledge and experience of those beyond the walls of the academy. And if scholars talk only to each other, their voices will, ultimately, echo in vain, for what they know is of little value unless it is put to use by all of us.

The papers that compose this book were first presented in a symposium of the Center for Austrian Studies at the University of Minnesota. The book has the same purpose as the symposium which produced it, namely, to bring the results of the authors' deliberations to a wider circle of interested people. All of us, not just scholars, need to understand our past if we would profit from its wisdom, be warned by its follies, and learn anew to abhor wickedness as our past reminds us of it.

The transformation of symposium-papers into a book became a more protracted task than the editor at first anticipated. The authors of the papers, and the publisher of this volume, Professor Donald Daviau, not only brought their impressive knowledge and skills to the writing of the work, but they have also shown great forbearance, for which the editor wishes to thank them most warmly.

The publication of these papers would not have been possible without the support of the Austrian Ministry for Foreign Affairs and the Austrian Cultural Institute in New York. In those offices, we are especially indebted to the understanding and cooperation, over a number of years now, of Section Chief Dr. Peter Marboe, of the Ministry, and Director Dr. Wolfgang Waldner, of the Institute. Over the years they have given welcome material support from their offices for many scholarly projects and they have also sustained scholars by their personal encouragements as well. The editor offers them his sincerest expression of gratitude.

William E. Wright

Deephaven, Minnesota
April 1994

Austria, 1938-1988: Anschluss and Fifty Years

Table of Contents

Introduction	1
From Reich to Republic *by Gerald Stourzh*	15
Reflections on the Anschluss by an American Eye-Witness *by R. John Rath*	47
Prelude to Anschluss: the Great War and the Sheltered International and Domestic Consensus *by Bruce Pauley*	57
Was the Authoritarian Christian, Corporate State an Effective Means of Resisting National Socialism? *by Isabella Ackerl*	71
The Austrian Writers' Response to National Socialism Between 1933 and 1938 *by Donald Daviau*	91
Austrian Universities and the Anschluss *by Walter Höflechner*	119

Triumph and Neglect: Austrian *Hochschulen* and the Anschluss
by John Haag ... 135

Between Stalingrad and the Night of the Generals: Popular Opinion in the "Danubian and Alpine Regions." 1943-1944
by Evan Bukey ... 167

Conscience and Obedience
by Gordon Zahn ... 197

Tirol and the Austrian Resistance in the Last Years of the War
by Radomír Luža ... 209

Perception of the Anschluss after 1945
by Anton Pelinka ... 223

The Political Effects of the Anschluss on the Austrian Second Republic
by Melanie Sully ... 237

A Jewish View of the Anschluss and the Second Republic
by Paul Grosz ... 253

Interpreting the Anschluss
by Lonnie Johnson ... 265

Austria Then and Now
by Wolfgang Waldner ... 295

Introduction

William E. Wright

If these essays had been written a decade earlier, they would have been cast in a very different spirit. Austria's recovery from the devastations, social as well as physical, of World War II elicited a great deal of admiration and praise from those who watched the Second Republic grapple with its problems. Admiration was all the greater because the fell ghosts of the First Republic, which one could reasonably fear would haunt the Second, were quickly laid by the rebuilders of the restored state. To be sure, the leaders of postwar Austria were people who had helped conduct the affairs of the First Republic, which had brought ruin to Austria, but they seemed to have accomplished that rare feat: They had learned from their history. As Benjamin Franklin said, Dame Experience keeps a dear school, and Austrians had indeed paid a very high price for the tuition of experience since the demise of the Habsburg empire, but at least the lessons were well learned and put to use in the years after 1945. It did not come effortlessly, but Austrians worked their way from one success to another.

The most striking accomplishment, in light of the precedents of 1918 to 1938, was their mustering the will and courage to lay aside the bitter animosities that had so deeply divided them politically in the First Republic. In those parlous times the parties had come to think of themselves as *Lager*, and their members regarded the other side as enemies, not just political rivals. The brief government by coalition that served until the peace was made and the constitution written, was always an uneasy one, its participants harboring stubborn suspicions that foretold an early end to that kind of government. But when the coalition was ruptured, and the Christian Socials took the reins of government, it was not the advent of the kind of government whereby one party governs while the other serves as the loyal opposition. The opposition, whether in office or out, was not just to be outvoted; it was to be *overcome*. The débâcle of the First Republic, the hardships, incarcerations, and exiles of the period 1938-1945, and the presence of occupying armies after 1945, however, showed the leaders of both sides the folly of antagonism and the imperative of cooperation. The coalition governments of 1945-1966, although not paragons of virtue and harmony, nevertheless established standards of political responsibility and civility that made for stable government and a framework within which the wounds and destructions of war could be healed and repaired and social amity could grow.

Just as the old political parties had taken new departures, so did the socio-economic institutions of Austria. The labor unions and the chambers of commerce, industry, and agriculture, along with representatives of government, in the initially informal and later more formal (but extra-constitutional) Social Partnership (*Sozialpartnerschaft, Paritätische Kommission für Preise und Löhne*) agreed among themselves on the setting of prices and wages and saved Austria not only many hours and days of economic loss from strikes, and made the Austrians' *Wirtschaftswunder* possible, but also powerfully influenced social attitudes for the better.

The class antagonisms that had seemed before to be so irreconcilable then had an example of reconciliation to ameliorate the social hostilities that had poisoned Austria in the First Republic. That is not to say that Austria became a new Elysium, but differences would be worked out in regular ways, not in street scuffles, *Wirtshaus* brawls, or violent strikes—and certainly the notion of partisan armed forces fighting in the streets, some of the ugliest happenings in the First Republic, was no longer imaginable. Austrians could think of themselves as one society, not several different societies pitted against each other.

The question of their identity has long plagued Austrians. Could they be anything other than a part of a great empire or a Greater Germany? Were they an identifiable—and viable—entity politically? Economically? Culturally? Social peace, political coalition, and economic cooperation, made it possible for them to think of themselves as an entity and as successful and viable. The exigencies and challenges of first the German occupation and then the Allied occupation made them feel less German and gave them a common purpose in facing the Allies. Moreover, it all worked so well that they were able to win their independence and release from the occupation in 1955, at the time, given the conditions of the Cold War, an astonishing accomplishment. With illuminating understanding, Gerald Stourzh portrays the unfolding of the process of the Austrians' sense of self-consciousness, from an imperial people to a people of the republic, from being vaguely part of a larger nation to becoming distinctly a separate people of a small state.

When coalition government gave way to one-party government in 1966, first to the Austrian People's Party and then, in 1970, to the Socialist Party, the successions were conducted in a proper parliamentary fashion, and the party out of office was not the enemy but the loyal opposition. Not only was Austrian politics mature and functioning, but Austrians were economically prosperous and socially untroubled. When Pope John Paul I called Austria an *Insel der Seligen*, (island of the blessed) few Austrians would then have argued with that description. Austrians could be justly proud of their achievements and confident in their ability to continue in their happy ways. They would be able to enjoy the fruit of their endeavors with a nearly pardonable sense of self-satisfaction.

However, although that fruit wore a bright and healthy cover, it concealed a worm within. In all the work and preoccupation of rebuilding and constituting their postwar state and society, the Austrians had unconsciously—and at times quite consciously—

thrust aside the unhappy and sometimes embarrassing memories of the recent past, especially those of the years 1938-1945. No people enjoys evoking ugly memories or even unhappy memories, and Austrians are no exception. Moreover, they had been excused from having to grapple with theirs—or believed that they had been excused—by the Allies' Moscow Declaration of 1 November 1943. It had declared Austria to be the first victim of Hitler's aggression, and victims are not responsible for what occurs. And, if Austria had been incorporated into *Grossdeutschland*, there was no Austria left then to be responsible for anything. Therefore, one could simply get on with the work of the present, unencumbered by the past. But the Austrians, who so enjoy their nostalgia for a more remote past should, of all people, know that the past is unavoidably present in and is the stuff of the present. Without the past, the present is incomplete. And if the task of the present is to define and assert one's identity and place in the world, then one must know, come to grips with, and reconcile oneself to one's past.

For four decades most Austrians suppressed the need to assess, judge, and be accountable for their recent past. Until the 1960s, history stopped in the schools at 1918. Few elders wished to tell the young people about what they had experienced in their own younger days. A few historians concerned themselves with *Zeitgeschichte*, but there was little if any public discussion of what took place from 1938 to 1945. Wrongs not admitted do not have to be righted; injuries unrecognized do not have to be remedied. It is understandable that a people would want to shun such memories, but to do so exacts a price.

It was as if the Austrians' suppressed memories of the recent past had lain beneath the surface like some volatile, explosive material, waiting for a spark that would ignite it. The spark was struck in 1986 during the electoral campaign for the Austrian presidency, when Kurt Waldheim's "brown"—that is, Nazi—past was made an issue. It was as if someone had turned the key to Pandora's box. In a trice the examination of Waldheim's conduct and whereabouts during the war became a general and very heated examination not just of Waldheim's but of *Austrians'* conduct during the years of 1938 to 1945. The sharpness of the accusations and counter-accusations among themselves and the vehemence of the reaction to foreigners' perceptions and comments showed that time and suppression had done nothing to diminish the power of the memories. Austrians were coming to their *Vergangenheitsbewältigung* late, but they were not escaping the rigors of the exercise.

One of the more painful elements of the process was that of seeing the perception of Austria in the eyes of the world undergo a swift, radical change. The land of great music, of idyllic Alpine scenery, of *gemütlich* but somehow also industrious people, much admired for domestic success and trusted in international diplomacy, had become a land of erstwhile accomplices in all the evils of the Nazi regime and of people who perhaps were themselves still unregenerate Nazis. Austrians' sense of identity, of self-worth and self-confidence was much too new and fragile not to be wounded by such a wrenching turn of affairs.

The essays in this book reflect that change. There is nothing to be found here of the laudatory, uncritical commentary that until the last few years so pleased and encouraged Austrians. The authors here are bent on looking at and describing and explaining what the Anschluss was, how it came to pass, and what subsequent influence the events of the Anschluss period would have. They do not fancy themselves to be either adversaries or champions; they are, rather, critical observers whose remarks are tempered by a decent sympathy. They are participants in the Austrians' venture upon *Vergangenheitsbewältigung*. It is not untoward that Americans and others partake in the effort, for a people's past is composed of others as well as of itself; and how a people comes to grips with its past is a procedure that includes relations with others, in the past as well as in the present. It is worth noting that, on balance, the Americans, the one Englishwoman, and the Austrians are about equally critical and equally sympathetic in their treatment of the issues. Indeed, without identifying names, one might have difficulty in discerning which essays were written by Austrians and which by others. That is as it should be.

The works here range from the account of first-hand experience of an American scholar, John Rath, in Vienna during the very hours of the Anschluss, to a look about at current Austria, with a glimpse ahead by the director of the Austrians' cultural institute in the United States, Wolfgang Waldner. From Rath's account one gets a sense of the confusion and apprehension abounding during those days. From Waldner's words one senses the new Austrian, now aware of and acknowledging his past and confident that he can make a future better than his past was.

In looking back to see how the Anschluss came about, Bruce Pauley points out that it was a perilous thing to be a small state in Central Europe in the interbelline period. The general framework of the European system went with the winds of the Great War, and in the readjustments that came after the war, there was little that was propitious for Austria. The large states also suffered considerable dislocation and were in no condition, or were not disposed, to support Austria, the remnant of a defunct empire. The large states, which determined the course of events, had other much more pressing matters to attend to, or, in the case of Germany, posed a threat to Austria after 1933. There would be no help for Austria, too weak internally to face foreign threat alone.

Isabella Ackerl shows how, in the last five years in Austria of the period before the Anschluss, the experiment in authoritarian government failed to maintain the polity and rendered Austria even more vulnerable to Anschluss. In the Central Europe of those times, it was widely thought that democracy was a weak form of government and that some form of authority, uninhibited by democratic deliberations and decision-making, was necessary to maintain the social order. In the Austrian case there was the added buttress of the Church to the corporative authority. The result was, however, even deeper division in society, with a large portion of the populace profoundly disaffected. Belated attempts to re-engage that disaffected element offered a classic example of too little and too late.

If people in political life did not prepare Austria for defense against Anschluss, the people of the literary world did no better. Donald Daviau recounts how Austrian writers did not foresee the dangers of Nazism in Germany as an immediate threat to Austria. Many of them were still wrapped up in their nostalgia for the old world they had known before the war and did not see the present very clearly. Therefore, when the Germans occupied Austria, they were shocked by the new reality, and there was a mass exodus of those who could get out. Of those who remained, many tried to accommodate and survive, but the Austrian literary garden was a parched earth indeed.

Another group of keepers of the culture failed Austria when they were the most needed. Walter Höflechner and John Haag tell the dolorous story of how the universities and their faculties and student groups did not just falter in an attempt to strengthen Austria against Nazism and Germany; they betrayed Austria by paving the way for the Anschluss to Nazi Germany. The process of Nazifying the higher schools was already well begun even before the Anschluss. It is a sorry thing when those persons in a society who are most responsible and well equipped to withstand intellectual and moral subversions like Nazism become, instead, the very ones who lead the subversion. There exists a chilling photograph of students crowding the ramp in front of the Rudolfinum in Vienna, hands upraised in the Hitler salute, *weeks before* the Anschluss. One finds no comfort in the poetic justice whereby the Nazis nearly destroyed the integrity of the institutions whose members, in large number, so avidly helped to introduce Nazism into Austria.

The public at large came, in time, to accept their lot as Germans and to bear the hardships and disappointments of the war. But Austrians never got good reports from the Gestapo concerning their fervor for their German cousins, and when the news was as disastrous as it was from Stalingrad, the grousing and discouragement were even greater. Nevertheless, there was still a sense of commitment to Hitler even into 1944. Evan Bukey examines the turns in public opinion in Austria during the years of 1943 and 1944 and finds that Austrian public opinion ran about parallel to that of Germans in the so-called "Altreich." It is interesting to note that the Moscow Declaration, which was designed to arouse Austrian resistance to Germany, seemed to have little, if any, effect on Austrian attitudes toward Germans or the war. Bukey further points out that Austrians, like Germans in general, were shocked and outraged at the attempted assassination of Hitler on 20 July 1944. Although Austrians suffered fatigue, despair, resentment, and sorrow in the later years of the war, it was not until the very end that they, like the Germans, began to lose faith in Hitler.

While the great majority of Austrians simply went along and tried to make their own personal ways in the circumstances in which they found themselves—and many did so quite happily at first— there were those who were prepared to resist the German occupiers and Nazism. Radomír Luža relates the example of the resistance in the Tirol, where, alone among Austrian cities, Innsbruck was seized by the resisters from the German army garrisoned there and was flying the Red-White-Red flag when the American troops entered the city. Here, Austrians had liberated their own city from the Germans. Elsewhere the efforts of the resistance were more modest, in part because Austrian resisters labored under peculiar handicaps that other resistances did not experience: their language was the same as the occupiers and therefore no handicap to those who would ferret them out; they had no government in exile to aid and encourage them; they got precious little encouragement from the Allies until the very last of the war; and, not least of the problems they faced, technically, and in the eyes of many of their countrymen, they were Germans and, therefore, traitors, not heroic resisters against a hated foreign conqueror.

Gordon Zahn takes the example of Franz Jägerstätter, who was decapitated for refusing to serve in the *Wehrmacht*, to search through the troubling questions of morals and ethics in civil obedience and disobedience. When is it time *not* to render unto Caesar that which Caesar thinks is his due? How is one obliged—even against the cautionary advice of the clergy, who are supposed to be the very vessels of morality—to refuse to obey wicked governors? What might have been the outcome if there had been many more who thought like Franz Jägerstätter and many fewer who thought like Kurt Waldheim, who "just did his duty"?

Anton Pelinka traces the evolution of the ways in which Austrian leaders saw the Anschluss and how they wanted the outside world, especially the Allied powers, to see it. It was important to depict the Anschluss as what the Moscow Declaration said it was: an act that made Austria the first victim of German aggression. Austria could not then be tainted with the guilt that the Germans bore, and it could not be expected that Austria should pay a price in reparation for German damage to lands invaded or bombed during the war. In 1955, at the signing of the State Treaty that set Austria free of the occupation, restored her sovereignty, and allowed her to join the community of nations again as a full-fledged member, the Austrians wanted to delete that part of the preamble to the treaty which referred to Austria's part in the war on Germany's side. Austrians did not want to return to the community under a shadow of guilt, as if they were rehabilitated malefactors; they wanted to be accepted as innocents rescued. And they prevailed upon the Allies to accept their offered interpretation of the Anschluss and its consequences.

The experiences of the years 1938-1945 colored Austrian political notions and practices in the Second Republic in many ways, and Melanie Sully outlines how some of those influences have been manifested. Whether in determining the legal considerations of the Concordat with the Church, the acceptability of ex-Nazis into Austrian political parties, or the suitability of Kurt Waldheim as a candidate for the presidency of Austria, the record of the Anschluss years lurked in the background and leaped forth at times to have a great impact on the course of politics. The celebrated Waldheim affair is only the most recent and striking representation of the persistence and volatility of the issue.

Finally, Lonnie Johnson presents a general, overall review of the various ways in which Austrians have explained the Anschluss to themselves and to the world and he sketches the effects these explanations have had in Austrian public opinion since the war. The Anschluss had as one of its earliest effects, paradoxically, the engendering of a sense of national identity and separateness from Germans. It exonerated the state of Austria from culpability for the war and its attendant monstrosities, and that notion served, for a time, to cloak Austrian *individuals* and cover their personal culpability for participation in war crimes of various degrees of savagery. But, ultimately, leaders like Chancellor Franz Vranitzky, and then the populace at large, began to conclude that the *state* was a victim of superior force, but that many individual Austrians were most willing accomplices, and that fact must be recognized as part of their history. Recent polls of opinion have shown that the number of Austrians who think of themselves only as victims is shrinking, while the number of those who admit the element of complicity is increasing.

After reading these essays, one is impressed by the extent to which the Anschluss has cast a long, somber, deeply affecting shadow over Austrian life from then to now. One is also impressed with the complexity of the issues surrounding the event and its aftermath. As in most human affairs, it is difficult to sort out the rights and wrongs, the noble and the base, the deeds and the myths, the causes and effects. For example, it was universally assumed by the people who had interests involved, including Hitler himself (there were no polls to read people's minds then), that the great majority of Austrians would have voted *Ja* in Chancellor Kurt Schuschnigg's announced plebiscite to maintain Austria's independence from Germany. Yet, the progress of the invading German army was marked by cheering throngs along the way. Had the populace become, overnight, avid German patriots and Nazi sympathizers?

There is a now-famous (or infamous) photograph of the Heldenplatz on 15 March 1938, when Hitler addressed a teeming crowd of possibly 200,000 people, announcing the "return" of Austria to the Reich. This photograph is offered in evidence to prove that Austrians were enthusiastic accomplices to the Nazi evil. But there were at least another 1,400,000 Viennese who were *not* on the Heldenplatz. Of the 200,000 how many had been brought in by busses from Niederösterreich on purpose to make an impressive show? How many of those on the Platz were of that famous Viennese breed, the "Adabeis," who will attend *any* spectacle? How many were there because they had been dismissed from school or work expressly to attend the speech? How many of those present were fearful, or at least skeptical, but wanted to see for themselves what sort of creatures the man Hitler and his minions were? Is the picture, in itself, then, proof of anything?

It is argued that Austrians joined the Nazi party in greater percentage than "Reichsdeutsche," and that is proof of their culpability. But the number still represented only a very small percentage of the whole population, as was also the case in Germany proper. It has been pointed out that Austrians were disproportionately numerous in the administrations of the concentration camps and extermination camps, but still the number is microscopic in relation to the total Austrian population. In addition to the great number of Jewish Austrians who suffered so terribly or lost their lives, there were many non-Jewish Austrians who were arrested and imprisoned in concentration camps, possibly in greater percentage to total population than the "Reichsdeutsche" who were in the camps, but they were still only a very small part of the whole Austrian population. More telling are the accounts of the great number of Austrians who gleefully profited from "Aryanization," or the overwhelming portion of the population who simply accepted the role of obedient, loyal Germans and did the Reich's business without demur. But there were some who resisted (without gaining thereby much credit from their compatriots, one is sad to report) and many who silently disagreed and disobeyed when they could. It is generally accepted that the period of the Anschluss was also the period when Austrians became most acutely aware of their national identity; how does this square with the charge that Austrians were enthusiastic Germans?

If it is daunting for others to try to sort it all out and draw satisfying conclusions, the Jews of Austria have an even more taxing exercise in deciding what it means to them as Jews and as Austrians. What was, only a couple of generations ago, the most flourishing Jewish community in Europe was completely destroyed. It was destroyed by people of the very culture in which they lived and which owed so much of its creation to its Jewish fellows. The destruction was accomplished with a ferocity and cruelty for which it is difficult to find parallels in our time. What terribly conflicting feelings must a person have in saying, "I am an Austrian—and a Jew." Is there *any* explanation, judgment, or conclusion that could be satisfactory or assuage those troubled feelings? And what can an Austrian Jew say to others about what it means to him to try to come to terms with that past and, maybe even more difficult, with this present and the way contemporaries see that past. Paul Grosz, without claiming to speak for all Austrian Jews, does offer some observations on his own views of the Anschluss and the Second Republic. He would be the first to say that no one person's thoughts, or words, can compass the whole of what it has meant to be a Jew of Austria.

This book is concerned with a troubling phenomenon of history. Like the daily news, history is more likely to be concerned with the troubles of a people than anything else because troubles more sharply mark the landscape of history than do other features. But, so far, the human race has survived its many troubles and has, from time to time, even enjoyed a small triumph or two. One may hope that Austrians are now on the way, not to a triumph but to a healthy examination of their major trouble, the Anschluss and its consequences, and to an assimilation of the examined phenomenon into their history. It is encouraging to see the widespread discussion and debate on the issue that has taken place and is still taking place in Austria. Some of the discussion and debate takes place outside of Austria, too. A small part of it is to be found here.

From Reich to Republic[1]

Gerald Stourzh

In his much-read memoirs, Bruno Kreisky relates that in 1933 he became chairman of the Reichs Education Committee (*Reichsbildungsausschuss*) of the Socialist Working Youth. And on New Year's Eve of 1934, he reports, he traveled to Brno (Brünn) to the first Reichs Conference (*Reichskonferenz*) of the (illegal) United Socialist Party.[2] Why, eighteen years after Austria had become a republic, the term "Reichs Committee," why "Reichs Conference"? Kreisky makes no comment about this nomenclature which is as familiar to older Austrians as it is strange to the younger ones. Or had the socialists, perhaps, by using the term *Reich*, terminologically anticipated the Anschluss to the German Reich? Not at all. It has to do with an old Austrian heritage. Also in the conservative camp during the *inter bellum* period there were diverse "Reichs" institutions like the Imperial League of Austrians, the *Imperial Post* (*Reichspost*), and a uniformed formation of the 1930s, the Ostmärkische Sturmscharen, had a "Reichs" directory with Kurt Schuschnigg as "Reichs Leader."

But numerous other quite apolitical organizations of the First

---

[1] This essay is a slightly revised version of a paper which Professor Stourzh presented in the symposium from which all these papers are taken. It first appeared in print in his book of the same title, *Vom Reich zur Republik*, published in Vienna by Edition Atelier in 1990. The translation from German to English is the work of the editor of this volume.

[2] Bruno Kreisky, *Zwischen den Zeiten. Erinnerungen aus fünf Jahrzehnten*, (Berlin, 1986), pp. 124 and 239.

Republic styled themselves likewise as "Reichs" organizations. The Viennese telephone book of 1933—a most instructive lesson on the history of the mentality of the First Republic—shows around forty such titles, from the "Reichs Institute for Mothers' and Infants' Welfare" to the "Reichs Association of Midwives of Austria" to the "Reichs Association of Austrian Printers and Newspaper Workers." The "Reichs Organization of Austrian Merchants," the so-called "Reichsorga" was well known. The prefix "Reichs" (Imperial) served to denote "all-Austrian" during the entire period of the First Republic until 1938, when the interpretation changed. The telephone book of 1937 still showed the "Reichs Association of Jewish Legitimists of Austria"—but such an entry would not remain long. Instead, in the spring of 1938, there was a "Reichs Commissioner for the Reunion of Austria With the German Reich" and a "Reichs Governor" (*Reichsstatthalter*) in Austria, with a different frame of reference, and from 1939 on there was a Reichsstatthalter in each of the seven "Reichs Districts" (*Reichsgaue*) of the "Eastern March" (*Ostmark*), as the Nazi government denominated Austria.

Indeed, manifestly so strong was the uninterrupted memory of the "Imperial" (*Reichs*) organizations that stemmed from old Austria, and remained current until 1938, that apparently even in the first months of the Second Republic, in 1945, that introductory word was still used. In any case, there is to be found, under the date 25 September 1945, in the documents of the Office for Foreign Affairs of the State Chancellory, a file of Norbert Bischoff concerning an intervention by the political representative of the French occupation force, Envoy Louis de Monicault, with the following content: On the previous day Monicault asked Bischoff how there could be in the Austrian People's Party a "Reichs Party Directory" (*Reichsparteileitung*) and other "Reichs" bodies. Bischoff answered Monicault that he too had wondered about that, did not know the details of the matter, but believed that he remembered that the bodies in question already carried this epithet in the First Republic, apparently as an inheritance from the

Monarchy. Thereupon the French diplomat remarked, "this may well be, but today the term 'Reichs' has gained a different, unpleasant connotation, and it would be very good if this word were omitted," otherwise an official "possibly imperative" démarche could ensue, "which all parties concerned would certainly wish to avoid." Bischoff added that one could see from this "the extraordinary anger which follows the slightest manifestations behind which even a vestige of a connection to Germany could be supposed." Right away on the next day, 26 September 1945, Heinrich Wildner, General Secretary of the Foreign Office, could put a quick follow-up report in the files: "State chairman [for Lower Austria] Figl informs that the objectionable title was abolished."[3]

I would like to propose, in admittedly pointed fashion, that it was just thus and then, not earlier, in November 1918, that the history of Austria *finally* became a republican history, rather than a "Reichs" history ("Österreichische Reichsgeschichte" was a required subject for law students until the middle of the 1930s!). This thesis I would like to offer for discussion: It was not until then and there that Austrian self-awareness finally freed itself from the "Reichs" notion, replete with so many different conceptions. It was only then that the way was open for an Austrian self-consciousness—not unlike that of Switzerland—that was able to overcome exaggerated political divisions and to integrate small-statehood and a democratic republic.

"To what extent was Austrian self-consciousness colored—and damaged—through the many variations and often very complex structure of the conception of Austria at a given time?" Erich Zöllner, the dean of writers of Austrian history, posed this question in an essay on "Forms and Variations in the Idea of

---

[3]Österreichisches Staatsarchiv, Archiv der Republik, Staatskanzlei/Amt für Auswärtige Angelegenheiten 1945, Zl. 1368-pol/45.

Austria" (1965), which should be required reading for all to whom Austrian history is important.[4]

The idea of Austria—and along with it Austrian self-consciousness—suffered the strongest mutations especially in the period from 1866/1867 to 1945. Still today we can feel the afterquakes of the ruptures and doubts of those eight decades. Before the outbreak of the war of 1866, the Empire of Austria was, with around 650,000 square kilometers, the largest European empire after Russia, and with a part of its kingdoms and provinces (and, as a glance at Trieste shows, its cities!) was a member of the German Confederation. With the Compromise of 1867, Austria slipped into a "situation of permanent crisis," as Zöllner describes it.[5] The non-Hungarian part of the monarchy, "Cisleithania," in common speech, and increasingly in official usage, designated as "Austria," comprised then only around 300,000 square kilometers. Fifty-one years later that Austria, as a part of the monarchy, expired. There came into being a republic that at once declared itself to be a part of the German Reich (Anschluss), a republic in which one was at first very uncertain as to what name to give it. After October 1919, according to the demands of the Allies, the republic was named "Republic of Austria," and comprised finally about 84,000 square kilometers. In 1938 this small Austria disappeared from the map. An Austrian social scientist, Franz Borkenau, in no wise sympathetic with National Socialists, wrote in the emigration from London in

---

[4] Erich Zöllner, "Formen und Wandlungen des Österreichbegriffs." In: Erich Zöllner, *Probleme und Aufgaben der österreichischen Geschichtsforschung* (Vienna, 1984), p. 14.

[5] Erich Zöllner, "Perioden der österreichischen Geschichte und Wandlungen des Österreich-Begriffs bis zum Ende der Habsburgermonarchie." In: Adam Wandruszka and Peter Urbanitsch, eds., *Die Habsburgermonarchie 1848-1918*, vol. III, *Die Völker des Reiches* (Vienna, 1980), p 29. Now see also Erich Zöllner, *Der Österreichbegriff. Formen und Wandlungen in der Geschichte*, Sammlung Österreich Archiv. (Vienna, 1988).

1938, "Austria, insofar as a forecast is possible, belongs to the past."![6]

After seven long years, from the perspective of 1938 as if by a miracle, the republic rose again. If one compares the enormous changes within eight decades in what "Austria" signifies with the stability in this whole period of the politically and territorially unchanging Switzerland, one can measure the difficulties in adequately presenting the continuities as well as the discontinuities of Austrian history. Remarks about three "waves of discontinuity" in the concept of Austria and Austrian self-consciousness—after 1867, after 1918, and after 1938—follow and will be concluded with considerations on problems in the history of the Austrian republic.

Why did the concept of Austria fall into a "situation of permanent crisis" with the Compromise of 1867? The historian Alfred von Arneth formulated the dilemma most significantly. It had to do with whether Hungary would take its place *in* Austria or *alongside* Austria.[7] In fact, it was alongside Austria. Only temporarily did the notion of "West Austria" surface in the Viennese press as a denomination for the giant non-Hungarian part of the monarchy. Symbolic for the transition from the old to the new was that Kaiser Franz Joseph sanctioned two laws on the same day, 21 December 1867, in which the adjective "Austrian" is used with two entirely different meanings: In the Compromise Law, concerning the common affairs of all the lands of the "Austrian Monarchy," this word included in the title of the law also the lands of the Crown of St. Stephen. At the same time, Franz Joseph signed the constitutional law on general rights of citizens,

---

[6]Franz Borkenau, *Austria and After* (London, 1938), p. 319. Otto Bauer's statement is well known, "Austria was." It is to be found in the article, "Österreichs Ende," of spring 1938 (*Der Kampf*, no. 4, 1938). In: Otto Bauer, *Werkausgabe*, vol. IX (Vienna, 1980), p. 844.

[7]Alfred von Arneth, *Aus meinem Leben*, vol. II (Stuttgart, 1893), pp. 199 and 200.

a law that governed the "Austrian" citizenship of only the non-Hungarian lands. Dualism was for contemporaries a stronger reality than we today realize. For example, if one wished to divorce, the difference between Austrian and Hungarian citizenship was considerable! Dualism has still today bizarre consequences for the teaching of history in Austria. We learn—and know—very little about Hungarian domestic politics in the time of dualism. When we teach and learn foreign policy of the monarchy, we have the whole empire in mind; when we teach and learn about internal history, we have quite predominantly only one half in mind! Also the Habsburg imperial idea after 1867 was fragile. The Reichsrat in Vienna was, after 1867, responsible for just half of the monarchy. Franz Joseph's exertions to create a title of "Imperial Chancellor" with which to compass both halves of the empire (a title which existed in Vienna four years earlier than in Berlin, namely in 1867, with the appointment of Beust) could not be continued because of Hungarian opposition. In other ways also the Hungarians were successful in their efforts to fight against the idea of "Reich" for the combined monarchy. The reduction of the name "Austria" to mean Cisleithania became accepted more quickly and earlier than we today accept, even in official use (not first in 1915, as is frequently to be read; on this issue there are interesting sources). This reduction was, however, not complete. Within the compass of dynastically stamped "black-yellow" Reichs patriotism, the name Austria lived on as the name for the whole monarchy, as in the anti-Hungarian reform project of the Romanian Aurel von Popovici concerning the "United States of Great Austria in 1906—and, especially, into the present time in the literary exaggeration of Kakania in the work of Robert Musil.

Is it cavilling to approach Musil's Kakania with the historian's probe? It is well known that we read in Musil that Kakania, "named itself in writing the Austro-Hungarian Monarchy and had itself called Austria, that is, by a name which it had ceremoniously set aside but held to in all matters of feeling." Is that a dream; is that reality? At least for the nearly ten million Magyars that was in no way true! Is it cavilling to point out that Musil took the part for the whole when he reported on the Kakanian emergency clause, with the help of which one could get along without parliament, without mentioning that this applied only to the Viennese, not, however, to the Budapest parliament. Is it cavilling to point out that Musil's remark, "Before the law all citizens were equal, but not all were equally citizens," is, for the period after 1867, downright false? No one knew this better than the Jews of the monarchy, and I dare to declare that, in Franz Theodor Csokor's drama, *3 November 1918*, the Jewish Regimental Doctor Grün, with his "Earth from Austria," more profoundly grasped a reality of Kakania than Musil's chapter on Kakania, namely the Jewish one. Is it, finally, cavilling to remind that Musil himself, in his article of March 1919 on the Anschluss to Germany, with biting acuity attacked Austrian culture, branded it as "a fault in the perspective of the Viennese point of view," although his Kakania itself strongly reflected that point of view.?[8]

The crisis in the concept of Austria, and in the Austrian self-consciousness, was acute after the fall of the monarchy. Karl Renner's first proposal of a constitution in October 1918 was, at first, for a Free State, "Southwest Germany." The *Innsbrucker Nachrichten*, which conducted a poll in spring of 1919 for an appropriate name for the state, rejected not only the name "Austria" but also "German-Austria": "We and the world know now only that we are not Hungary and also not Czech-, Polish-, or

---

[8] Robert Musil, "Der Anschluß an Deutschland (March 1919)." In: Robert Musil, *Gesammelte Werke,* ed. Adolf Frisé, vol. VIII (Reinbeck, 1978), pp. 1039 and 1041, cited by Fritz Fellner, "Die Historiographie zur österreichischen Problematik als Spiegel der nationalpolitischen Diskussion" In: Heinrich Lutz and Helmut Rumpler, eds., *Wiener Beiträge zur Geschichte der Neuzeit,* vol. IX (Vienna, 1982), p. 41. The citations from the Kakania chapter are taken from Robert Musil, *Der Mann ohne Eigenschaften.* In: Adolf Frisé, ed., *Gesammelte Werke in Einzelausgaben* (Hamburg, 1952), p. 34.

South Slavic-Austria—rather German-Austria, as if there were such a thing as the others. Yes, it did not occur at all to the others to continue to use the tainted old name." How long had it been since one could be proud of the name "Austria," questioned the newspaper; the coming generation should not be burdened with it: "One dances again—even in Innsbruck—and, one hopes, will beget children again, to which dancing will be a good preparatory exercise; but these children will think and live differently from us and our parents. Build them a new house, in which they will be able to be happy; but do not name it with a romantic name from days gone by." The poll of the newspaper produced quite original suggestions (here only a selection): Upper Germany, German Mountain Empire, Danube-Germany, Eastern Hold, East German Confederation, German March, Teutheim, Treuland, Peace Land, German Peaceland.[9]

As the Allies rejected the name "German-Austria," Renner expressed his preference for a republic of the "German Alpine Lands" because the name "German-Austria" implied that "all Germans of the former Austria" were united and formed a state; since the Sudeten Germans were separated from Alpine Germans by the Treaty of St. Germain, that no longer was accurate. Sullenly, the First Republic accompanied the requirement to name itself the "Republic of Austria" with the constitutional anchoring, in October 1919, of the German language as the language of state (still today valid constitutional law) with the justification— thus the supporting argument—that thereby "our character as a German national state" will[10] be given expression. Rightly, the

---

[9]*Innsbrucker Nachrichten*, 6 and 8 March 1919; see also Friedrich F. G. Kleinwaechter, *Von Schönbrunn bis St. Germain* (Graz, 1964), pp. 145 and 146.

[10]Renner's comment on the state name "German-Austria" for a state that would comprise Sudeten and Alpine Germans. In: *Stenogr. Protokolle der Konstituierenden Nationalversammlung*, 29. Sitzung, 6 September 1919, p. 776; on the supporting argument for the law on the form of state of 21 October 1919 (StGBl. Nr. 484) in which the German language is introduced as the language of state, cf. Kleinwaechter, *Von Schönbrunn bis St. Germain*, pp. 148 and 149.

Salzburg historian, Gerhard Botz, averred that it is unclear how widely the Anschluss idea was actually present in the broad masses of the population, especially among the workers and peasants, if indeed its influence was not often exaggerated.[11] It should be added that in the first years after 1918 it was primarily the mentality "Let him who can save himself where he can" which dominated: the direction was not only toward Germany, as shown by Tirol's doubtful attempt to save South Tirol through proclamation of a neutral Republic of Tirol, or the Voralberg movement for Anschluss to Switzerland. Indeed, "German-feeling" possessed the intellectuals and the politicians with few exceptions (as Heinrich Lammasch, who at that time already drew the analogy of little Austria to Switzerland, an analogy that was used, moreover, many times by Karl Renner, among others, after Hitler's seizure of power in 1933).

Two examples, that today may shock: Hans Kelsen wrote in 1926 that it was a "morally unbearable condition that six and a half million people were drawn together in a community that was bereft of any inner sense, any political concept." Kelsen—in any case without understanding for the historical maturity of the Federal Lands—stated: "Neither historical nor national, nor religious, nor cultural grounds are there that can justify this Austria, that is nothing but an arbitrary scrap of land, left over after the victors have satisfied their territorial desires."[12] In the same year of 1926, Sigmund Freud explained in an interview that his lan-

---

[11]Gerhard Botz, "Das Anschlußproblem (1919-1945) aus österreichischer Sicht." In: Robert Kann and Friedrich Prinz, *Deutschland und Österreich. Ein bilaterales Geschichtsbuch* (Vienna, Munich, 1980), pp. 182 and 183. See also Erik Bielka, "Wie viele Österreicher waren in der Ersten Republik für den Anschluß an Deutschland?" *Geschichte und Gegenwart*, vol. VII, 1988, pp. 38-50.

[12]Hans Kelsen, "Zur Anschlußfrage." In: *Republikanische Hochschul-Zeitung*, vol. II (Munich, 1926), Book 1/2, pp. 1 and 2. Citation in my study "Hans Kelsen, die österreichische Bundesverfassung und die rechtsstaatliche Demokratie." In: Gerald Stourzh, *Wege zur Grundrechtsdemokratie* (Vienna, 1989), p. 317.

guage was German, his culture was German; he considered himself German in spirit until he noticed the growth of anti-Semitic prejudice in "Germany and German Austria." Thereafter he preferred to call himself a Jew.[13]

The dominance of a "German" consciousness(in which the language-cultural, and in many the ethnic [völkisch], sense of belonging together outweighed the state-political as well as the elements of cultural socialization beyond language) was promoted in the last decades in Cisleithanian-Old Austria by a development of great impact: more and more the conviction grew that the "ethnic groups" (Volksstämme) were the factors that had the right to make the decisions in public life. A Czech politician, Josef Kaizl, had demanded in Prague that "only on the basis of concurring decision of both ethnic groups" could laws henceforth come into being.[14] The famous Moravian Compromise of 1905 rested on this principle. The struggle for the "assets" (Besitzstand) of the "ethnic groups" (Volksstämme) (thus the political vocabulary of Austria around 1900!) brought with it Karl Lueger putting in the city statute of Vienna, in 1900, the oath for acquiring citizenship, averring that the candidate will maintain "the German character of the city" to the best of his ability.

From the events of 1918 and thereafter, this primacy of the "ethnic group" became effective. A new concept, that of "ethnic citizenship" surfaced, also welcomed by Ignaz Seipel, but this idea led, at several institutions of higher learning in the First Republic, including in 1930-1931 the University of Vienna, to the establishment of the obligatory association of students according to "Nations," whereby the "German student nation" excluded Jews and half-Jews. God be praised, the Constitutional

---

[13] Sigmund Freud in an interview with George S. Viereck, citation in Peter Gay, *Freud, Juden und andere Deutsche* (Hamburg, 1986), p. 112.

[14] Citation in Gerald Stourzh, *Die Gleichberechtigung der Nationalitäten in der Verfassung und Verwaltung Österreichs 1848-1918* (Vienna, 1985), p. 14.

Supreme Court put an early end to this evil[15]

Considering the dominance of "German-feeling" that permeated so many areas of life in the First Republic, it seems all the more imperative to put the frequent criticism of the theme of the "second German state" of the Dollfuss-Schuschnigg era into a broader context. After Hitler's seizure of power in Germany, the Social Democrats—and this is too seldom noted—were hard at it in defense of the thesis of a second, "better" German state. In an article, "Austria's Mission," in the "Worker on Sunday" (supplement to the *Arbeiter Zeitung* of 15 October 1933, unsigned, but Otto Bauer's authorship cannot be precluded) there is stated: "A German land of Freedom, a German land of the mind and culture—that Austria should be." On the previous day Otto Bauer, in the name of the party representatives, laid before the Social Democratic Party Convention a text according to which the working class would be ready at any time to "defend the independence and the freedom of the Austrian people (sic!) against German national fascism (sic!)," when (in addition to the guarantees of democracy, of civil rights, and the social achievements of the working class) "this republic, in a time when the German people in the Reich have fallen under the bloody rule of a barbaric despotism, fulfills the mission for the whole German nation to preserve a place on one part of German soil for the

---

[15] See the outstanding dissertation of Brigitte Fenz, *Volksbürgerschaft und Staatsbürgerschaft. Das Studentenrecht in Österreich 1918-1932* (unpublished dissertation, University of Vienna, 1977) as well as by the same author, "Zur Ideologie der 'Volksbürgerschaft'—Die Studentenordnung der Universität Wien vom 8. April 1930 vor dem Verfassungsgerichthof," *Zeitgeschichte*, V (1977/78), 125-145. For a contemporary criticism of the racist structure of the "Gleispachschen" student regulation of the University of Vienna see: Herbert Stourzh, "Studentenrecht und Christentum," *Menschenkämpfer*, VI, no. 3 (5 February 1932), 4, 5.

upward-struggling German working masses."[16]

The thesis of a "better" German state was also not specific to the Dollfuss-Schuschnigg regime.[17] Indeed, in order to steal a march on the National Socialists, a black-red cooperation, if it had ever come to pass, might have made use of such a thesis. That is not contradicted by the fact that in the time from 1933 to 1938, through the mobilization of an Old Austrian-oriented sense of tradition, precisely in Catholic and regime-loyal youth groups a strong Austrian self-consciousness was promoted—quite aside from the ideas of the circle around Ernst Karl Winter, Alfred Missong and Hans-Karl Zessner-Spitzenberg, and Coudenhove-Kalergi's use of the principle of nation, valid from Switzerland to North America, with regard to Austria.[18]

It was decisive for the general situation of the year 1933-

---

[16]Otto Bauer's authorship of the article, "Austria's Mission," is very probable, just as the cited text of the party representation (*Arbeiter Zeitung*, 15 October 1933) bears Otto Bauer's handwriting. Still in the spring of 1938, after the engrossment of Austria, Bauer used the formulation for Austria as the "abode of German freedom," if the Social Democrats and the Christian Socials had come to cooperate. Otto Bauer, *Werkausgabe*, IX (Vienna, 1980), pp. 837 and 838.

[17]A one-sided interpretation of the second German state thesis in the Dollfuss-Schuschnigg regime, which does not take proper account of the historical context, is to be found in Anton Staudinger, "Zur 'Österreich'-Ideologie des Ständestaats." In: *Das Juliabkommen von 1936* (Vienna, 1977), pp. 198-140.

[18]Cf. especially Richard Coudenhove-Kalergi, "Geburt einer Nation," *Pan-Europa* (February 1935), cited in Kurt Skalnik, "Auf der Suche nach der Identität." In: Erika Weinzierl and Kurt Skalnik, eds., *Geschichte der Ersten Republik*. vol. I (Graz, 1983), p. 19. The formulation of the Austrian nation in the thirties was a notion of struggle in the battle against National Socialism, which surfaced in Catholic publications years earlier than in communist publications. A first (unsigned) article, "Austrian Nation," appeared in the organ of the Schuschnigg-led Ostmärkischen Sturmscharen's, *Sturm über Österreich*, no. 13 (16 July 1933). Coudenhove-Kalergi's article dated from February 1935. Ernst Karl Winter expressed himself on the Austrian nation in his writing, "Monarchie und Arbeiterschaft," of 1 October 1936. The articles of the communist, Alfred Klahr, appeared in March and April of 1937. Cf. also Wolfgang Häusler, "Wege zur österreichischen Nation," *Römische Historische Mitteilungen*, XXX (1988), 381-411.

1934 that Chancellor Dollfuss adopted, as has been rightly stated, the conviction of Mussolini that "the only method promising success in stabilizing Austria against the dynamic of National Socialism" would be the attempt "to take away from the competition the weapon of anti-Marxism."[19] A representative of the wing of government that most radically defended the Mussolini line formulated its political strategy considerably more drastically: "We can beat National Socialism in Austria by 'out-Hitlering' (*"überhitlern"*) it." Thus spoke the ideologue of the Heimwehr Movement, Odo Neustädter-Stürmer, in a discussion of the governing parties at the end of March 1933. This was a frightfully erroneous estimate of the situation that, from the outset, made impossible a closing together of the governing parties and the Social Democrats.[20]

It should not be forgotten that at first there were still areas in which, even after the dismissal of parliament by the Dollfuss government, the Christian Socials and Social Democrats cooperated against the National Socialists. In the Lower Austrian legislature the Social Democratic representative, Leopold Petz-

---

[19] Jens Petersen, "Konflikt oder Koalition zwischen Christlich-Sozialen und Sozial Demokraten?" *Österreich in Geschichte und Literatur*, XVI (1972), 432. I am following in this segment several of my works on the pre-history of the "Anschluss," among others, my memorial address on 11 March 1988 on the occasion of the memorial ceremony of the Lower Austrian legislature and government, published under the title "Österreich im 20. Jahrhundert—Umbrüche und Konstanten." In: *Niederösterreich '38-'88*, in *NÖ-Schriften*, XVI (Vienna, 1988), 21-32, as well as my article, "Der Weg zur Einverleibung Österreichs." In: Klaus Hildebrand, Jürgen Schmädeke and Klaus Zernack, eds., *Die Entfesselung des Zweiten Weltkriegs und das internationale System*. Veröffentlichung der Historischen Kommission zu Berlin (Berlin, New York, 1990), pp. 213-221.

[20] In a discussion of the majority parties on 25 March 1933, in Walter Goldinger, ed., *Protokolle des Klubvorstandes der Christlich-Sozialen Partei 1932-1934* (Vienna, 1980), p. 204. Schuschnigg attested, in another connection, to Neustädter-Stürmer's "purely fascistic ideas." Kurt Schuschnigg, *Im Kampf gegen Hitler* (Vienna, Munich, Zürich, 1969), p. 169. Neustädter-Stürmer committed suicide in March 1938.

nek—later the husband of the daughter of Crown Prince Rudolf—cried out in June 1933: "Hitler-Germany is conducting war against Austria." Christian Socials and Social Democrats together enacted provincial constitutional laws against the National Socialists, even up to 31 January 1934![21]

The years from 1934 to 1938 were years of disjunction and alienation of the three divisions of the Austrian population. Different initiatives toward the bringing together of the "Fatherland Front" camp and the defeated camp of February 1934—the names of Ernst Karl Winter, Alfred Maleta, and later Richard Schmitz may be cited—failed in part because of the bitterness of the defeated and in part because of the lack of interest or unwillingness of the most important decision-makers. Federal Chancellor Schuschnigg was—even up until the eve of Berchtesgaden—a decided braker. Even on 10 February 1938 Schuschnigg said: "Accompanying the Marxists in combatting the National Socialists," was to be rejected absolutely; his argument was that one would come "onto the side of Czechoslovakia and therefore into international isolation."[22] In any case, Austria already found itself increasingly in isolation, at least since 1936.

In January 1936, Mussolini gave over Austria to being made a satellite of the German Reich. Mussolini recommended to the German ambassador in Rome an agreement between Germany and Austria whereby Austria "would be formally a completely independent state, practically a satellite of Germany." Mussolini saw great advantage for Germany and Italy in that "Germany would obtain a reliable satellite while at the same time German-

---

[21]Hermann Riepl, *Der Landtag in der Ersten Republik* (Vienna, 1972), (Part I of the work *Fünfzig Jahre Landtag von Niederösterreich*), p. 365.

[22]Cited in Everhard Holtmann, *Zwischen Unterdrückung und Befriedigung— Sozialistische Arbeiterbewegung und autoritäres Regime in Österreich 1933-1938* (Vienna, 1978), p. 239.

Italian mistrust would be disspelled."[23] The years from 1936 to 1938, under the aegis of the July Agreement, agreed to not exactly on the advice of Mussolini, but under his pressure, were years of "controlled accommodation" toward the Third Reich, in the hope of winning time and in the hope of not letting a certain accommodation become creeping or galloping satellization

In spite of everything, it should not be forgotten that in the years from 1933 to 1938 there resounded in Austria again and again clear, strong public criticism of the National Socialist system, which was already in power in the neighboring German Reich. The fiasco of the National Socialist *Putsch* of July 1934, with its international response concerning the murder of Chancellor Dollfuss, was, in fact, Hitler's only failure in foreign policy between his seizure of power and the unleashing of the war. Very clear voices were to be heard from Austria during these years. The German Catholic philosopher Dietrich von Hildebrand, who fled from National Socialists to Austria, published, and caused to be published, astonishing things in the periodical *Der christliche Ständestaat*—he actually wanted to call it *Das neue Österreich*. Von Hildebrand attacked in the sharpest way the most profoundly anti-Christian blood and racial teachings of National Socialism. Hildebrand assaulted the tendencies of Catholic anti-Judaism without mincing matters. Alfred Missong conducted a courageous polemic against the book of Bishop Alois Hudal, which built bridges between National Socialism and the Church. Herbert Stourzh stated a very clear word on the true nature of National Socialism in the autumn of 1934: "It did not require first the Berlin and Munich murders and the shameful deed of 25 July to recognize National Socialism as national bestiality and to show Germany's supposed rising in the sign of the swastika as in reality Germany's abasement." Ernst Karl

---

[23] Report of the ambassador, Ulrich von Hassel (Later a victim of the 20 July vengeance), reprinted in Esmonde Robertson, "Zur Wiederbesetzung des Rheinlands 1936," *Vierteljahreshefte für Zeitgeschichte*, X (1962), 189.

Winter and Josef Roth also wrote in this periodical; it made no secret of its rejection of the slogan about a "second German state."[24]

The *finis Austriae* of March 1938 was an act of force brought on from the outside (12 February 1938 in Berchtesgaden) and finally decided on 11 March as a result of Schuschnigg's decision to hold a popular referendum, which provoked Hitler in the extreme. That which was played out between 12 February and 11 March 1938 in mobilizing and galvanizing the Austrian National Socialists was a result of Hitler's demands of 12 February, and in the last phase—the seizure of power by Austrian National Socialists in the provinces in the evening hours of 11 March 1938—a result of Hitler's and Göring's ultimative reactions to the plan for a popular referendum.[25]

With all of its great weaknesses, the planned popular referendum was a challenge to Hitler and an act of resistance. The words of Schuschnigg, "We submit to force," bespeak a historical reality, and I see no occasion to revise the judgment of the English historian, Francis Carsten: Hitler's conquest of March 1938 "was only in part to be attributed to Austrian National

---

[24] Cf. among others Dietrich von Hildebrand, "Die letzte Maske fällt," issue of 8 July 1934; Alfred Missong on Bishop Hudal's book, "Die Grundlagen des Nationalsozialismus," issue of 29 November 1936; Herbert Stourzh, "Deutscher Mensch oder deutscher Unmensch," issue of 7 October 1934.

[25] That (among other things) "the meeting of the chancellors in February 1938" foreshadowed "the evolutionary way to a joining [of Austria] to the German Reich" is an interpretation to which I cannot subscribe; it is to be found in Erwin A. Schmidl, *März 1938. Der deutsche Einmarsch in Österreich* (Vienna, 1987), p. 256. Also in this work the strongly suggestive acceptance of the possibility of an Austria become National Socialist, but nevertheless maintaining a certain independence (pp. 103, 107-108) stands in stark contradiction to the National Socialist slogans, "Heim ins Reich" (home into the Reich) or "Ein Volk, ein Reich, ein Führer" (one people, one empire, one leader). A more realistic presentation of the provisional character of the so-called "plans for personal union" is to be found in Gerhard Botz, *Die Eingliederung Österreichs in das Deutsche Reich.* 2nd rev. ed. (Vienna, 1976), pp. 32-39, especially p. 39.

Socialists and much more to German pressure and to the military might of the Third Reich."[26] That which is said here is not disproved by the phenomenon of mass psychosis in the days following 11 March. The historian Klemens von Klemperer has said rightly that the discrepancy between the majority which Schuschnigg's plebiscite would have brought, as is generally accepted, and the overwhelming enthusiasm on Heroes' Square on 15 March and the National Socialist plebiscite of 10 April is too striking not to be examined further.

> In the course of events following 11 March," wrote Klemperer, there set in a "natural dynamic of crisis accompanied by an increasing terror that was beyond all rational explanation, to be understood only through means of mass psychological explanation. The situation was like an earthquake that suddenly makes the arm of the seismograph swing wildly. Only later does the crisis-psychosis abate again and give way in the course of a sobering to a new normality, in which, once again, rational positions are bared, such as identification with a new regime, accommodation, opportunism, rejection, resistance and opposition.[27]

The history of Austria from 1938 to 1945, in the NS-time or Nazi-time, has been written in the past decades with a certain

---

[26]Francis L. Carsten, *Faschismus in Österreich* (Munich, 1978), p. 291. In 1988 the German historian Franz Müller wrote: "The concept 'Anschluss,' in its original quality, had precious little in common with the actions of March 1938. Therefore, the use of the term in this connection appears to be unsustainable from a scientific point of view." Franz Müller, "Franz von Papen und die deutsche Österreichpolitik in den Jahren 1934 bis 1938." In: Thomas Albrich, Klaus Eisterer, and Rolf Steininger, eds., *Tirol und der Anschluß. Voraussetzungen, Entwicklungen, Rahmenbedingungen 1918-1938* (Innsbruck, 1988), pp. 377f.

[27]Klemens von Klemperer, "Diskussionsbeitrag auf einem Symposion der Österreichischen Akademie der Wissenschaften im Februar 1988." In: Gerald Stourzh and Birgitta Zaar, eds., *Österreich, Deutschland und die Mächte--internationale und österreichische Aspekte des "Anschlusses" von März 1938* (Vienna, 1990), p. 465.

emphasis. In the first instance it was written as the history of the victims and persecuted, of those driven into emigration, of heroes of the resistance, of the gradually disillusioned—and also as the history of the Nazi criminals. The step-by-step destruction of the name "Austria"—from the former "Ostmark" to the "Reichs districts of the Danube and Alpine provinces," because to Hitler even "Ostmark" designated too much unity—has been depicted in many ways. It would be entertaining to seek out the few names that preserved the word "Austrian" during the whole Nazi time. There are some! The "First Austrian Savings Bank" (Die Erste Österreichische Spar-Casse) preserved its name, and the federal press lasted out seven long years as the "Austrian National Press" (Österreichischer Landesverlag); thousands of school report cards of the National Socialist time bore in the bottom margin the printer's mark "Austrian National Press." Indeed, a striking aspect of the history of the seven years—affecting millions of people in Austria—was first taken in hand in the most recent years, beginning with the works of Gerhard Botz and Ernst Hanisch: the history of accommodating. It is so difficult to investigate because accommodation had not only many faces but also many motives, from accommodating as camouflage, as alibi for accepting the unavoidable, accomodateing to something ultimately understood, to the accommodation of the fellow traveller—the nuances were innumerable.[28]

Three snapshots of "accommodating" in Austria after the Anschluss:

1. Under the date Gloggnitz, 1 November 1938, Karl Renner wrote a postscript to the foreword of his brochure on "The Founding of the Republic of German-Austria, the Anschluss and the Sudeten Germans": "The present work was finished and given to the printer as in the dramatic course of a few weeks,

---

[28]Gerhard Botz, *Wien vom "Anschluß" zum Krieg,* 2nd ed. (Vienna, Munich, 1980); Ernst Hanisch, *Nationalsozialistische Herrschaft in der Provinz Salzburg* (Salzburg, 1983).

through the unparalleled perseverance and energy of the German Reich's leaders, united with the farsighted, wise statecraft of Great Britain, with the sacrificial self-control of France and the heroic resignation of Czechoslovakia, with the negotiating assistance of Italy, without war and war's sacrifices, as one may say, overnight, the Sudeten German problem was completely solved." Renner opined further, the "Munich Agreement closes a painful chapter of history, in that it liquidates for all time the Danubian Monarchy and leads to the end of the national state principle in Central Europe." In his conclusion Renner praises the powers participating in the Munich Agreement: "The tetrarchy of the western Great Powers has treated in the stead of the League of Nations." These were, then, Chamberlain's England, Daladier's France, Mussolini's Italy, and Hitler's Germany—the "tetrarchy of the western Great Powers"! An offprint copy of this (unpublished) brochure was, on the orders of Adolf Schärf, kept under lock in the International Institute for Social History in Amsterdam until 1970, although the communists possessed a copy and published excerpts from it on Renner's eightieth birthday in 1950, fourteen days before his death.[29]

At a Renner-Symposion at Gloggnitz in October 1984, I was concerned to point out the phenomenon of time-assessment, instead of laying into Renner with upraised forefinger, which is quite easy to do. We know that 1945 followed 1938. If, however, someone had said to Renner on 1 November 1938 that seven years and seven weeks later he would be elected president of the Republic of Austria, he would have looked at that person disbelievingly and without understanding. One may remind of the words, just cited, of Franz Borkenau in April 1938: "Austria,

---

[29]Renner's brochure can be seen, among other places, in the library of the Institute for History of the University of Vienna, in the Documentation Archive of the Austrian Resistance (Dokumentationsarchiv des österreichischen Widerstandes) in Vienna, and in the archives of the International Instituut voor Geschiedenis in Amsterdam.

insofar as a forecast is possible, belongs to the past." From this perspective of the coming-to-an-end, of the finality—which is today unimaginable, not to be recaptured—can Renner's words be understood. All the more should our special respect indeed be paid to those who early on, and against the stream of the times, risked their lives for "Austria," and also often enough lost them.

2. Second snapshot—15 January 1940. In the Church of St. Charles there took place the burial of the deceased Cabinet Director of the President of the First Republic, Dr. Josef Freiherr von Löwenthal. Two former presidents, Michael Hainisch and Wilhelm Miklas, were present. It is reported (in a still unpublished source)[30] that, after the condolences, Hainisch went away on foot toward Resselpark, while Miklas got into a state vehicle assigned to him (a large Daimler with two swastika-flags). In fact, we know from Walter Goldinger's article on Miklas that Hitler, in March 1938, decreed that Miklas be allowed full income, an official dwelling, and an official automobile. Miklas, according to Goldinger, "accepted the temporary demise of the state of Austria and accommodated himself to the governing circumstances." This does not indicate that Miklas did not suffer a good deal; his correspondence with Arthur Seyss-Inquart in April 1938, published years ago by Ludwig Jedlicka, but little known, shows his scruples as to whether he should vote "ja" on 10 April. Under the subtle threats of Seyss-Inquart's pressure, Miklas decided (according to a letter of 7 April 1938), "even now in an hour heavy with destiny, as a German obeying his own most intimate sensitivities, and, not last, also obeying the call of the Austrian archbishops and bishops, not to separate myself from the German-Austrian people when they declare

---

[30] In a note of the later ambassador Dr. Josef Schöner, dated 16 January 1940. For permission to use this note, I owe thanks to Frau Rita Schöner.

themselves for reunion with the German Reich."³¹ Miklas lost three of his sons in the war; the fiancé of one of his daughters died in a concentration camp.

3. Third snapshot—21 December 1940. Anton von Webern, against whose music the people in power conducted a vendetta, calling it degenerate art, wrote to a friend enlisted in the armed forces about a discovery he (Webern) made in the papers of Stefan George.

> I would like to tell you further that I have made very eminently interesting discoveries in Stefan George: in 'Stern des Bundes,' in which he gives a lesson that now to a large extent has become reality—but already in 1914!!! and in the 'New Reich' (1921) in which basically things are named directly: he speaks about the 'true symbol' on the 'people's banner.'!!!³²

His biographers, Hans and Rosaleen Moldenhauer, write that then von Webern saw "in George the prophet of a new German

---

³¹Walter Goldinger, "Wilhelm Miklas," in Friedrich Weißensteiner, ed., *Die österreichischen Bundespräsidenten. Leben und Werk* (Vienna, 1982), pp. 82-120. The correspondence with Seyss-Inquart of April 1938 published as addendum to: Ludwig Jedlicka, "Verfassungs- und Verwaltungsprobleme 1938-1955." In: *Die Entwicklung der Verfassung Österreichs vom Mittelalter bis zur Gegenwart.* Institut für Österreichkunde (Graz, 1963), pp. 138-141. In a note from May 1939, written by Miklas himself, he was, for the time being, "by virtue of a well-meaning word from the Führer, so to say, the last German-Austrian put under protection as a historical monument." In a note from 12 April 1938, Miklas says, circumspectly, concerning the events of 11-12 March 1938, that he capitulated "somewhat after midnight to the conquering Austrian revolution of the NSDAP, that is, to the political movement of my own German-Austrian people"; the apologetic character of this expression must be reckoned with regard to the moment in time in which it was written. Published in Rudolf Neck, "Wilhelm Miklas und der "Anschluß" 1938." In: *Arbeiterbewegung-Faschismus-Nationalbewußtsein*, Helmut Konrad and Wolfgang Neugebauer, eds. (Vienna, Munich, Zürich, 1983), pp. 99-113, here p. 113 as well as p. 106.

³²Hans and Rosaleen Moldenhauer, *Anton von Webern. Chronik seines Lebens und Werkes* (Zürich, 1980), p. 480 (to Josef Hueber).

generation, through Providence, as he believed, united behind a chosen leader." These lines from George's "The New Reich" fascinated Webern:

> Er sprengt die ketten fegt auf trümmerstätten
> Die ordnung, geißelt die verlaufnen heim
> Ins ewige recht wo großes wiederum groß ist
> Herr wiederum herr, zucht wiederum zucht, er heftet
> Das wahre sinnbild auf das völkische banner
> Er führt durch sturm und grausige signale
> Des frührots seiner treuen schar zum werk
> Des wachen tags und pflanzt das Neue Reich.[33]

At same time Webern corresponded with friends in the emigration in Switzerland and consorted with a Jewish friend until the friend went underground as a "U-Boat." [Ed. note: People who went underground to escape the attentions of the authorities were called, and called themselves, "submarines."] In the middle of the war in Vienna he introduced the Bavarian composer, Karl Amadeus Hartmann, to a work of Arnold Schönberg. Webern spoke "so glowingly of the work that I felt like the person that Virgil led through heaven and hell," reported Hartmann back home. Indeed, he reported also that Webern earnestly advocated the opinion "for the sake of dear order, *every* authority must be respected and the state in which one lived must be recognized at any price. His goodwill toward those who would press him to the wall is incredible."[34] The majority of Webern's children and nieces and nephews were close to the National Socialist movement; a son-in-law was an SA man, his son Peter von Webern

---

[33]Ibid., p. 481. "He breaks the chains, to the ruins brings / order, drives the lost home / to the eternal law where great is anew great / Lord again lord, / discipline redoubled disciplined, he affixes / the true symbol to the people's banner / he leads through the storm and eerie signals / of the dawn his loyal followers to the work / of the bright day and plants the New Reich."

[34]Ibid., p. 492.

was an illegal [Editor's note: "Illegals" were those Austrians who joined the NSDAP before the Anschluss and were members of the party while it was outlawed in Austria.] and wrote still on 31 January 1945 from Znaim that one must fight and work "until the victory is ours." (He died shortly thereafter as the result of a wound suffered in an air raid) [35] Webern considered it expedient that a bust of Gustav Mahler "that for more than a decade had held a place of honor in his home, be banned to the seclusion of his bedroom in order that it escape the watchful eyes of Nazi-sympathizers."[36] In Vienna proscribed, Webern was nevertheless allowed in 1943 to travel with his works to a concert in Switzerland. Webern returned to Vienna, where he continued to be proscribed. Few histories have yet so vividly depicted the schizophrenic existence that people could lead during the Nazi period as the Moldenhauers' biography of Anton von Webern.

Walter Goldinger, the biographer of Miklas, reports that "He developed plans for pilgrimages in the Greater German Reich and, still in March 1945, saw not even a glimmer of a resurrection of Austria, rather only the threatening clouds that were approaching the West from the East. As so many Austrians, he subscribed to the romantic notion of Austrian demands for leadership in Germany.[37]

The Reichs-romance played a great role in Austria of the first decades of this century; a contemporary sceptic—although Catholic and legitimist—Ernst Karl Winter, even criticized it as "Reichs-mysticism."[38] *Das Neue Reich* was not only Stefan George's volume from 1921 that fascinated Webern; that was

---

[35]Ibid., p. 544.

[36]Ibid., p. 482.

[37]Goldinger, *Miklas*, ibid., p. 120.

[38]Ernst Karl Winter, *Monarchie und Arbeiterschaft* (supplement 1 to the *Wiener Politische Blätter*, 1 October 1936), republished in Karl Hans Heinz, *E. K. Winter. Ein Katholik zwischen Österreichs Fronten 1933-1938* (Vienna, Köln, Graz, 1984), p. 270.

also the name of a Catholic periodical, *Das Neue Reich und seine Begründung* as well as the title of the main chapter in Karl Renner's book on the foundations and the goals for development of the Austro-Hungarian Monarchy of 1906! In the transformation from monarchy to republic, from a great empire to a small state, in the vacillation between independence and Anschluss, the Reichs-romance bloomed.[39] Seipel's words from 1928, that the Austrians were, according to their whole nature, "Great State People," and that it is no great task for the inhabitants of the Carolingian Eastern March and the heirs of the conquerors of the Turks "to till our own little garden and stand against the incursion of the foreigner," are often cited.[40]

The Reichs-romance offers the key to Austrian self-consciousness in those transitional decades from the demise of Old Austria until the genesis of the Second Republic. It existed in different variations, and it would be a mistake to connect them all to Hitlerism and the Third Reich. It existed in the Catholic camp, and the Catholic Convention in Vienna in September 1933 overflowed with invocations of a romantic Reichs-idea. It existed in a confessionally unfettered variation in the historical works of Heinrich von Srbik, and it is not astonishing that the successors of Srbik are imbued with a special interest for the project of the German History Museum in Berlin. There were, in a continuation

---

[39] The work by Klaus Breuning, *Die Vision des Reiches. Deutscher Katholizismus zwischen Demokratie und Diktatur (1929-1934)* (Munich, 1969), is outstanding and has two informative segments on Austrian publications, pp. 25-38 and 253-265. A Catholic Reichs-idea was strongly expressed in Schuschnigg's speech before the general German Catholic Convention in Vienna on 9 September 1933, published as a brochure under the title, "Kurt Schuschnigg, Die Sendung des deutschen Volkes im christlichen Abendlande" (Vienna, 1933).

[40] Seipel in a letter to Wilhelm Bauer on 31 July 1928, cited in Viktor Reimann, *Zu groß für Österreich—Seipel und Bauer im Kampf um die Erste Republik* (Vienna, Frankfurt, Zürich, 1968), pp. 190-193.

of the "Forty-Eighter" tradition, also Social Democratic Reichsromantics.[41]

Otto Schulmeister has described in the collective volume, *Vom Reich zu Österreich*, what "Reich" could signify to generational contemporaries of the (Catholic) youth movement of the 1930s: "Reich—that rings today like a romantic-pubescent extravagance; that the word occurs in Austria, has something to do with universalistic demands, indeed, the name could be a word of destiny, that has completely paled away. In any case, one thing it did not mean to us in the 1930s: Hitler, the Third Reich, the National Socialist regime. Messianism, German, especially Austrian mission were bound together in the conception of a renewed political order for the small-state survivors of a world that seemed to have slipped off the tracks and become pointless."[42]

"Small-state," "pointless"; after the Third Reich and the Second World War it was not that any more. "We are Austrians again." This entry from a Viennese diary (unpublished) from April 1945 characterizes a thousand-times-lived experience. The rediscovery and retrieving of confidence that had been lost, that perhaps only through the loss became worthwhile or new and higher valued—all this is a considerable component of the Austrian self-consciousness after 1945.

It is in order today to oppose the new lie about the so-called "life's lie" of the Second Republic. There are still enough members of the "generation of 1945" who are able to witness that they experienced, and how much they experienced, the reestablishment of Austria after 1945 as a "liberation." The writer of these lines, even when he was just fifteen, sixteen years old can

---

[41] Cf. among others Ernst Panzenböck, *Ein deutscher Traum. Die Anschlußidee und Anschlußpolitik bei Karl Renner und Otto Bauer* (Vienna, 1985); further, Günter Fellner, *Ludo Moritz Hartmann und die österreichische Geschichtswissenschaft* (Vienna, Salzburg, 1985), especially pp. 269-270.

[42] Otto Schulmeister, "Reifeprüfung auf Tod und Leben." In: Jochen Jung, ed., *Vom Reich zu Österreich* (Salzburg, 1983), p. 155.

testify to this also. The experience of the rebirth of Austria in 1945 was for him a fundamental experience that marked his entire unfolding life. It is time to take a stand against the new fad: "All (or almost all) Austrians were for the Anschluss, Nazis," etc.[43] The cultivation of identity, the state- and nation-building of the Second Republic, as Gerhard Botz has rightly written, was successful not through uniting, but through distilling from a larger collection of political sovereignties the continued existence of a more or less strong cultural connection with other nations."[44] "Austria," wrote the most significant political thinker of the Danubian Monarchy in the nineteenth century, Josef von Eötvös, "is to be regarded as entirely a product of history."[45] Naturally, Eötvös had in mind the Empire of Austria. Indeed, that is valid even today. Austrian history was never the history of an ethnic or linguistic entity; it was always, and is today, the

---

[43]Cf. *supra* pp. 11 and 12, as well as Gerald Stourzh, "Die Außenpolitik der österreichischen Bundesregierung gegenüber der nationalsozialistischen Bedrohung." In the collective volume, *Österreich, Deutschland und die Mächte* (as in *supra*, footnote 10), p.179.

One should point out a singularity of the Hitler referendum of 10 April 1938, with its ominous 99.73% yes votes in Austria, because it is almost always overlooked: those persons designated Jews or "effective Jews" according to the National Socialist laws—those, as a National Socialist functionary wrote, who "are presented as normal citizens in the previous (i.e., Austrian) lists" (!) were not eligible to vote; nor were those in protective custody or who were political opponents admitted to the electoral registry; nor were Gypsies. This indicates that, conservatively estimated, many more than 150,000 adult Austrians, according to a probably exaggerated estimate by G. Botz, even 8% of the pre-Anschluss qualified Austrian voters—and exactly those who would, in a free election, almost exclusively vote "no"—were not even allowed to the polls. Then the ominous 99.73% looks quite different! Cf. also the reference in *"Anschluß" 1938*, published by the Dokumentationsarchiv des österreichischen Widerstandes (Vienna 1988), pp. 471f., 490-494, and 523.

[44]Botz, *Anschlußproblem*, p. 179. (see footnote 10 *supra*).

[45]Josef Freiherr von Eötvös, *Die Garantien der Macht und Einheit Österreichs*, 3d. ed. (Leipzig, 1859), p. 85. The book at first appeared without the author's name.

history of lands brought together and in many ways grown together[46] The more than four decades of history that have passed since 1945 also count as part of the history of Austria. Within one to two generations much has changed. When two Austrians—in England, let us say—speak German with each other, and they are asked: "Are you German?" most Austrians under sixty years of age would answer spontaneously: "No, we are Austrians." Fifty or sixty years ago, the answer would probably have been more complicated, something like: "Yes, but from Austria," or "We are German-Austrians."

Two things should be made clear.

First, neither the historical and juridically grounded conviction of the forcible end of Austrian independence in March 1938, nor the development of an Austrian consciousness of identity in the past four to five decades should prevent us from seeing a common moral responsibility of Austrians and Germans during the National Socialist time. On the most humiliating thing done by compatriots in this century, in this land to their Jewish fellow humans, I would just like to report the words of Chief Rabbi Dr. Israel Taglicht as he was forced to wash the street in his prayer-gown in Vienna,"I wash God's earth—if it thus pleases God, it pleases me also." Here, in shame for what was done, in reverence for such love of God, we all can only fall silent.[47]

---

[46]Cf. also Gerald Stourzh, "Der Umfang der österreichischen Geschichte." In: Herwig Wolfram and Walter Pohl, eds., *Geschichte Österreichs. Probleme ihrer Darstellung*. Veröffentlichungen der Kommission für die Geschichte Österreichs der Österreichischen Akademie der Wissenschaften (Vienna, 1991).

[47]On this subject see also Herbert Rosenkranz, *Verfolgung und Selbstbehauptung—Die Juden in Österreich 1938-1945* (Vienna, 1978), p. 23, as well as Thomas Chaimowicz, "'Lacht nicht, ich wasche Gottes Erde.' Als Jude und Legitimist im Wien von 1938." In: Thomas Chorherr, ed., *Anatomie eines Jahres* (Vienna, 1987), pp. 292-299. To the most important publications on the outbreak and consequences of unbridled anti-Semitism that would no longer be held in check by the norms of equal civil rights, as they obtained in Austria until 11 March 1938, one numbers: Jonny Moser, "Die Katastrophe der Juden in Öster-

Although in the years most recently passed much has been caught up in Austrian historiography, the systematic assimilation of the National Socialist time into Austrian republican history remains on the agenda of historical science in Austria. It will be important to pay attention to the moment in time of the inner rediscovery of Austria after 1938. The magnificent poem to Austria by Gerhard Fritsch begins with the words:

> Eitel genannt belächelt ausposaunt
> bezweifelt totgesagt, verraten verboten.[48]

So difficult is it, indeed impossible, for us to put ourselves in that place and time, given the current fundament of untroubled Austrian self-consciousness of contemporary Austrians, that we must, more than we wish to, take the word "totgesagt" ("pronounced dead") more seriously as it describes the time from spring 1938 to the outbreak of the war—despite praiseworthy examples to the contrary in the Resistance and in the Emigration. The anti-National Socialist freedom movement of the Augustinian Chorherr, Karl Roman Scholz, called itself at first the "German Freedom Movement"; only at the outbreak of war did

---

reich—ihre Voraussetezungen und ihre Überwindung." In: *Der Gelbe Stern in Österreich,* Studia Judaica Austriaca, vol. V (Eisenstadt, 1977), pp. 67-134; Gerhard Botz, *Wohnungspolitik und Judendeportation in Wien 1938 bis 1945. Zur Funktion des Antisemitismus als Ersatz nationalsozialistscher Sozialpolitik* (Vienna, Salzburg, 1975); Hans Safrian und Hans Witek, *Und keiner war dabei—Dokumente des alltäglichen Antisemitismus in Wien 1938* (Vienna, 1985). The eerie conventionality of Adolf Eichmann's words are hardly known in Austria: "Long live Germany. Long live Argentina. Long live Austria. Those are the three lands with which I am most closely bound. I shall not forget them," cited in Hannah Arendt, *Eichmann in Jerusalem—Ein Bericht von der Banalität des Bösen* (Munich, 1964), p. 300.

[48]"Vainly named, smirkingly blared forth / in doubt pronounced dead, betrayed, forbidden." Gerhard Fritsch's poem to Austria, *Dieses Land,* composed in 1966 on commission of the periodical, *Die Furche,* on the occasion of the National Holiday, is contained in Fritsch's *Gesammelte Gedichte* (Salzburg, Otto Müller), and has been many times reprinted.

Scholz make the change of name to "Austrian Freedom Movement." Even then his group was in search of a Greater Austria, not yet for a small Austria. It does not derogate from the courage of Karl Roman Scholz, and our respect for his martyrdom, when we ponder the moment of the inner re-discovery of Austria. Before his execution in 1944, Scholz composed these lines:

> Ich grüße dich, mein Österreich!
> Euch Freunde! und das schöne Wien!
> Gott schirme und geleite Euch
> zu einer bessren Zukunft hin![49]

Second, it is also to be made clear that the Republic of Austria since 1945 is not a part of a trifurcated Germany, as the distinguished historian in Kiel, Karl Dietrich Erdmann, in a now famous speech in April of 1985 proposed: "Three states—two nations—one people."[50] A "German history since the partition," that would be composed from three states that arose from the collapse of the Third Reich (and that is Erdmann's notion) appears to be extremely problematic. A German history fashioned in that manner, of a "tripartite Germany," hypothesizes a "normal year" as a point of departure, the year 1938, and the Greater German Reich as the framework for what is to be considered Ger-

---

[49] "I hail thee, my Austria! / you friends! and beautiful Vienna! / God protect and guide you / to a better future." On the change of name of the Scholz group, see Edda Pfeifer, *Beiträge zur Geschichte der österreichischen Widerstandsbewegung des konservativen Lagers 1938-1940. Die Gruppe Karl Roman Scholz, Dr. Karl Lederer und Dr. Jakob Kastelic*, (unpublished dissertation, University of Vienna, 1963), p. 93. The poem, *Ich grüße dich, mein Österreich* is reprinted in Franz Stundner, "Das katholische Lager." In: *Widerstand und Verfolgung in Niederösterreich 1934-1945*, vol. III (Vienna, 1987), p. 78.

[50] Karl Dietrich Erdmann, *Drei Staaten—zwei Nationen—ein Volk? Überlegungen zu einer deutschen Geschichte seit der Teilung* (Kiel, 1985). Republication, among others, in the small volume, Karl Dietrich Erdmann, *Die Spur Österreichs in der deutschen Geschichte. Drei Staaten—zwei Nationen—ein Volk.* Manesse Bücherei, vol. XXVII (Zürich, 1989), pp. 7-37.

man history since 1945. The separation and reestablishment of the Republic of Austria in 1945 bore a fundamentally different character from that process of division that led to the establishment and final consolidation of the Federal Republic of Germany and the German Democratic Republic. It is noteworthy that the years-long practice of speaking of "both" German states or of "two" German states, in the last few years has been replaced by reference to "three" German states or even, as with Erdmann, to "tripartite Germany." This is what I describe as a tendency toward a "re-engrossment" of Austria; it may not be impossible that this change of speech has underlying motives that are akin to the disappointed hopes for re-unification in the Adenauer era. Three German states were perhaps less painful to speak of than just of "both" German states, whose re-unification was not foreseeable. One German people in three German states? How is this thesis of Erdmann's to be reconciled with the preamble to the constitution of the Federal Republic of Germany, in which is written: "The whole German people is charged, in free self-determination, to accomplish the unity and freedom of Germany"? Are we included in that?

The thesis of "tripartite Germany" overlooks, in any case, a connection that has been growing ever closer for four decades, the one existing among German Swiss, the Federal Republic of Germany, and Austria in all areas of linguistic culture—in the realm of literature, the press, the theatre, universities and sciences, as well as in the areas of medicine and especially television. How far, over and above that, does the Second Republic of Austria show structural analogies to Switzerland, in the finally positive acceptance of small-state consciousness, in the acceptance of permanent neutrality—this is also quite lost if a conception of "German history after 1945" draws in Austrian but cuts out German Switzerland.

The overlappings, the contiguities, the occasional fusions of later and most recent Austrian and German history are complex; we study them, we recognize them, we do not suppress them.

Let us do this as good neighbors, and let us not subsume the one under the other.

From Reich to republic—the transition was a complex one, as the reader of the foregoing pages may well gather. Twice in the first half of our century has history transported Austria from a Reich to a republic: from the Reich of the Habsburg Monarchy into the First Republic, and from the Greater German Reich into the Second Republic. The final transition, from the consciousness of Austrians as "Grand State People," as Ignaz Seipel once expressed it during the First Republic,[51] to the affirmation of the small-state republic, was a stubbornly difficult one. The transition was not yet successful after 1918; it was successful only after 1945. With many a frightening glance into the mirror of its own history, but in the consciousness of a firm identity, Austria of 1994 should be in a position to face the fundamentally and manifoldly radically changed Europe of the 1990s. We very much wish it for Austria.

---

[51] See note 29 *supra*.

Reflections on the Anschluss by an American Eyewitness

R. John Rath

A few minutes before 8:00 p.m. on March 11, 1938, Chancellor Kurt von Schuschnigg announced that he was "yielding to force" and resigning as chancellor of Austria. That same night my good American friend George Shuster, former associate editor of *Commonweal* and later president of Hunter College, spent most of the night convincing Nazi patrols, composed largely of teenagers, that they should allow him to return to Vienna from Graz. Shuster had been asked by the Austrian chancellor, who no longer knew what Austrian officials he could trust to make an unbiased report, to travel to western and southern Austria in his own American car, chauffeured by one of the chancellor's drivers, to sound out public opinion and report to him personally on the strength of National Socialism in the Tirol, Carinthia, and Styria.

A couple of months later my closest Austrian friend in 1937-1938, Alexander Issatschenko, personal secretary of Baron Hans von Hammerstein-Equard, Austrian state secretary for cultural propaganda, explained to me when I visited him in Ljubljana why I had not seen him in Vienna the last two or three weeks before March 11. Warned that Austrian Police President Michael Skubl was using a series of speeches he was delivering in Denmark, Norway, and Sweden as a cover to make some kind of secret deal with the National Socialists, the chancellor had sent Issatschenko to check Skubl's movements. My friend followed Skubl until he went to a Berlin nightclub for a secret meeting with Hermann Göring, whereupon Issatschenko returned to

Vienna to bring this information to the Austrian head of state.

Although there had been forebodings about a possible coup after rumors leaked out that Chancellor Schuschnigg's meeting with Hitler at Berchtesgaden on February 12, practically no one, not even convinced Austrian Nazis, felt that the end would come so soon. Perhaps we should have been more apprehensive over Austria's future than we actually were when we learned about Arthur Seyss-Inquart's appointment as Minister of Interior and Edmund Glaise-Horstenau's as Minister of Defense. Yet we were not especially perturbed, since we had heard that Schuschnigg regarded Seyss-Inquart, a personal friend of his, as one of the most trustworthy of all the German national leaders. As for Glaise-Horstenau, he was an archivist, the director of the Kriegsarchiv, and as a historian I naively believed that an archivist could always be trusted. How wrong I was. Since the Minister of Interior controlled the security forces and official communications with the provinces, the Nazis were now in a position to nullify any defensive measures Schuschnigg might undertake to protect Austria. A few hours after he was appointed minister Seyss-Inquart was on his way to Berlin to confer with Hitler.

From the outset Seyss-Inquart worked hard to undermine Austria's defenses. He repeatedly countermanded Schuschnigg's orders against the Nazis and personally took part in Nazi demonstrations. In pursuance of carefully laid out plans, large groups of Nazis would congregate at specific points in a town or city, prominently wearing *Hakenkreuz* insignia and loudly chanting Nazi slogans. In all other parts of the town no single person could be found wearing Nazi badges at that particular time. Frequently, after one of the demonstrations, baskets full of discarded *Hakenkreuz* emblems could be found on the streets.

The new Minister of Interior began systematically to disable the police and security forces, some of whom had secretly been pro-Nazi all the time. Pressure was put on governmental officials, businessmen, professionals, students, in fact, persons from all walks of life, to join the Nazi Party so that they would be able to share the spoils or avoid trouble after Hitler took control of the country. Friends and acquaintances whose loyalty to the government I had never suspected now began to talk openly about what a fine leader Hitler was. Other Austrians panicked. In increasing numbers frightened people were preparing to emigrate. Theaters, restaurants, and cafés became increasingly empty.

Then suddenly the supporters of Schuschnigg's government were electrified. After long days of silence, on February 24 Chancellor Schuschnigg made a rousing speech in parliament in which he essentially declared: "So far and no farther!" His words were greeted with frantic applause, not only in parliament but by hordes of people jammed together in front of the building. I shall never forget how excited and happy many of us were to see Schuschnigg on top of the Burgtor, obliquely across the Ringstrasse from the parliament, waving to an enthusiastic crowd below. At that moment my wife and I—and no doubt many Austrians—felt that Austria could be saved.

The Nazis reacted furiously to the chancellor's challenge, especially in Graz, where, at a Nazi demonstration of twenty thousand attended by Seyss-Inquart, plans were made for another gathering of sixty-five thousand Nazis in defiance of the government's ban on meetings. Meanwhile the police and civil service were torn asunder by the conflicting orders of the chancellor and the minister of interior. By early March the Nazis had effectively destabilized Austria to the point where the chancellor could no longer count on the loyalty of his key officials or the reliability of the police or the army.

It was at this critical moment that Schuschnigg took his last desperate gamble to save Austria. In a speech at Innsbruck on March 9 he called for a plebiscite on Sunday, March 13, for Austrians to vote on whether or not they were in favor of a free and independent Austria. We "innocents abroad" became deliriously happy, for we knew that, according to the estimates of nearly all foreign observers then in Austria, only one-third of the Austrians actually wanted union with Germany, while two-thirds were opposed. (Of course, in some individual cities such as Linz, Graz, and Innsbruck the pro-Nazi element was much stronger.) It must be admitted that only about one-half of the anti-Anschluss populace actually supported the Schuschnigg government. Yet many of the other half, the Social Democrats, who had been bitterly alienated by the February 1934 civil war, came out in force to demonstrate against the Hitlerites during the last few days before that fateful March 11th.

In actual fact, calling on a plebiscite proved to be the worst thing the chancellor could have done. The challenge was a slap in the *Führer's* face which he could not have left unanswered, for the results would definitely prove the falsity of the Nazi claims that ninety-some percent of desperate Austrians longing to return to the Reich were being held in chains by the Schuschnigg dictatorship. Up to then Hitler had been employing salami-tactics, merely hoping to undermine the government to the point where the German-nationals and local Nazis could gradually take more and more control and then ask for some kind of arrangement with Germany that would lead to eventual absorption by the Reich.

Now that Hitler's hand was forced, he acted swiftly, decisively, and violently. To him the plebiscite was clearly an attack on his prestige. Göring regarded it as a definite violation of the Berchtesgaden agreement. On the 10th, Hitler ordered the two army corps commanders who were to play a leading role in an attack on Austria to draw up operational plans to cross the Austrian border. Early on the 11th the Germans closed the border at Salzburg. Emissary after emissary landed at Aspern throughout the course of the day. After several ultimatums had been handed to him Schuschnigg resigned just before a final time limit expired at 8:00 p.m. Mussolini had refused to accept all telephone calls from Vienna; the French government was unable to act because it was undergoing another cabinet crisis; and the British refused to act without the French.

Immediately after listening to Schuschnigg's speech we hurried over to the Shusters. We found Doris in tears. She had not heard a word from her husband since he had started on his semiofficial trip on behalf of the federal chancellor. While anxiously awaiting his return we lamented the fate of the Austrian people. None of us expected ever to be able to come back to an Austria that was not an integral part of the Third Reich.

Shuster finally arrived in the wee hours of the morning, and the Raths returned to their own living quarters. Two or three hours after we managed to get to bed I was awakened by a telephone call from George Shuster asking me to help him smuggle Ernst Karl Winter, a former vice-mayor of Vienna, out of Austria. The plan was to take him to a monastery near the Hungarian border in the hope that the monks would hide him until he would be able to sneak across the frontier. We went in Shuster's car with United States insignia. The chauffeur was one of former Chancellor Schuschnigg's. Our plan was for me to make the first effort to convince security guards at checkpoints that George and I were wealthy Americans who had hired a guide (Winter) and driver to show us art collections in the Burgenland—a weak ruse since there were very few art treasures in the part of the Burgenland through which we were driving. It was risky for George to show his passport since the German government had refused to grant him a visa because of books he had written about the treatment of Catholics by the Nazi government. We were stopped every ten or twelve kilometers by gendarmes heading bands of ten to fifteen Nazi youngsters. At Bruck, a city through which we had to pass on our return trip, we were questioned by a polite, middle-aged gendarme, surrounded by the usual claque of juveniles with Nazi arm bands. He was the first official we ran across who did not limit his questioning just to me. Seeing that I was unsuccessful, George tried to persuade him that Winter was just a guide, again in vain. Winter now had to pull out his identity papers. Fortunately for us, the gendarme was a decent, civilized old-line Austrian security officer. When he saw Winter's papers he exclaimed, "Ach, Vizebürgermeister!" but then added, "Fahren

Sie fort." Nonetheless, our mission was unsuccessful. Two monasteries near the Hungarian border refused to hide Winter since local Nazis had threatened to set them on fire the previous evening. On the way back to Vienna from the second monastery we stopped for a while in a clump of trees near the border debating whether we should leave Winter there in the hope that he could find his way to Hungary or take him back to the capital. The issue was decided by a wagon pulled by a couple of oxen. Since we did not know whether the driver might report what he saw to the local Nazis, there seemed to be nothing to do but take Winter back home.

In Vienna the Nazis launched a campaign of terrorism the very moment Chancellor Schuschnigg resigned. The day Shuster and I vainly tried to smuggle Winter out of Austria, my wife, Isabel, went to Herzmansky, the largest department store on Mariahilferstrasse, which was Jewish-owned, to buy some needles and thread. Nazis were all around the store intimidating people and trying to prevent them from entering it. Inside were a lot of terrified clerks with no customers. On that same day, and many others, we saw Nazis rounding up Jews and other anti-Nazis and forcing them to scrub off pro-Austrian insignias and slogans from the sidewalks, while they jeered and kicked and caned them if they were too tired or hesitated to work at the feverish pace demanded of them. In other places I saw Nazi SA or SS men shutting down and seizing Jewish-owned shops. These and other brutal acts perpetrated by the Nazis demonstrated only too well that when it comes to a matter of survival, or in some cases, just of getting ahead, the line separating man from beast is a faint one if it exists at all.

Minute plans had been devised long before March 11 in regard to which patrol was to arrest a particular person immediately after the Nazis gained control of the government. Schuschnigg himself was incarcerated in the Metropole Hotel in Vienna for eighteen months before he was sent to Dachau. Fifteen years later he gave me a fascinating account of the childish pranks concocted by his guards at the Metropole to torture him whenever he tried to sleep. A large number of other officials were also arrested during the next few days. For the deliberate purpose of engendering an atmosphere of fear among opponents of the new regime, warnings were often circulated that certain persons would soon be incarcerated. For example, one night one of our acquaintances came to our living quarters to implore me to come quickly to her home. When I arrived I found her family engaged in an emotional debate over whether her brother should immediately try to escape by swimming across the icy waters of the Danube to Czechoslovakia or whether he should momentarily just try to hide himself in Austria. He had been threatened with arrest because five years earlier some secret pro-Nazi on a work detail had overheard him denounce Hitler as a "Schweinehund." Frightened Jews were resorting to foolhardy means to get out. My tutor who had given me a dozen or so lessons in Italian, since we were planning to go to Italy in May, implored me to divorce Isabel and marry her. She promised that after she obtained the United States citizenship she naively believed that all spouses of United States citizens automatically acquired she would raise no objection if I would then divorce her and remarry Isabel. (She was truly desperate!)

The fear engendered by the numerous arrests and other acts of violence greatly augmented the effectiveness of the Nazi technique of propaganda. All cultural outlets—public meetings, schools, newspapers, magazines, books, music, theater, art—were systematically used to instill a limited number of highly emotion-evoking phrases into the minds of the people. One of our American friends, a piano student, was forbidden to perform in an all-Mendelssohn concert that had been arranged for a couple of weeks after the Anschluss. She was even prohibited from continuing to play any Mendelssohn numbers. When she complained loudly about this censorship, she was finally allowed to continue practicing, but her teacher admonished: "Aber spiele leise, sehr leise!"

It is obvious that the Nazi-staged plebiscite on April 10, 1938, was a fraud and that 99.73 percent of the Austrians were not in favor of union with Germany, as the Nazis claimed. As reported to us by Austrian friends who voted, the Nazi election-officials repeatedly intimidated voters. Conditions at the polls amounted to open voting. Moreover, a "no" vote meant only one thing: danger for any voter who dared to express open opposition to Nazi policies and practices. Then, too, evidence indicates that the votes often were never actually counted.

Be that as it may, it is obvious that by the middle of April substantially more than one-third of the Austrian people, perhaps even a majority, approved of union with Germany. Cardinal Innitzer's appeal to the Austrians to vote in favor of union was not without influence. The two-prong campaign of intense, emotional propaganda combined with frightening terror was achieving noticeable results. Before we left Austria for Italy early in May, 1938, various of my Austrian friends who had been strongly anti-Nazi before March were already beginning to voice sentiments such as: "Yes, I am not in favor of Hitler, but he is right when he . . ."

But there were ways to counter Nazi terrorism, as Isabel and I found out while playing a minor role in the underground during the brief interval between the Anschluss and the time we left Austria. Since the Shusters were *personae non grata*, they found it prudent to leave Vienna a few days after March 11th. They entrusted us with sixty-five documents concerning the treatment of the Catholic Church in Germany. They were of such a nature that, as George admonished, if the Nazis got hold of them quite a few heads would roll, and Isabel and I might possibly be in considerable trouble. They also put in our hands money left behind by various persons who had fled and could not take it with them. By the latter part of April we had over a quarter of a million marks in our custody. George assured me that everything would be picked up before we left Austria.

As for our minor role in the underground, as innocent

Americans we could function best by warning persons that orders had been issued for their arrest. A secret operative within police or Gestapo headquarters would procure the information and pass it on to a confidant, who would hand it to us. How? Not by telephone, for lines were constantly being tapped. Not in person. The porter in every house in the city was a potential Gestapo agent, and many were. Nor by exchanging information while quietly walking in a park or secluded alley. We had learned about various instances when Gestapo agents would separate such persons and ask them individually what they had been talking about. There was only one safe way: go to a café that was a popular Nazi hangout, join in the fun, and pass on the information *sotto voce*.

As May began to approach we became more and more nervous about all the things left in our custody, since we had many weeks earlier bought our tickets and made all other arrangements to leave in early May for Italy via Budapest and Ljubljana. Finally, on 9 April 1938, when Hitler made his second speech in Vienna, the person whom Shuster had promised would pick up the incriminating testimony and money arrived in our living quarters. He was Max Jordan, the NBC head for Central and Southeastern Europe, who had come to Vienna to supervise the broadcasting of Hitler's speech. During his free moments he went around Vienna collecting money for persons who had fled and getting valuable or incriminating papers. He mixed them up with the transcripts of the *Führer's* speech and took them to his plane at Aspern Airport, which was filled with hundreds of Gestapo agents and policemen. I have always felt that foreign journalists were among the genuine, unsung heroes of the underground.

Now we had only one more reason to worry: how to get all my research notes and quite a few books back to the United States. While the archival documents and volumes on early nineteenth-century Italian-Austrian history would probably be regarded as rather harmless by a German customs agent, the few notes and considerable number of books I had dealing with the Schuschnigg era, most of which were on the Nazi *verboten* list, would definitely arouse the suspicions of an even half-alert customs official. On the day of our departure for Hungary we took all these notes and books and all our other belongings with us in eleven suitcases, some of them quite large. I was especially worried when we approached the border and I saw how thoroughly the Germans custom officials were checking the passports and examining every cubic centimeter of the contents of the baggage of the first occupants in our compartment with whom they talked. Finally our turn came. Almost involuntarily, when the official asked me what I had been doing in Austria the past nine months I pulled out a letter provided me by the Social Science Research Council addressed to "whomever it may concern" expressing the thanks of the foundation for any assistance that might be given to me in my research. The letter had a nice gold-embossed seal in the lower left-hand corner. Sensing that the official who questioned me was a lower rank bureaucrat who knew no English and who would very likely be greatly impressed by a gold seal, I handed it to him without saying a word in reply to his query. It worked like a charm. The official not only did not open a single one of our eleven bags, but he apologized profusely for holding up the train while he continued making careful searches of the bags of all the other passengers.

After we crossed the border into Hungary a young girl in our compartment, who had been asked by the border officials if she were Jewish, broke into tears and sobbed most of the way to Budapest. Although Hungary was anything but a free, democratic country, Isabel and I really celebrated that night in the Hungarian capital. Among other things, we drank toasts to a gold-embossed seal on a letter of introduction. That seal was to provide the world with another historian at the expense of an unhappy, disgruntled, and, in this case, unsuccessful, northwestern Kansas wheat-farmer. Broke as we were, I could never have afforded spending another year collecting material for another thesis.

Prelude to Anschluss: The Great War and the Shattered International and Domestic Consensus

Bruce F. Pauley

Put in the simplest terms, the annexation of Austria by Nazi Germany occurred in March 1938 because a majority of the European governments and people did not feel politically, militarily, or, perhaps most important of all, morally committed to maintaining the Paris Peace Settlement. This lack of consensus was especially apparent in Austria, where most of its people during much of the interwar period denied not only the legitimacy of the international boundaries drawn up at St. Germain, but also had serious doubts about their own democratic government.

The prewar international consensus was by no means as universally accepted as it would appear in the hindsight of a nostalgic postwar generation. None of the Balkan states accepted the status quo; of the Great Powers, Russia and Italy in particular had imperialistic ambitions. Yet none of the Great Powers wanted a drastic overhaul in the international boundaries of Europe and no one questioned the legitimacy of the governments of the other Great Powers to the extent that they wished to foster revolutions or see states disappear.

Within Austria-Hungary there were certainly many people desiring political or social reform, or both, especially among the intelligentsia. It is extremely doubtful, however, whether a majority of the Habsburg subjects repudiated the very existence of the Dual Monarchy; and only among the Italians of Austria and the Serbs of Hungary and Bosnia and Herzegovina is it possible that a majority wished to secede. By contrast, postwar national minorities usually believed that an improvement in their status could come only with the destruction of the state into which they had been unwillingly incorporated.

Of all the Austro-Hungarian nationalities (unless Jews are counted as such), the German-speaking people were undoubtedly the most loyal to the Habsburg dynasty and state. Only the followers of Georg von Schönerer's minuscule Pan-German party had any desire to secede and join the German Empire and they lost heavily in the elections of 1907.[1] Even Social Democrats, though eager for political and social reform, did not advocate the destruction of Austria-Hungary or wish to see its dynasty replaced with a republican form of government. Zionism was also a tiny and declining faction among German-Austrian Jews.

The emperor-king, Franz Joseph, though hardly a charismatic figure, had become, after a shaky start in the Revolution of 1848, the Italian War of 1859, the failed constitutions of the early 1860s, and the defeat by Prussia in 1866, a beloved and almost universally revered symbol of authority by German and non-German-speaking Austro-Hungarians alike before the end of the century. He was almost "vergöttert" as one elderly woman in Burgenland told this writer in 1958.

Postwar Europe in general and Austria in particular present a picture which at every level contrasts sharply with the prewar era. The Paris Peace Settlement was rejected by the defeated states, above all Germany, Austria, Hungary and the Soviet Union. However, even victorious powers such as Italy and Great Britain did not accept its arrangements as just and permanent.

Fundamental disagreements during the interwar years even extended to the question of how the victorious states should maintain their security. France and Italy, along with the new or

---

[1] Andrew G. Whiteside, *The Socialism of Fools: Georg von Schönerer and Austrian Pan-Germanism* (Berkeley and Los Angeles: University of California Press, 1975), pp. 241, 282.

greatly enlarged countries of East-Central Europe—Poland and the Little Entente states of Czechoslovakia, Romania, and Yugoslavia—defined security in terms of traditional power politics, i.e., land and strategically defensible borders; the Anglo-Saxon powers looked to their navies or the League of Nations, or both. Consequently, the Italians successfully claimed the Brenner Pass along with 225,000 German-speaking South Tiroleans, and the Czechs, with strong French support, succeeded in making the Sudeten Mountains their northern boundary along with well over three million German-speaking Austrians.

The many one-sided uses of non-ethnic criteria to establish boundaries created injustices, and the injustices created insecurity in those states which were stuffed with disgruntled national minorities. President Wilson's ideal of self-determination was so abused that the intellectual and moral foundations of the peace were undermined, causing major difficulty during the interwar period in arousing popular support for the forceful maintenance of the Paris Settlement. By ceding nearly four million German-Austrians along with vital natural resources to Austria's neighbors, the Allies also contributed significantly to the Austrians' growing conviction that their country could recover the lost territories and become *lebensfähig* only through an Anschluss with Germany.

France was consistently and adamantly opposed to an Anschluss at the Paris Conference and throughout most of the remainder of the interwar years, although never to the point of being willing to give a binding military guarantee to Austria. By contrast, the passivity and equanimity with which Britain and the United States accepted the German annexation of Austria in 1938 can already be seen in their reluctant agreement to Austrian independence in 1919. They had opposed France's desire to annex the Rhineland so vehemently that a *quid pro quo* elsewhere seemed necessary. Besides, the Anglo-Saxon powers were no more anxious than France to see postwar Germany larger than the prewar Empire. But many delegates from the English-speaking powers left the conference with guilty consciences;[2] and in the following years their governments were by no means unequivocally hostile toward the Anschluss.[3] Britain's attitude toward Austria was also influenced by its desire to avoid involvement in continental affairs in general, especially those east of the Rhine River. The United Kingdom's commitment to the Empire and its unwillingness to take any action in Europe without the approval of the Commonwealth states, together with its inadequate armaments, especially for land-based combat, conflicted with its traditional policy of "holding the balance of power."

France, although certainly far more committed to the status quo in East Central Europe than Britain, could not reconcile its need to come to the aid of Poland and the Little Entente with the defensive mentality implied in the building of the Maginot Line and in the strictly defensive support the French government received from Great Britain. In the end, France's eastern allies were to be treated more like liabilities than assets.[4] And what held true for France's eastern allies was doubly valid for neutral Austria.

The bitter irony of the Anglo-French acquiescence to the Anschluss in 1938 is that the western democracies were willing to give to the imperialistic Nazi dictatorship that which they had steadfastly denied to the democratic Weimar Republic which had desperately needed some diplomatic victories to shore up its popularity. Italy's foreign policy also suffered from a lack of

---

[2]Charles Seymour and Harold B. Whiteman, Jr., eds., *Letters from the Paris Peace Conference* (New Haven and London: Yale University Press, 1965), p. 268; F.L. Carsten, *The First Austrian Republic 1918-1938: A Study Based on British and Austrian Documents* (Hants, England: Gower/Maurice Temple Smith, 1986), p. 6; Harold Nicholson, *Peacemaking 1919* (New York: Grosset and Dunlap, 1965; originally published in 1933), pp. 165, 187, 193.

[3]Carsten, p. 130.

[4]A.J.P. Taylor, *The Origins of the Second World War* (2nd ed., New York: Fawcett Premier Book, 1966), pp. 39, 42-43.

consensus over fundamental principles. For years Mussolini thought it essential to maintain Austrian independence in order to protect Italy's new conquest in the South Tirol. This policy was epitomized by his military demonstration on the Brenner during the July *Putsch*. On the other hand, he was unwilling to defend Austria unilaterally, especially if such a commitment interfered with his other goals in foreign policy. Ultimately, he was torn between his desire to make satellites out of Austria and Hungary and his passion to enlarge his African empire. When he opted for the latter by invading Ethiopia in October 1935 he had to acknowledge Hitler's preponderant influence in Austria in the July (1936) Agreement, although he did so with misgivings and some equivocations.[5]

The Little Entente countries and Poland were even less a barrier to the Anschluss than the Great Powers of western Europe. Distracted internally by huge, irreconcilable minorities and (with the partial exception of Czechoslovakia) by their economic backwardness, they were equally divided in their foreign policies. The Little Entente could agree only on preventing a Habsburg restoration and a revision of Hungary's boundaries. Only Czechoslovakia showed much interest in stopping the Anschluss, but even it was more concerned about a return of the Habsburgs.[6] Ardent Hungarian revisionism and Austrian legitimism—modest as the latter was—prevented the formation of a Danubian bloc of states which might have opposed German expansionism.[7] Poland merely hoped that Hitler's appetite for revisionism would be appeased in Austria.

The Soviet Union, as one of the losers in the postwar settlement, criticized the treaties for years, including the prohibition of Anschluss. After Hitler's seizure of power, however, the

---

[5] Alfred D. Low, *The Anschluss Movement, 1931-1938, and the Great Powers* (New York: Columbia University Press, 1985), pp. 385, 411.

[6] Ibid., pp. 225-226.

[7] Ibid., p. 167.

Soviet government realized that Austria was the key to German domination of Central Europe and expansion into southeastern Europe. The Soviets, therefore, along with their comrades of the numerically tiny communist party in Austria, reversed their stand on the Anschluss and even went so far as to insist that there was a separate Austrian nationality. This shift in policy, however, was not accompanied by any military commitment to Austria.[8]

American ambassadors to Austria were alarmed by the growing German threat to Austrian independence, but they simply took for granted that stopping Hitler was the duty of Britain, France, or Italy, and certainly not that of the United States.[9]

Thus, Hitler's Germany was the only major European power which had an unambiguous foreign policy, even if Hitler was flexible and opportunistic in the tactics he employed. If Britain, France, Italy, and the Little Entente—not to mention Poland, the Soviet Union and the United States—lacked a consensus among themselves, internationally, or domestically, about the Anschluss, Hitler suffered from no such ambivalence.

From the start of his political career in 1919, or at the latest from the time he wrote the first volume of *Mein Kampf* in 1924, he made the Anschluss his first objective of foreign policy.

> German-Austria [Hitler wrote on the first page of *Mein Kampf*] must return to the great German mother country and not because of any economic considerations. No and again no: even if such a union were unimportant from an economic point of view; yes, if it were harmful, it must nevertheless take place. One blood demands one Reich.[10]

Until the Anschluss itself took place in 1938, Hitler never lost sight of this long-term goal. To be sure, Hitler did not allow

---

[8]Ibid., pp. 296, 308, 314.

[9]Ibid., p. 334.

[10](Boston: Houghton Mifflin, 1943; originally published in 1927).

the Anschluss question to distract him from what he regarded as other more pressing issues. Until 1933 his primary concern was gaining political power; thereafter it was rearming Germany. As for Austria itself, his first goal was to control the Nazi party even if it meant allowing it to split over his renunciation of the South Tirol. Once in power, Hitler soon realized that an Anschluss was not possible as long as Germany was militarily weak. Consequently, he postponed the annexation indefinitely in favor of the more subtle and realistic policy of *Gleichschaltung*, i.e., a Nazified Austria, which he hoped would not alarm the proponents of Austrian independence.

To implement such a policy required considerable patience on Hitler's part and a willingness to restrain the more restless, and at times reckless, Austrian Nazis. The need for such a policy of restraint became especially apparent after Hitler had tolerated the disastrous July *Putsch* in 1934 when the Austrian Nazis outraged world public opinion by assassinating Chancellor Engelbert Dollfuss. Hitler speeded up the process of *Gleichschaltung* only well after the remilitarization of the Rhineland and the signing of the July Agreement, both in 1936.[11]

By February 1938 Mussolini had moved into Hitler's camp, British officials had hinted that they would not object to a peaceful Anschluss, and the *Führer* had gained a firm grip on the *Wehrmacht*. Although Chancellor Schuschnigg's ill-fated call for a plebiscite on 9 March set in motion the process which led to the German invasion three days later, there is little reason to doubt that a German annexation, overt or disguised, was only a matter of time by then, and probably a short time at that.

---

[11] For details on Hitler's policy toward Austria see Bruce F. Pauley, *Hitler and the Forgotten Nazis: A History of Austrian National Socialism* (Chapel Hill: University of North Carolina Press, 1981), pp. 52, 112, 133-137, 223-224. This book has been translated and revised by the Österreichischer Bundesverlag in Vienna under the title, *Der Weg in den Nationalsozialismus: Ursprünge und Entwicklung in Österreich* (1988).

If the lack of a consensus about Austrian independence—except on Hitler's part—was the decisive factor in the German annexation, a lack of any domestic consensus among the Austrian people on their country's independence, or even the form of government, was at least a contributing factor.

To say that Austria was *Der Staat, den keiner wollte*[12] (the state that nobody wanted) would be an exaggeration. Nevertheless, it is certainly true that few if any Austrians in the winter of 1918-1919 were enthusiastic about this new creation. And if the same might be said of the Third French Republic in 1870, there is still the difference that Austria's economy prevented many of its citizens from changing their minds.

This is not to suggest, however, that most Austrians were ardent advocates of the idea of Anschluss from the beginning to the end of the First Republic. Support for a union with Germany was strongest among the Social Democrats (SDAP) and the Greater German People's Party (GDVP) and never more than lukewarm among the Christian Socials (CSP). Indeed, the party's most influential leader, Ignaz Seipel, strongly opposed the idea, although he was not above paying lip service to it for political reasons.[13] And sentiment for Anschluss among the Social Democrats and Greater Germans tended to be mutually exclusive: the stronger the Social Democrats were in Germany the less eager were the Greater Germans for an immediate Anschluss. Likewise, the more influential German nationalists became in Germany, the less interested was the Austrian SDAP in the union. This policy culminated in the SDAP eliminating the Anschluss from the program once the Nazis attained power in Germany, a policy also followed by the Christian Socials. Support for the Anschluss was

---

[12] The title of the popular book by Hellmut Andics (Vienna: Verlag Herder, 1962).

[13] Low, p. 26: Klemens von Klemperer, *Ignaz Seipel: Christian Statesman in a Time of Crisis* (Princeton: Princeton University Press, 1972), especially pp. 114-117, 192-194, 301-306, 312-319, 327-328.

also generally low in Austria during times of political or economic crisis in Germany as, for example, in 1923.

Hitler's electoral victories between 1930 and 1932, along with his *Machtergreifung* the next year, made Austrian pan-Germans all the more excited about the prospects of an Anschluss, and caused them to shift their support from the GDVP, and to a lesser extent from the semi-fascist paramilitary *Heimwehr,* to the Austrian Nazi party. Although the Austrian Nazis were more fanatically pro-Anschluss than any of the other Austrian parties had ever been, and although they successfully contributed to the actual German annexation in 1938, there were far fewer Austrians who supported the Anschluss idea in early March 1938 than did in the winter of 1918-1919.

If the Austrian people and the political parties never simultaneously and unanimously favored a union with Germany, unfortunately neither did they ever unanimously oppose it. Even such apparent defenders of Austrian independence as Chancellors Dollfuss and Schuschnigg were not consistently and unambiguously opposed to the Anschluss. Both stressed that Austrianism was merely a special form of Germanism.[14] In other words, as abroad, there was no domestic consensus either for or against the Anschluss. Making matters worse, and contributing to Austria's inability to resist the Anschluss, was a lack of consensus about the form of government.

The Social Democrats were convinced supporters of the new republican regime. Indeed, they were all too prone to refer to the state as "our republic" thus equating socialism and republicanism in the eyes of anti-socialists. Moreover, their willingness to use obstructionist tactics in the National Assembly, their use of force to break up party meetings of the opposition in the early days of the new state, their denunciation of political opponents, and, finally, their loose rhetoric about a proletarian revolution and class dictatorship, hardly contributed to an atmosphere of mutual

---

[14]Low, p. 190; see also Pauley, p. 159.

respect and toleration that democracies need to survive.[15]

The CSP, along with the *Heimwehr* and the League of Front Fighters, had no enthusiasm for the new republic; many of their members preferred a restoration of the Habsburgs, an idea which was almost hysterically opposed by the Little Entente. Still others favored some form of authoritarian or even dictatorial government. The *Heimwehr* was divided between a pan-German wing, particularly strong in Styria, which favored a dictatorship, and a more moderate Catholic wing which staunchly defended Austrian independence. Conservatives in general were too willing to believe radical Socialist words rather than moderate Socialist deeds. And like the Socialists they placed the vested interests of their constituents above the common good of the country. Austrian politics was infused with a religious fervor in which rival parties were regarded not as honest, if mistaken, opponents, but as heretics to be eliminated by fair means or foul. Thus, there was little chance of the Austrians presenting a united front on the Anschluss or anything else, for example, questions of social welfare or church-state relations.

Ultimately, this lack of consensus helped Dollfuss succeed in allowing the parliament to "dissolve itself" in 1933 and made way for civil wars of February and July 1934. These events, in turn, made possible the establishment of the corporative state in 1933-1934. Despite the elimination of the political parties, including Dollfuss' own Christian Socials, and the creation of the supposedly all-encompassing "Patriotic Front," the new authoritarian regime was even more unpopular than the democratic one it replaced. Evan Bukey recently described the corporative state as supported only

> by the remnants of the Christian social movement.... It

---

[15]Klemperer, p. 227; Alfred Diamant, *Austrian Catholics and the First Austrian Republic: Democracy, Capitalism and the Social Order, 1918-1934* (Princeton: Princeton University Press, 1960), pp. 78, 80, 120.

> operated on an ad hoc basis with little regard to long-range goals. It depended primarily on the force of tradition without, however, providing a father figure to attract the masses or resolve their conflicts."[16]

Indeed, a major cause for the lack of a domestic consensus in Austria during the First Republic was the absence of any individual or institution which could take the place of Franz Joseph as an object of loyalty. Neither the presidents nor still less the chancellors enjoyed much respect outside their own political parties. And in any event the executive powers of both offices were severely restricted until the establishment of the corporative state. Even then, Dollfuss and Schuschnigg were not the objects of the reverence enjoyed by Franz Joseph or the blind faith inspired by the charismatic Adolf Hitler. By the same token, Vienna, now an independent province and ruled by socialists, no longer won the same respect and loyalty from the more conservative federal states as it had during the monarchy.

The First Republic, for the most part, even lacked issues that might have at least created a negative consensus. In the empire, Czech, Italian, and Slovene demands for autonomy had unified the German-Austrians as did the occasional Hungarian demands for independence. In the postwar secessionist states of Poland, Czechoslovakia, Romania, and Yugoslavia the question of national minorities created one of the few centripetal forces for the dominant nationalities which controlled the government. But after 1918 the issue of nationality was dead in Austria, except in Carinthia. Only the issue of the South Tirol provided a rallying cry, but it was not enough to overcome the chronic political divisiveness. Lacking common enemies, the Austrians turned against each other.

The closest the Austrians came to a negative consensus was on the "Jewish problem." All the political parties and social

---

[16] Evan Burr Bukey, *Hitler's Hometown: Linz, Austria, 1908-1945* (Bloomington: Indiana University Press, 1986), p. 139.

classes of Austria were anti-Semitic to one degree or another. The SDAP was the only party to reject anti-Semitism as an official program and to accept people of Jewish origin into positions of leadership. In practice, however, professing Jews did not become party leaders. Moreover, the party denounced Jewish capitalists in political cartoons in a way which was scarcely distinguishable from those used later by the Nazis. The CSP accepted Jewish converts into its ranks, but not into positions of leadership and consistently denounced Jewish cultural and economic influence. The GDVP and the pan-German wing of the *Heimwehr* promoted a racial anti-Semitism which was every bit as vicious as that found in Nazi propaganda.[17]

If there was nearly universal agreement in Austria over the extremely vague principle of Jewish "domination," this was scarcely the kind of consensus which could ward off the Anschluss. Far from repelling most Austrians, therefore, the anti-Semitic policies of the German Nazis after their seizure of power almost certainly appealed to a great many citizens of the Alpine republic. Indeed, some Austrians such as the leader of the Christian Socials' *Arbeiterverein*, Leopold Kunschak, complained that the early anti-Semitic legislation of Nazi Germany was too mild![18] Austrian anti-Semites needed no encouragement from Germany to humiliate Jews in the streets of Vienna immediately after the Anschluss or to burn down synagogues during the pogrom known as *Kristallnacht* in November 1938.

Curiously enough, the lack of a positive domestic consensus extended even to Austria's 200,000 Jews who could reach no agreement on their future role in the country or on how to

---

[17]For a discussion of this negative consensus on anti-Semitism see Bruce F. Pauley, *From Prejudice to Persecution: A History of Austrian Anti-Semitism* (Chapel Hill: University of North Carolina Press, 1992).

[18]Hermann Holzmann, "Antisemitismus in der österreichischen Innenpolitik 1918-1938. Der Umgang der drei politischen Lager mit diesem Phänomen" (University of Vienna: *Diplomarbeit*, 1986), p. 56.

respond to the growing Nazi menace. Liberal, assimilated Jews wistfully hoped that Hitler was a passing phenomenon which Jews could survive through patience, enlightenment of their gentile compatriots, and by reaffirmations of their loyalty to Austria. Zionists saw salvation in cultivating a separate Jewish culture and eventually by emigrating to Palestine. Orthodox Jews thought the times simply proved the need for a return to traditional Jewish religion and values.[19]

Jews as a whole, especially those not in positions of leadership in the Social Democratic party (which was outlawed after February 1934), were undoubtedly more supportive of Austrian independence and the Dollfuss-Schuschnigg regime than any other group in Austria.[20] Yet it is more than doubtful whether this support was of any real benefit to either the government or to Austrian independence. Comprising less than three percent of the country's population, the Jews hardly represented a major source of popularity. Furthermore, the Jews' support of republican government supplied Nazis in both Austria and Germany with useful propaganda.

Thus, when Hitler made his decision to invade Austria late in the evening of 11 March, he faced a country and a world which lacked any consensus on the necessity of continued Austrian independence, not to mention lesser domestic questions. The Austrian government, its Socialist opponents, and surprisingly, even the Austrian Nazis all did oppose a German military invasion at least and favored the continuation of some form of Austrian autonomy. But there was no consensus on which party or person should lead Austria or on what the form of government should be.[21] This lack of a domestic or international consensus

---

[19] On Jewish responses to anti-Semitism see Bruce F. Pauley, "In the Shadow of Death: Austrian Jews and the Nazi Threat," *Shofar* (Spring 1987), 28-43.

[20] Ibid., pp. 34-37.

[21] For a more detailed discussion of this question see Pauley, *Forgotten Nazis*, pp. 193-215.

therefore enabled Hitler to invade and annex Austria without a single shot being fired by Austrians or by soldiers of any other state.

It is one of history's greatest ironies that Hitler, who was so easily able to annex Austria because of a lack of an opposing consensus, helped create the very consensus which has made the Second Republic a success. Seven years of Hitler's government, and 427,000 unnatural deaths in World War II[22] were substantial, although not solely determining, reasons for creating a new consensus in Austria and in the world for an independent Austria ruled by a democratic government.

---

[22]Fritz Molden, "Austrian Resistance: Phantom or Reality." Paper delivered at the Center for Austrian Studies, University of Minnesota, 14 May 1988. Cf. Helga Leitner, "Demography and Population Problems," in Kurt Steiner, ed., *Modern Austria* (Palo Alto, California: The Society for the Promotion of Science and Scholarship, 1981), p. 76.

Was the Authoritarian, Christian, Corporative State an Effective Means of Resisting National Socialism?

Isabella Ackerl

The term "authoritarian regime" in an Austrian context is applied to the Dollfuss and Schuschnigg governments. The period concerned can be exactly delineated: it lasted from 4 March 1933 to 11 March 1938. The designation "authoritarian" was not imputed to these governments by later historians but derives from a definition propagated by Dollfuss himself. The fourth day of March 1933 was the day on which the Austrian parliament was suspended; the twelfth day of March 1938 saw the armed forces of Nazi Germany enter Austria.

The neat chronological dividing lines which mark off this period of the history of the First Austrian Republic should not obscure the fact that its ideological roots can be traced back to the earlier democratic era. Those years of constitutional government had nurtured what may broadly be identified as two types of roots for the authoritarian regime which succeeded it. The one type consists of judicial factors, aspects of the constitution and other legislation, which, interpreted loosely, paved the way for an authoritarian form of government. The other type of root comprises political factors; it must be conceded that the Dollfuss regime could count on huge resources of anti-democratic sentiment on the right of the political spectrum.

The "Austrian Revolution," as Otto Bauer[1] termed it, had in fact been no more than an attempt to accomplish a nineteenth-century bourgeois revolution. And yet influential sections of the Austrian population adopted a wait-and-see, or even a mistrustful, attitude towards the innovations of 1918, which had after all brought about a democratic constitution and important social legislation. The caution with which people viewed the newly proclaimed republic was heightened by political tendencies in the twenties which were by no means confined to Austria.

Political groups in Austria which were calling for a strong leader could count on material and ideological backing from like-minded supporters abroad—above all in Germany and Italy and to a lesser extent in Hungary. The economic depression which was affecting the whole of Europe was grist for the mill of the anti-democratic groups. Slogans which spoke of apathy and disillusionment towards democratic and parliamentary institutions did not fall on deaf ears. It would, however, be entirely wrong to conclude from this that a majority of Austrians had had enough of democracy. The truth is that a minority managed to avail itself of the more effective methods—and, above all, of the means—of imposing its wishes on the rest.

The 1929 constitutional reform, which had emerged after a protracted process of bargaining, significantly strengthened the powers of the federal president. In juridical terms this opened the door to the establishment of presidential rule. But Austria did not take this path. The immediate and decisive occasion for the elimination of democratic procedures was an essentially minor law dating from the era of the First World War. The 1917 *Kriegswirtschaftliches Ermächtigungsgesetz* (War Economy Powers Act) had been invoked time and again in the postwar years without the slightest breach of the constitution and with the

---

[1] Otto Bauer, *Die Österreichische Revolution* (Vienna, 1923).

endorsement of all the parliamentary parties.[2] It was only when the governing coalition set its sights on dismantling the democratic institutions that this law provided the starting-point for five years of unconstitutional rule. These events bring one to pose the question: how was this possible?

On 4 March 1933 the Austrian parliament was conducting a heated debate on a work stoppage by the country's railroad workers. In the course of the debate a procedural technicality produced an impasse: all three parliamentary presidents (equivalent to the Speakers of the Chamber) tendered their resignation, with the result that the session could be neither continued, nor terminated, nor reconvened. With a minimum of good will this dilemma could easily have been surmounted; but the Dollfuss government took advantage of it to bypass parliament and institute authoritarian rule, invoking the War Economy Powers Act to legitimize its actions. Having once applied the Act in a broad interpretation which was juridically untenable, the Dollfuss regime continued to cite it as the basis for its future infractions of the law of the land.

The decision to institute authoritarian rule was taken not by the cabinet as a whole but by a small group of politicians from the Christian Social Party. Not even Federal President Wilhelm Miklas was consulted. But Miklas acquiesced in the step taken by his fellow Christian Social Party members, thus setting a precedent. In the course of the next few years Miklas proved a weak president, reluctant to offer any resistance. His only protests took the form of private correspondence which made no impact.[3]

---

[2]Gernot D. Hasiba, "Das kriegswirtschaftliche Ermächtigungsgesetz (KWEG) von 1917. Seine Entstehung und seine Anwendung vor 1933," in *Aus Österreichs Rechtsleben in Geschichte und Gegenwart. Festschrift für Ernst C. Hellbling zum 80. Geburtstag* (Berlin, 1981), pp. 543-565.

[3]Hilde Verena Lang, "Bundespräsident Miklas und das autoritäre Regime 1933-1938" (diss. University of Vienna, 1972?); Walter Goldinger, "Wilhelm Miklas," in Friedrich Weissensteiner, ed., *Die österreichischen Bundespräsidenten. Leben und Werk* (Vienna, 1982), pp. 82-120.

At this point one needs to examine the stance adopted by the partners of the coalition because one must not forget that the Dollfuss cabinet was made up of three right-wing parties and, up to March 1933, had a majority of only one seat in parliament. The groupings represented in the Dollfuss cabinet were: the Christian Social Party itself; the *Landbund für Österreich*,[4] a rural-democratic, corporate-based party; and the *Heimwehr*,[5] the right-wing paramilitary organization. In its basic ideological orientation the *Heimwehr* saw itself as a fascist group closely modeled on its Italian counterpart. Strictly speaking, the *Heimwehr* could not be called a political party in any conventional sense of the term, it adhered too strongly to its paramilitary character and took too little interest in formulating an ideological stance. The *Grossdeutsche Partei* (The Greater German Party), for over ten years the middle-class partner in coalition with the Christian Social Party, had revoked its alliance with Dollfuss in 1932, largely as a result of differences in the field of foreign policy.[6]

One must consider the question: to what extent could Dollfuss count on the backing of his own party and of his coalition partners when he set about dismantling the institutions of consti-

---

[4]Angela Feldmann, "Landbund für Österreich," (diss. University of Vienna, 1967); Adam Wandruszka, "Der Landbund für Österreich," in Heinz Gollwitzer, ed., *Europäische Bauernparteien im 20. Jahrhundert* (Quellen und Forschungen zur Agrargeschichte, XXIX; Stuttgart, 1977), pp. 587-602; Charlotte Heidrich, *Burgenländische Politik in der Ersten Republik. Deutschnationale Parteien und Verbände im Burgenland vom Zerfall der Habsburgermonarchie bis zum Beginn des autoritären Regimes (1918-1933)* (Studien und Quellen zur österreichischen Zeitgeschichte, IV, Vienna, 1982); Günther R. Burkert, "Der Landbund für Österreich. Die Partei der Bundesländerpolitiker" (unpublished paper, conference of Wissenschaftliche Kommission zur Erforschung der Geschichte der Republik Österreich, 24-25 October 1983).

[5]Walter Wiltschegg, *Die Heimwehr. Ein unwiderstehliche Volksbewegung?* (Studien und Quellen zur österreichischen Zeitgeschichte, VII; Vienna, 1985).

[6]Isabella Ackerl, "Das Ende der christlichsozial-grossdeutschen Regierungskoalition," in Ludwig Jedlicka and Rudolf Neck, eds., *Vom Justizpalast zum Heldenplatz. Studien und Dokumentationen* (Vienna, 1975), pp. 82-94.

tutional rule? Undoubtedly, a considerable majority within the Christian Social Party was in favor of authoritarian government. This group was made up not only of industrial interests but also of members of that generation which, young and preponderantly Catholic, felt it had been cheated of its chances to make a career in a larger national context and tended to see itself as having been dispossessed by the new republic. A prototype of this generation was Kurt Schuschnigg, minister of justice under Dollfuss and subsequently chancellor. It was he who, as a member of the authoritarian government, was responsible for the punctilious and dispassionate implementation of such far-reaching judicial reforms as the reintroduction of the death penalty.

At the same time, the Christian Social Party also harbored considerable bodies of opinion loyal to democracy. These were located partly in the provinces, partly in the Christian labor movement. As study of the minutes of party organization meetings shows,[7] any protests from these quarters were rapidly silenced, in some instances even with the consent of the established Church. By the summer of 1934 the Christian Social Party had so completely succumbed to its passion for emulating the cult of the *Führer* that it acquiesced in its own dissolution.[8]

Dollfuss could count almost unconditionally on the support of the *Heimwehr*, which was aware that, under democratic rule, it would never have risen above the status of a minor party.

Only the loyalty of the *Landbund* remains to be considered. It was the *Landbund* members in the cabinet who held out longest in defense of democratic principles. And it was they, the adherents of a national-liberal party representing the interests of the farming community, who used the term "breach of the consti-

---

[7] Walter Goldinger, ed., *Protokolle des Klubvorstandes der Christlichsozialen Partei, 1932-1934* (Studien und Quellen zur österreichischen Zeitgeschichte, II; Vienna, 1980).

[8] Ibid., Vorstandsitzung, 14 May 1934, pp. 361ff.

tution"[9] and lambasted the regime's unconstitutional methods of government at cabinet sessions. They were to be given only half a year in which to voice their opposition. By the autumn of 1933 Dollfuss had succeeded in ridding himself of their unwelcome criticism, replacing the *Landbund* ministers by more subservient individuals.

On the basis of the above, one might be tempted to imagine that the abolition of democratic rule in Austria was the product of a minutely planned and highly sophisticated conspiracy. Certainly the authoritarian regime, in its incipient stages at least, was manifestly determined to eliminate democracy as a thorn in the government's flesh. On the other hand, no conclusive evidence has come to light to show that it deliberately and consistently pursued this objective in practice. In other words, all those measures designed to suppress political opposition after the abolition of parliamentary government may be attributed not to a preconceived strategy but rather to improvisation within the political vacuum created by the absence of any significant response from circles within the opposition.[10]

The first decrees issued by the Dollfuss government on the basis of the Wartime Economy Powers Act were directed against the political opposition on both the right and the left wings; the blanket prohibition of parades and meetings and the introduction of preemptive censorship applied equally to both camps.[11] It should be noted, however, that the Dollfuss government initially described these measures as being aimed exclusively at the National Socialists. In early 1933 the Nazis, with massive support from abroad, launched a broad-based campaign of propaganda

---

[9]*Protokolle des Ministerrates der Ersten Republik,* Kabinett Dollfuss, Tom. 3, Ministerratsprotokoll (MRP) 871, 4 May 1933, p. 32.

[10]Ulrich Kluge, *Der österreichische Ständestaat, 1934-1938. Enstehung und Scheitern* (Vienna, 1984).

[11]Dollfuss, Tom. 3, p. 17, MRP 861, 22 and 23 March 1933.

against the Austrian government and went so far as to resort to terrorist methods.

Sepp Straffner, a parliamentary delegate representing the Greater German People's Party, who had been the last of the three speakers to resign, made a last-ditch attempt to save democracy and parliament. When he tried to summon the other delegates to a parliamentary session, the government intervened, ordering the police to use force to prevent the delegates from gathering.[12]

Although the regime was reluctant to seek a way out of the procedural impasse and had already issued a large number of decrees, there could have been a juridical solution to the problem. The subcommittee of the main parliamentary committee could have been convened and the issue brought before the Constitutional Court. The Vienna Municipal Council, whose autonomy in financial matters had been the target of several decrees, lodged a protest with the Supreme Court. It was widely assumed that the court would find in favor of the Council and against the government, whereupon the latter resolved to abolish the Constitutional Court. Those judges who owed their positions to the nomination of the Christian Social Party were induced to resign, leaving the decimated bench without a quorum and hence paralyzed. Hardly surprisingly, the judges who had stepped down were not replaced. This marked the point of no return in the Dollfuss government's progress into unconstitutionality. Up to that point constitutional rule could still have been restored. Henceforth, there was, to all intents and purposes, no way of going back which would not have entailed a loss of face for the members of the government.[13]

The subsequent measures adopted by the government pur-

---

[12] Dollfuss, Tom. 2, MRP 851 and 852, pp. 393-416, 7 and 9 March 1933.

[13] Archiv der Republik (AdR), Bundeskanzleramt (BKA) Z1. 7.045-Pr. 1933; see also Historische Einführung zu Ministerratsprotokolle, Kabinett Dollfuss, Tom. 3, p. xii

sued just one goal: to prohibit every form of political activity by the opposition. On 31 March 1933 the Republican *Schutzbund,* the social democratic paramilitary organization, was outlawed.[14] In late May of the same year the Communist Party was banned from political activity.[15] When on 19 June 1933 a hand grenade attack was perpetrated against a group of Christian-German gymnasts near Krems on the Danube, the government used the incident as a pretext for issuing a decree prohibiting the National Socialists from indulging in political activity.[16] The Nazis knew, however, that they could rely on the backing of the German *Reich* and continued undeterred their militant opposition to the regime.

As the elimination of the one-time political parties from Austria's public life progressed, it became evident that a vacuum was being created. At the same time, resistance to the National Socialists—the need for which was being used by the government as a pretext for the repressive steps it was taking against the left wing—would have required broader-based support than that which the partners in coalition were able to muster by themselves. Dollfuss established the Fatherland Front which, modeled closely on the "patriotic fronts" existing in other countries, was to serve as a rallying point for the politically homeless.[17] In its early stages the Fatherland Front, imposed upon the country by decree, proved too anemic to attract more than a few people. It was only in the wake of the so-called "Racetrack Speech" on 11 September 1933,[18] in which Dollfuss, heavily swayed by his

---

[14] Bundesgesetzblatt (BGBl.) 97/1933.

[15] BGBl. 200/1933.

[16] BGBl. 240/1933.

[17] Irmgard Baernthaler, *Die vaterländische Front. Geschichte und Organisation* (Vienna, 1971).

[18] The so-called "Racetrack Speech" (*Trabrennplatz-Rede* of 11 September 1933 is published in Klaus Berchtold, *Österreichische Parteiprogramme 1866-1966* (Munich, 1967).

recent meeting with Mussolini in Riccione, proclaimed the Christian, authoritarian, corporative state, that a consensus of sorts began to rally 'round the apolitical Front movement. By this stage, Dollfuss had secured the strong backing of industrialists who had been won over by the regime's policies and saw in the unfettered application of government by decree the promise of far-reaching change, first and foremost in the social field. While organizations which supported the government began *en masse* to join the Fatherland Front, nothing was being done to lend it a more pronounced profile. For a while it existed side by side with the old Christian Social Party, which, by its abject pandering to the regime's policies, was fast digging its own grave. In the spring of 1934 it acquiesced in its own dissolution.

From the early summer of 1933 onwards, Austria was turned into a police state on the pretext of the threat from the National Socialists. The only difference between the methods of police control in Austria and those which existed in other countries lay in the realities of their political implementation: traditional Austrian laxity somewhat blunted their effectiveness. The main steps which led along the path to a police state were: the concentration of responsibility for law enforcement in the hands of the minister of security; the creation of "detention camps" for interning political opponents without a judicial warrant or trial;[19] and the transformation of the judiciary into a body subservient to the wishes of the government. This latter was a daunting task; the judiciary was traditionally liberal in outlook and was reluctant to connive in infractions of the law of the land. Minister of Justice Kurt Schuschnigg, however, was one of Dollfuss's most loyal henchmen and used all his considerable expertise to erode the structures of the constitutional state. It was he who provided the legislative tools with which to straightjacket the system of magistrates' courts and to infiltrate judicial proce-

---

[19]Gerhard Jagschitz, "Die Anhaltelager in Österreich (1933-1938)" in Jedlicka and Neck, eds., *Vom Justizpalast zum Heldenplatz*, pp. 128-151.

dures, a step which effectively curtailed the independence of the judiciary. And it was Schuschnigg who, allegedly in conformity with the constitution, reintroduced the death penalty.[20]

Another major assault on civil liberties was conducted not on the political nor on the judicial but on the social front, and this proved to have a very real impact on the life of the individual. The still very precarious system of social welfare that had been instituted after the end of the First World War was progressively dismantled. The system was modified in its basic structure so that the legal claim to a minimum of social security was abolished and replaced by benefits provided for supporters of the government.[21]

Until the events of February 1934 the regime was partially successful in convincing foreign governments that the measures described above were necessary adjuncts of its resistance to the National Socialist threat. After the brutal elimination of left-wing opposition in February 1934, this argument was no longer plausible. As a result, Austria found itself deprived of backing when it confronted its real enemy, the Third Reich. Italy's pledge of support for Austria's independence held good only as long as its *sacro egoismo* did not necessitate a change of policy.

The Dollfuss cabinet soon realized that the Social Democratic institutions abolished in the wake of the events of February 1934 would have to be replaced by new ones. The government generally agreed that organizations must be created to rally the supporters of the Social Democratic Party; it deluded itself into thinking that this might be a way of gathering widespread support amongst the working class.

---

[20] BGBl. 505/1933.

[21] Emmerich Tálos, "Sozialpolitik im Austrofaschismus," in Emmerich Tálos and Wolfgang Neugebauer, eds., *Austrofaschismus. Beiträge über Politik, Ökonomie und Kultur, 1934-1938* (Vienna, 1984), pp. 161-178.

A single, general trade union was established by decree[22] to provide a framework for the representation of working-class interests at least in the field of labor legislation. It is not surprising that the supporters of the Social Democratic Party refused to join. It was only in later years that a few workers enrolled in the general trade union, either under the pressure of material hardship or to improve their occupational prospects.

The hasty, if clumsy, attempts which the Dollfuss regime made to find a basis for dialogue with the labor movement suggest that the government was not altogether sure it was on the right path in its treatment of the working class. Ernst Karl Winter, a Catholic whose friendship with Dollfuss dated back to the war, was one of the first men who, while not rejecting the government's course, offered his services as an honest broker. With nothing other than reconciliation in mind, he conducted tentative talks with leading left-wing officials and a large number of workers themselves. It seemed at first as though his efforts might not be in vain; he did, after all, enjoy the support of the Christian labor movement. Winter was appointed Third Deputy Mayor of Vienna to invest him with a degree of official authority. But the *Heimwehr* and the Fatherland Front viewed his activities with profound suspicion, and it was not long before intrigues and countermeasures undermined Winter's exertions. He had to admit defeat when the Christian labor movement withdrew its support from him.[23]

There were, however, more far-sighted politicians in the ranks of the government who realized how important a role the

---

[22] Dollfuss, Tom 6, MRP 926, 2 March 1934, pp. 61-68; BGBl. 132/1934. Regarding the Christian workers' movement see Christl Kluwick-Muckenhuber, *Johnny Staud. Ein Leben für die Arbeiterschaft* (Vienna, 1969) and Anton Pelinka, *Stand oder Klasse? Die christliche Arbeiterbewegung Österreichs, 1933-1938* (Vienna, 1972).

[23] Ernst Karl Winter, *Christentum und Zivilisation* (Vienna, 1956), esp. pp. 388-402.

labor movement could play in the fight against National Socialism. Alfred Maleta, later president (speaker) of the lower chamber of parliament, was one. At the time he was an official of the Chamber of Labor and wrote a book detailing the shortcomings of the regime's policies.[24] Maleta's views proceeded from the tenets of Catholic social dogma and were notable for advocating far-reaching tolerance and respect for one's political opponents. His Social Working Group, an organization whose purpose it was to bring about reconciliation, was ultimately frustrated in its efforts by the inability of Chancellor Schuschnigg to countenance any opinion which diverged from his own bizarre, romantic vision of a second, superior German state in Austria.

Once Dollfuss in his "Racetrack Speech" of September 1933 had proclaimed a whole new ideological basis for the Austrian state, the government was faced with the problem of bringing the constitution into line with these concepts. One objective of the planned constitutional reform was, of course, to legitimize the breaches of the constitution which had been perpetrated so far. Another was to incorporate the substance of the encyclical *Quadragesimo anno* and the concept of vocational corporative structures in the constitution. The idea of the corporative state was by no means a newcomer to Austria's domestic political scene; born in the nineteenth century, it had in times of crisis repeatedly been cited by anti-democratic elements as a possible alternative state structure. The school that had formed around the university lecturer Othmar Spann had also pledged its allegiance to the concept of the corporative state, while dictatorial regimes abroad were citing the same body of ideas in attempting to legitimize their exercise of power. In Austria there were no unequivocal precedents to work from, and the cabinet was by no means of one mind over the question of the substantive definition of the corporative state. The constitution which, after months of deliberation, was finally submitted to the rump parliament for rubber-

---

[24] Alfred Maleta, *Der Sozialist im Dollfuss-Österreich* (Linz, 1936).

stamp endorsement, had been completely purged of democratic elements.[25] Both legislative and executive powers were now entrusted solely to the government; the newly created representative bodies were not supplied their membership by public ballot, and they were accorded only consultative functions. The bogus endorsement of the new constitution by parliament provoked protests from the Greater Germany Party, which, since it had not been proscribed, remained the only surviving party from the democratic years to vote against the violation of the constitution.[26]

The new anti-democratic constitution failed to generate sufficient impetus to infuse the concept of the corporative state with life, and its practical realization barely got off the ground; by 1938 only two vocational corporative groups had been established by law (civil service and agriculture and forestry). It is therefore inaccurate to speak of Austria between 1933 and 1938 as a corporative state.

It is not intended here to deal in detail with the attempted coup by the National Socialists on 25 July 1934.[27] It did not effect a change in the system. Kurt von Schuschnigg, who succeeded Dollfuss as chancellor, insisted that he was retaining both the style and the spirit of his predecessor. The propaganda-machine invested Dollfuss with the status of a martyr. The cult of personality which grew up around him, often enough embarrassingly inept in itself, demonstrated the authoritarian regime's moral bankruptcy. Schuschnigg implemented no formal changes

---

[25]Dollfuss, Tom. 6, MRP 929, 13 March 1934, pp. 124-139; MRP 930, 20, 21, 24, 26, 28 and 29 March 1934, pp. 140-292; MRP 938, 14, 16, 17 and 18 April 1934, pp. 399-529. Dollfuss, Tom. 7, MRP 939, 24 April 1934, pp. 4-9, 27-74 BGBl. 1/1934.

[26]Rudolf Neck, "Die Entwicklung der österreichischen Verfassung bis zum Sommer 1934," in *Das Jahr 1934: 25 Juli* (Veröffentlichungen der Wissenschaftlichen Kommission, Tom. 3; Vienna, 1975), pp. 69-75.

[27]Gerhard Jagschitz, *Der Putsch. Die Nationsozialisten 1934 in Österreich* (Graz, 1976).

either to the constitution, to the Fatherland Front, or to the general trade union. Nevertheless, some differences in his style of government are apparent. Whereas the Dollfuss era had been characterized by a certain lackadaisical approach, Schuschnigg proved himself capable of consistent and purposeful action. While Dollfuss had been forced to rely completely on the loyalty of the *Heimwehr*, Schuschnigg decided that he could afford to dispense with its backing and embarked upon a systematic policy of eliminating it from the political scene. By the end of 1936 he had succeeded in neutralizing all of the pro-government paramilitary organizations and placing them under the aegis of the armed forces, leaving the Fatherland Front as the undisputed state party. This was consonant with Schuschnigg's outlook as a whole; in his heart-of-hearts he remained a monarchist.

As a figure of public charisma Schuschnigg ran his predecessor a poor second. Dollfuss had been able, by virtue of his simple and unaffected manner, to appeal to people and win them over. Schuschnigg's speeches were highly polished masterpieces of rhetoric steeped in intellectual frigidity. He never ceased to play the role of the university professor, whereas Dollfuss had been adept at playing the part of the popular tribune. This abrupt change in style had a certain impact on the climate of domestic politics; Schuschnigg never succeeded in establishing the basis for dialogue with those whose persuasions differed from his own. His German romanticism—his vision of a superior German culture emerging in Austria in the face of the Nazis[28]—was to be an unmitigated disaster for his country, leaving Austria as it did all the more prone to the aberrations of National Socialism. The Austrian nationalism which Dollfuss had begun to foster—albeit only tentatively and sporadically—petrified under Schuschnigg to a meaningless ritual which, given his infantile pandering to foreign prototypes, was totally devoid of any poten-

---

[28]Schuschnigg presented his arguments in his book, *Dreimal Österreich* (Vienna, 1937).

tial as a source of resistance. In light of the above it is barely surprising that no period of the First Republic seems to be so shallow, so culturally vacuous as the years between 1934 and 1938.

The repertoire of repressive measures directed against political opponents remained unchanged under Schuschnigg, except insofar as he attempted to stage spectacular show-trials which he hoped would definitively discredit the opposition. But, as it turned out, these trials achieved a quite different effect: neither in the *Schutzbund* trial nor in the large-scale trials of Socialists in 1936 was the prosecution able to produce incriminating evidence against the indicted Social Democrats.[29] Indeed, the court proceedings effectively put the government on trial for its violation of the constitution.

Another significant feature of these show-trials was that they were conducted exclusively against members of the left-wing opposition. The agreement of July 1936 had accorded the National Socialists far greater political scope, and they could count on the backing of a major power which was threatening reprisals, an asset the Social Democrats had never been able to fall back on.

The establishment of the authoritarian regime was significantly facilitated by the person of Federal President Wilhelm Miklas, in office since 1928, who at no point availed himself of the scope for political initiative which the constitution accorded him. On the contrary, he proved to be a subservient tool of the cabinet. On occasion he entertained misgivings about the government's constitutional violations, but he never voiced public disapproval and confined his protests to his correspondence. His posthumous papers contain letters which describe the authoritari-

---

[29] See Everhard Holtmann, *Zwischen Unterdrückung und Befreiung. Sozialistische Arbeiterbewegung und autoritäres Regime in Österreich, 1933-1938.* (Studien und Quellen zur österreichischen Zeitgeschichte, I, Vienna, 1978), pp. 246-278.

an regime as exemplifying "Austro-fascism." He would have served his country better had he been more outspoken in public.[30]

How could an effective resistance to the totalitarian menace of National Socialism possibly have been generated by this hybrid political system? An Austrian historian, Gerhard Jagschitz, has described it as "the sum total of bourgeois revisionist and restoration policy towards the system instituted in November 1918."[31] Was the authoritarian regime ever capable of living up to its self-ordained purpose: to lead the unstinting fight against National Socialism? Or must a detailed study of its (indisputably inept) strategies of resistance justify one in passing a verdict of guilty on the corporative state? And if so, to what extent must it be convicted of committing negligent or even willful harm by underestimating the danger posed by the Third Reich?

The intrinsic weaknesses of the corporative state, its amorphous political landscape (which remains to be adequately researched), and the overall economic instability of Austria during the period paved the way for the emergence of an authoritarian regime which adopted effective measures only against certain sections of the political spectrum, but in the end proved incapable of safeguarding its own survival by exercising sufficient authority over its real opponent on the foreign political horizon.

Its abject emulation of other European dictatorships never rose above the status of shallow political posturing, which did more to bewilder than to unify the general public. The "German path" for Austria, which Schuschnigg envisioned, evinced so many embarrassing parallels with the system he claimed to be

---

[30]See Lang, "Bundespräsident Miklas," and Goldinger, "Wilhelm Miklas," cited *supra*.

[31]Gerhard Jagschitz, "Der Österreichische Ständestaat 1934-1938," in Erika Weinzierl and Kurt Skalnik, eds., *Österreich 1918-1938* (Graz, 1983), I, p. 498. The text reads: "Der Ständestaat stellt die Summe bürgerlicher Revisions- und Restaurationspolitik gegen das System des November 1918 dar."

defying that, far from strengthening the Austrian state, it undermined it. It was a miscalculation to appeal to an Austrian sense of national identity at a time when this sense of identity was riddled with self-doubt and anyway irrelevant to significant, immediate public concerns. For years the broad masses of the population had had to contend with unemployment and economic recession. These factors brought with them an increased susceptibility to messianic promises of work and food, and this exactly matched the rising popularity of the Nazis.

There can be no doubt that Schuschnigg—perhaps more than anyone else—was aware of the threat posed by the Third Reich. How else can we explain his attempts to break out of the foreign political isolation in which Austria found itself? Whereas Dollfuss had relied entirely on fascist Italy and its dictator Mussolini to guarantee Austria's independence, Schuschnigg made concerted efforts to establish a dialogue with the western European nations through the mediation of Czechoslovakia.[32]

It must be said, though, that he utterly failed to understand the intrinsic interests of the countries concerned. It was manifestly absurd to court Czechoslovakia's support and at the same time to give free rein to—and indeed to look benevolently upon—Habsburg legitimist agitation within Austria itself, which represented a dire threat to Czechoslovakia as a successor state. It was inevitably fruitless, on the one hand, to seek the backing of the western democracies for a sovereign Austria and, in the same breath, to describe Austria as a "German state" whose system of dictatorship closely resembled that in Germany.

The authoritarian regime never managed—nor even wanted—to avail itself of the international contacts maintained by those political groups within Austria whose concern was to save the state. The Social Democrats had close links with sister-parties

---

[32]On the other hand, when Schuschnigg published his book, *Im Kampf gegen Hitler. Die Überwindung der Anschlussidee* (Vienna, 1969), he did not even mention the name of Eduard Beneš.

in western Europe and with Czechoslovakia, but they were excluded from efforts to resist National Socialism. The Nazis for their part maintained ties with the Third Reich which posed an eminent danger for Austria, and they were allowed ever greater scope for their activities.

One of the greatest omissions of the authoritarian regime was to impose political impotence on Austria's ethnic and religious minorities which had a vested interest in the nation's survival. Neither the Slovenes nor the Czechs nor the Croats, nor, least of all, the Jews[33] were accorded true recognition under the corporative state. Although the constitution did not de jure condone any form of discrimination, day-to-day political life entailed blatant discriminatory practices. This is all the more deplorable and the acquiescence in anti-Semitism all the more abhorrent in light of the fact that it was Austria's assimilated Jews who were the most fervent supporters of the corporative state.[34]

While an overall verdict of guilty must be passed on the corporative state, one should not overlook the fact that Austria ranked at the very top of the list of National Socialist targets for subversion and that almost certainly even a functioning democracy would hardly have held out longer against Nazi aggression, especially in view of the balance of power in Europe and the prevailing economic conditions. Then again, not every factor which contributed to Austria's prostration in the face of National Socialism was a product of the years after 1933. At the very hour of the First Republic's birth, doubts had been voiced as to whether the new state could survive. And throughout the twenties there had been politicians from all camps who had advocated

---

[33]Silvia Maderegger, *Die Juden im österreichischen Ständestaat, 1934-1938* (Vienna, 1973).

[34]Isabella Ackerl, "Das Janusgesicht des christlichen Ständestaates. Die Erfolglosigkeit schizophrener Abwehrstrategien," in *Voll Leben und voll Tod ist diese Erde. Bilder aus der Geschichte der jüdischen Österreicher (1190-1945)* (Vienna, 1988), pp. 209-217.

annexation to Germany, invoking a heavily idealized vision derived from a nineteenth-century view of history and remaining unable and unwilling to adjust it to the realities of contemporary life.

Nevertheless, one should not conclude without pointing out a few positive aspects of the corporative state.

The sense of national awareness which it had tried to awaken may ultimately have proved counterproductive in the circumstances, but this incipient nationalism was, in the end, to pave the way for a different, healthier national identity. The resistance-movement and the rebuilding of Austria after 1945 proceeded from a new outlook which significant sections of the population had adopted towards the state.

The broad-based consensus on domestic political issues which facilitated the smooth institution of a democratic system in the immediate postwar years can also be traced back to ideas which had been in circulation in the corporative state.

The generation of politicians which took the reins after the Second World War proved capable of seeking solutions transcending immediate political interests and allegiances. This is true of sections of the trade union movement and of the Social Working Group upon which Alfred Maleta had left his stamp. The willingness to enter into dialogue with the political opposition had its roots in the era preceding March 1938, when the view of democracy as discussion was just beginning to emerge. In 1945, after seven years of enforced hiatus, this incipient development was continued.

The Austrian Writer's Response to National Socialism between 1933 and 1938

Donald G. Daviau

The ramifications of Hitler's appointment as chancellor in Germany in 1933 and the resulting consolidation of power in the hands of the National Socialists were not long in manifesting themselves in Austria both politically and culturally. Although the writers in Austria for the most part made a determined effort to ignore the political warnings—avoidance of reality has long been a tradition in Austrian literature—events rapidly escalated to the point at which writers could no longer avoid taking a stand. As Klaus Amann has documented in his recent book *Der Anschluß österreichischer Schriftsteller an das Dritte Reich,* the National Socialists had pursued a methodical policy of infiltrating literary and cultural organizations in Austria since 1928 and had succeeded to such an extent that the Nazification of literary life in Austria could be completed within twenty-four hours following the Anschluss on 11 March 1938.[1] The catalyst that brought this infiltration to public attention was the burning of books by German university students on 10 May 1933, a well-publicized event that was impossible to ignore. Since works of thirty-five Austrian authors from Richard Beer-Hofmann to Stefan Zweig were included, the incident caused a crisis of con-

---

[1]Klaus Amann, *Der Anschluß österreichischer Schriftsteller an das dritte Reich* (Frankfurt am Main: Athenäum, 1988, p. 50.

science among Austrian writers. Even though these anti-Semitic and anti-intellectual actions posed no immediate threat and were not regarded as dangerous for Austrians in any direct way, nevertheless these acts made themselves felt in the sense that every writer had to take a stand on them. For even though the German government disavowed any role in the book burnings, at the same time there was no repudiation of the students' conduct nor any apology.

The watershed occurrence for Austrian writers, with regard to the book burnings and the National Socialist campaign of anti--Semitism they represented, was the meeting of the Eleventh Congress of the International P.E.N. Club from 25 to 28 May 1933 in Ragusa (now Dubrovnik).[2] Here members of the Austrian delegation, Paul Frischauer, Franz Theodor Csokor, and Raoul Auernheimer, among others, introduced a resolution condemning the book burnings. The German delegation walked out in protest, joined by Grete Urbanitzky, the founder and secretary of the Austrian P.E.N. Club and head of the Austrian delegation; Felix Salten, who argued that he could not vote for a motion that would harm the income of his fellow writers who needed the German market for their livelihood; and Egon Caesar Corti, who even at this early juncture was a National Socialist by conviction.

Since nothing was decided at Ragusa and because of the sharp division within the Austrian delegation, the matter was subsequently debated in June 1933 at a P.E.N. meeting in Vienna, where a group of liberal authors, including Auernheimer, Csokor, Oskar Maurus Fontana, Ernst Lothar, Robert Neumann, and Friedrich Torberg, succeeded in passing a resolution defending intellectual freedom and condemning the abolishing of hu-

---

[2]See Hilde Spiel, ed., *Die zeitgenössische Literatur Österreichs* (Zürich, Munich: Kindler, 1976), pp. 19-23, and Klaus Amann, *P.E.N. Politik, Emigration, Nationalsozialismus. Ein österreichischer Schriftsteller Club* (Vienna:, Köln, Graz: Hermann Böhlaus Nachf., 1984), pp. 23-38.

man rights and the persecution of writers in Nazi Germany. The opposition to this motion remained firm, causing such Nazi sympathizers as Corti, Wladimir von Hartlieb, Robert Hohlbaum, Mirko Jelusich, and Franz Spunda to leave the meeting. A few months later Bruno Brehm, Emil Ertl, Hans von Hammerstein, Enrica von Handel-Mazetti, Franz Nabl, Othmar Spann, Dora Stockert-Meynert, Felix Salten, Karl Hans Strobl, Grete Urbanitzky, and the publisher, Paul Zsolnay, all resigned from the P.E.N. Club. This mass exodus virtually depleted the organization, leaving only Csokor, Auernheimer, Fontana, Frischauer, Jacob Neumann, and Robert Musil.[3]

Grete Urbanitzky, the secretary of the P.E.N. Club, justified her support of Hitler by portraying him as the last bulwark against Bolshevism; she joined other Austrian writers in urging readers and publishers in Germany to boycott those who had signed the P.E.N. resolution condemning the book burnings.[4] Auernheimer, who knew her well from working with her in the P.E.N. Club, described her affiliation with the Nazi party as follows:

> Mrs. Urbanitzky's heyday came when Mr. Felix Salten was chairman. Salten was an author of the Zsolnay Publishing House and so very soon was Mrs. Urbanitzky. She made the missing link between the appeaser Zsolnay and the growing Nazi party, to whose "ideology" she felt much attracted, overcompensating her racial minority complex by the strongest—and soon enough—socialist feelings. She belonged to the group of P.E.N. Club members who left the club demonstratively in June 1933 after the majority of the membership had approved the protest against the Nazi methods concerning literature, burning of books, racial persecution, and so on. Not at all terrified by these atrocities Mrs. Urbanitzky, in

---

[3] Franz Theodor Csokor, *Zeuge einer Zeit. Briefe aus dem Exil 1933-1950* (Munich, Vienna: Langen-Müller, 1964), p. 33.

[4] Klaus Amann, *P.E.N.*, p. 41: Also Klaus Amann, *Der Anschluß österreichischer Schriftsteller an das dritte Reich*, p. 80.

the last years before Hitler raped Austria, became an assiduous commuter between Schuschnigg Vienna and Hitler Berlin, where she was *persona grata* if not *gratissima*.[5]

Other Austrians also published statements against their own colleagues and countrymen as a means of currying favor in Germany. Hence, the consequences of this stand on principle by the P.E.N. Club members were serious, for the idealists who supported the resolution soon found themselves blacklisted and boycotted in Germany. They could no longer publish or lecture there, nor could their plays be performed, a severe economic loss. Whether it had been his true reason or simply a screen for his political convictions, Salten was correct in warning that confronting Nazi Germany would result in economic deprivation for Austrian writers. Salten's stand emphasizes what has always been true, namely, that Austrian writers need German publishers and German readers to survive, since there have always been more writers in Austria than the country could support by itself. Traditionally, more books of Austrian writers have been published in Germany than at home, a situation that is as true today as at the turn of the century, when all of the major writers appeared with the S. Fischer Verlag. To lose the German market and the German theaters was a major setback if one's living depended on literary income, for there was no replacement for that market. The issue became one of choosing between "gutes Geschäft oder gutes Gewissen," as Csokor expressed it.[6] Salten, unfortunately, did not even have this choice, despite his acquiescence; as a Jewish writer he had to flee to Switzerland in 1938 to escape arrest.

Csokor's case is also instructive in this matter, for he was offered the possibility of having his plays performed and his

---

[5] Unpublished statement prepared by Raoul Auernheimer. Document in this writer's possession.

[6] Franz Theodor Csokor, *Zeuge einer Zeit*, p. 24.

books published in Germany if he would withdraw his name from the protest.[7] For the National Socialists it would have represented a major coup to win over a writer of the stature and reputation of Csokor. But he refused to sell out to this form of bribery and held to his principles. Many others, however, were quick to endorse National Socialism in the hope of greater recognition at home by eliminating the competition of the Jewish writers and in the expectation of preferred treatment in Germany in the form of publications, performances, and readings. Accordingly, the authors most often invited to Germany during the 1930s included Anton Bossi-Fedrigatti (9), Bruno Brehm (17), Robert Hohlbaum (19), Mirko Jelusich (12), Karl Heinrich Waggerl (13), and Josef Weinheber (16).[8] All became members of the National Socialist *Kulturgemeinde* founded under the sponsorship of Joseph Goebbels on 4 June 1934 to replace the earlier *Kampfbund* which had been established in 1928 by Alfred Rosenberg and dissolved in November 1933. Others also joined the movement in the hopes of winning recognition in Germany, including Franz Karl Ginzkey, Paula Grogger, Max Mell, Franz Nabl, Josef Georg Oberkofler, Hermann Heinz Ortner, Joseph F. Perkonig, Karl Schönherr, Ferdinand Schreyvogel, and Heinrich Suso Waldeck, among others. All of them were rewarded for their political support by being favored and promoted in Germany, although not always to the extent that they had expected. Franz Nabl, for example, felt that he never reaped the advantages he had expected. Writers who did not join the *Reichsverband Deutscher Schriftsteller* were boycotted in Germany.

In 1936 a new National Socialist organization, *Bund der deutschen Schriftsteller Österreichs,* was founded in Austria to replace the decimated P.E.N. Club. It was modeled on the German *Reichsschrifttumskammer* and served the purpose of distin-

---

[7]Ibid., p. 54.

[8]Klaus Amann, *Der Anschluß österreichischer Schriftsteller an das dritte Reich,* p. 45.

guishing between reliable and unreliable writers. Max Mell served as the first president. In 1939 the *Bund* became an official branch of the *Reichsschrifttumskammer* with Hans Karl Strobl as president. Since a number of the members were former P.E.N. Club members, this organization despite its membership of known Nazi sympathizers maintained a veneer of respectability. The government's sponsorship in Germany combined with the collusion of journalists and academic critics enabled a number of these authors to receive state prizes during the 1930s; Richard Billinger, Hans Karl Ginzkey, Max Mell, Josef Perkonig, Josef Wenter, Theodor Mayer, Paula Grogger, Josef Georg Oberkofler, Hermann Heinz Ortner, Friedrich Schreyvogel, Karl Heinrich Waggerl, and Josef Weinheber were all officially honored. Furthermore, the public bought their books in large numbers, mainly historical novels, war novels, and reminiscences, as well as plays and novels in the tradition of *Heimatliteratur*. While these works did not necessarily espouse the *Blut-und-Boden* line of National Socialist literature, it was so close that it was difficult to differentiate between them. In some cases such literature contained the *Blut-und-Boden* themes in encoded fashion for the initiated. Not only were these narrative works widely read, but historical plays by National Socialist writers were also performed at the prestigious Burgtheater and Akademietheater. Thus the economic argument proves to be only a specious screen for the blatant anti-Semitism which in any case has always flourished in the provinces. Only Zweig had printings equal to those of Rudolf Hans Bartsch's *Zwölf aus der Steiermark* (1911) or *Das deutsche Leid* (1912), Ginzkey's *Der von der Vogelweide* (1912), or books by Bruno Brehm, Rudolf Greinz, Robert Hohlbaum, or Mirko Jelusich.[9] The issue was rather one of literary quality, which brought critical acclaim but not necessarily financial reward. Robert Musil, for example, lived much of his later life in penury supported by donations from friends and advances from his

---

[9]Ibid., p. 65.

publishers, while the works of Mirko Jelusich, whose National Socialist affiliation began in the *Kampfbund* in 1928, sold in editions ranging from 80 to 110 thousand copies.

Many of the prominent writers had begun producing literature acceptable to National Socialism during the 1920s to combat what was regarded as the pernicious influence of the predominately Jewish writers from Vienna—Beer-Hofmann, Hofmannsthal, Schnitzler, and Zweig—who were considered the leading writers of the time. Actually, this conflict between Vienna and the provinces was not new; it has a long history in Austria. One of the major campaigns at the turn of the century was aimed at overcoming the hostility between Vienna and the provinces, and this call was repeated in 1945, following World War II, to little avail.[10] The antagonism remains in evidence to this day in the continuing division between writers of the P.E.N. Club in Vienna and those of the *Autorenversammlung* in Graz. Because of the multiplicity of reasons motivating authors to join the National Socialist movement, considerable research is still needed on each author. Many certainly joined out of opportunism, feeling that the Jewish writers were receiving an unfair proportion of the prestige and acclaim as the best writers Austria had to offer, thus denying non-Jewish writers both reputation and monetary return. By seizing the opportunity to eliminate the Jewish competition they hoped to advance their own cause, just as people in every manner of job denounced their superiors in Germany to remove them and thus advance to a better position. Denunciation played a major role in the *Gleichschaltung*.

Although many Austrian writers opportunistically expected to gain economic advantage in Germany by joining the National Socialist program, at the same time, in the interest of fairness, it must be kept in mind that some of the authors joined the Nazi

---

[10]Donald G. Daviau, "Das junge und das Jüngste Wien," *Österreichische Gegenwart. Die moderne Literatur und ihr Verhältnis zur Tradition*. Wolfgang Paulsen, Hrsg. (Bern, Munich: Francke, 1980), pp. 81-114.

movement out of the conviction that the Anschluss was a long overdue action, for the idea of Anschluss has a lengthy tradition going back to 1867, when Germany expelled Austria from their union. The Schönerer movement of the 1880s had pursued Anschluss as a major goal. and Germany and Austria had been united in World War I, only to be forcibly separated again by the harsh terms of the Versailles Treaty.

Not only were efforts made to lure and drive writers into the National Socialist camp, but economic pressure was also exerted on the publishing houses to enforce the ban on anti-Nazi authors. Zsolnay, for example, was threatened with economic ruin by a boycott in Germany and had to transfer his loyal Austrian writers to publishers in Switzerland, while the firm was forced to publish Nazi writers like Urbanitzky. Actually, not much pressure was necessary, for Zsolnay had joined the group who departed from the P.E.N. Club in June 1933, and, according to Auernheimer, the publisher was more than willing to sell out his authors in order to retain his place on the German market:

> When Hitler seized power in Germany and prepared his seizure of power in Austria, these barriers [between the Austrian authors and the German reader] became gradually insurmountable. From this moment on Zsolnay tried to "appease" the Nazis by concessions. They were twofold: he published pro-Nazi writers and he avoided as far as possible publishing those authors who were undesirable according to the Nuremberg Laws or because of their democratic convictions. It was under his and mouthpiece Salten's influence that at the international congress of the P.E.N. Club at Ragusa, June 1933, any strong protest against the burning of books in Germany and other Nazi atrocities was withheld. In fact, Zsolnay publications were admitted to the "Reich" until the annexation of Austria. Shortly after this event Zsolnay . . . disappeared noiselessly from Nazified Vienna.[11]

---

[11] Report prepared by Raoul Auernheimer. Copy in this writer's possession.

Zsolnay's role was possibly more difficult than Auernheimer recognized, and the latter's strong indictment illustrates the need to examine each case individually. To stay in business at all, Zsolnay was forced to make compromises. For example, he was not able to be very helpful to Csokor, who in 1933 counted heavily on his friend and publisher Zsolnay for support after the German market was closed to him: "Gott sei Dank habe ich ja Dich, lieber Freund und Deinen Verlag."[12] Zolnay published Csokor's eulogy of old Austria, *Dritter November 1918* in 1936, even though it could not be sold or performed in Germany. The premiére was held at the Burgtheater in Vienna on 11 December 1937, thanks to the integrity of Director Roebbeling, who attempted as much as possible to keep the theater free of politics. For his efforts he was replaced the day after the Anschluss by Mirko Jelusich, who insisted that Roebbeling clear out his office and vacate the premises that very day.

Another major force working within Austria to undermine the literary and cultural life was that of the academic world; leading faculty members willingly endorsed National Socialism, either out of conviction or opportunism. Two of the major literary historians, Heinz Kindermann and Joseph Nadler, lent their prestige and talent to replacing the traditional Austrian literary canon with a new set of standards conforming to German policies. They praised literature for its political rather than its aesthetic merits and acclaimed works that fulfilled the purpose of gathering and strengthening followers of National Socialism rather than those which contained the traditional humanistic and humanitarian values. Similarly, the historian Heinrich Ritter von Srbik followed the National Socialist line in his works.

One force attempting to defend Austria's interests against the dominance of Nazi-influenced writers was Guido Zernatto (1903-1943), a staunch patriot who divided his talents between literature and politics. In 1929 Zernatto was called by Schuschnigg to

---

[12]Franz Theodor Csokor, *Zeuge einer Zeit*, p. 41.

become Secretary of the "Heimatblock," a forerunner of the party called the "Heimatschutz," which eventually was transformed into the "Heimwehr" paramilitary organization. Zernatto, a conservative Catholic, was dedicated to the concept of "old Austria," that is, to the traditional Austria that existed prior to the formation in 1918 of the "Staat, den keiner wollte." In 1934 he became Vice-President of the "Katholischer Schriftstellerverband," and in 1935 he was named Vice-President of the state-operated Austrian Bundesverlag, the leading Austrian publishing house for school texts. He also served as a member of the "Bundeskulturrat" overseeing the cultural activities of the state, with responsibility for formulating cultural policies that supported Schuschnigg's aims. When Prince Starhemberg, the leader of the "Vaterländische Front" became a liability to Schuschnigg because of his support for Mussolini's intervention in Ethiopia, Zernatto was invited to join Schuschnigg's cabinet as Secretary of State. He served in this capacity and headed the "Vaterländische Front" organization until the Anschluss.

In 1936 Chancellor Schuschnigg appointed Zernatto head of a new organization called *Neues Leben* with a broad charter covering leisure-time activities in Austria: culture, athletics, and travel. The following year the organization introduced a cultural journal under the same name, a publication made necessary in 1934 because one of the terms of the Non-intervention Pact Schuschnigg signed with von Papen in Germany was the relegalization of the National Socialist Party, which had been banned since 1933. Censorship was relaxed in general, and the still illegal Social Democrats were also able to increase their public activities. Hence, there was a critical need to combat such propaganda efforts by stressing the Austrian heritage, Catholic values, and the traditional life of the provinces. One purpose was to arouse Austrian patriotism and to keep Austria independent rather than to let it succumb to the annexational blandishments of the National Socialists, both in Germany and in Austria. The reception of *Neues Leben* was good, and circulation exceeded

300,000 copies, but the attempt came too late. Only the three issues of December 1937 and January and February 1938 appeared before the Anschluss ended its publication. Zernatto was even more adamant than Schuschnigg in his opposition to Anschluss, and he fought for the plebiscite until the last moment. Like so many others on the Nazis' list of political enemies, Zernatto had to flee, escaping first to Bratislava and eventually making his way to the United States, where he died in 1943.

As a result of the liberal policy on publication after 11 July 1936, Otto Basil, who had been thinking about a journal devoted to the arts since 1935, decided to proceed with the publication. Thus was born *Plan,* a periodical intended to serve as a voice of opposition to the aesthetic policies of both the "Vaterländische Front" and the National Socialists. The journal, devoted to art, architecture, and literature, proclaimed its intention of defending the integrity of the arts: "Our little journal represents—conceived aphoristically—the attempt to bring in manifest expression and in detailed presentation young and living art, that is, art struggling for meaning and expression in contemporary form to the reader."[13]

As an active socialist, Basil had developed *Plan* to oppose the literary trend that had come to dominate Austrian literature after 1933: provincial literature modeled on the *Blut-und-Boden* literature in Germany, which combined a strong sense of nationalistic fervor with an almost mystical belief in the strength to be gained from close ties to the land. The aesthetic program of the strongly Catholic, fascist-oriented "Vaterländische Front," while not to be identified with the National Socialist program, was nevertheless similarly oriented toward a glorification of the healthy life in the provinces as contrasted with the "decadence" of Vienna. Thus in general the "official" literary approach sanctioned by the Austrian government appeared not far removed

---

[13]Otto Basil, *Plan,* No. 1 (1938), inside cover.

from that of Germany. It was a question of degree more than of kind.

Like *Neues Leben,* only the three issues of *Plan* in December 1937 and January and February 1938 were published, and of these only the first was actually circulated. The second and third issues, which among other things emphasized workers' literature, were confiscated, and further publication of this socialist periodical was banned. Not a single copy of the last two issues survived. Basil was summoned to appear before the Gestapo in September 1938 and might have been sent to a concentration camp had it not been for Weinheber's intercession on his behalf. Basil was reduced to keeping a low profile during the war and, like Gütersloh, worked in a factory. After the war he revived *Plan* and intended to publish the names and biographies of more than seventy major authors who had joined the National Socialists, but he did not carry out this idea. The journal itself could not long be sustained, but Basil is nevertheless a noteworthy figure in the immediate postwar period for the important role he played, along with Rudolf Henz, Friedrich Torberg, and Hans Weigel, in helping to bridge the literary hiatus caused by the Anschluss.

Quite amazingly, despite the division within the P.E.N. Club during the 1930s and the German pressures placed on authors and publishers in Austria, few writers were still alarmed enough to flee the country. Partly this is a testimony to the secrecy with which the infiltration of the literary circles was carried out. The National Socialists' maneuvering was kept among sworn initiates and was not widely circulated. Additionally, a great deal of the conspiracy was accomplished orally to avoid having records or letters that could be traced. This situation was even more true after Dollfuß's ban of the National Socialist Party in Austria in June 1933, to which Germany responded with the "tausend Mark Sperre," a fee charged to Germans visiting Austria, as a means of hurting Austria's tourist business. The lack of written documentation makes the task of reconstructing this period extremely difficult, but considerable information can be gleaned, as Amann has shown. The need for a thorough examination is further shown in the ambiguous situations that have arisen. For example, a writer like Ortner is known to have collaborated with the National Socialists in the beginning, but at the end of the war he claimed to be a member of the resistance. The one may not necessarily preclude the other, for attitudes changed rapidly and radically within Austria after the country was occupied by the Germans.

Some writers left early, but essentially the feeling that everything would work out all right prevailed right up to the day of the Anschluss. One of the few who departed in timely fashion was Stefan Zweig, who always felt he could see the future more clearly than others. He worried about what he foresaw for Austria and emigrated to Great Britain in 1934, following a search of his home in Salzburg by police ostensibly searching for illegal weapons. This intrusion justified on a pretext made him realize that citizens had no protection against misused governmental and police power, and this recognition inspired his flight. He tried in vain to alert his friends and colleagues to depart as well, and he was depressed by the lack of concern that they displayed as they chided him for being a Cassandra. As late as 1937, in a letter to Felix Braun, Zweig lamented the total obliviousness to danger that he encountered among his friends and colleagues in Vienna. In 1938 he expressed his concern about the hopeless situation that he could see coming for the Jews.[14] Csokor also foresaw the need to emigrate, and he too felt that his friends ignored his warnings.[15] Yet he himself did not leave Vienna until 18 March, a week after the Anschluss.

The vast majority of writers waited until the very last minute

---

[14]Unpublished letter to Felix Braun of 3 June 1938. The unpublished letters are located in the Stefan Zweig Archives at State University of New York, Fredonia.

[15]Franz Theodor Csokor, *Zeuge einer Zeit*, p. 76.

to leave the country. In the early 1930s no one in Austria, including Zweig and Csokor, thought that Hitler would ever maintain himself in power, not to mention the possibility that he might ever annex Austria. The common view was that National Socialism would soon self-destruct of its own excesses. Even when Hitler became chancellor there was no worry about his influence in Austria. The covert infiltration that had begun in a formal way in 1928 went undetected, and it was not until after the Anschluss had actually taken place that people realized the gravity of the situation. Even those who wanted the Anschluss never dreamed of German occupation but thought that things within Austria would remain pretty much the same. No one ever imagined how rapid and thorough the takeover would be, how quickly the borders would be sealed, and how completely control would shift to Nazi hands. Also, there was still faith in the legal system. So confident was Auernheimer of protection in Austria, for example, that he returned to Vienna from Zürich the day after the Anschluss only to be arrested and sent to Dachau because of his activity in the P.E.N. Club and also because he had sent a copy of his latest book, *Wien - Bild und Schicksal* (1938) to Chancellor Schuschnigg with a handwritten dedication congratulating him for defying Hitler's order against the plebiscite on the question of annexation. Fortunately, Auernheimer could be released six months later through the intervention of the German writer Emil Ludwig and the American attaché in Berlin, Prentice Gilbert, a personal friend who had translated two of Auernheimer's plays into English. Others were not so fortunate; Peter Hammerschlag, Paul Kornfeld, and Jura Soyfer died in concentration camps. Writers like Egen Friedell (died 1938), Ernst Weiss (died 1940), and Stefan Zweig (died 1942) committed suicide because they could not cope with exile.

The exodus in 1938 to escape Hitler and National Socialism represented a virtual *Who's Who* of Austrian literature, including such writers as Leopold von Andrian, Franz Blei, Felix Braun, Hermann Broch, Max Brod, Ferdinand Bruckner, Franz Theodor

Csokor, Albert Drach, Alfred Ehrenstein, Erich Fried, Paul Frischauer, Fritz Hochwälder, Ödön von Horváth, Ernst Lothar, Robert Musil, Robert Neumann, Hertha Pauli, Josef Roth, Hilde Spiel, Fritz Torberg, Johannes Urzidil, Ernst Waldinger, Hans Weigel, Franz Werfel, Martina Wied, and Stefan Zweig. At present no exact figures are available on how many writers emigrated: the Dokumentationsarchiv des österreichischen Widerstandes in Vienna is engaged in an attempt to establish numbers and distributions. Depending upon who is counted as a writer, present estimates range anywhere from 150 to 400 authors who fled into exile to avoid either anti-Semitic persecution or political arrest. If one includes only those who earned their living as authors, the number is probably closer to the lower rather than the higher end of the scale.

Writers who did not leave early enough often had a difficult time arranging their departure and were usually forced to bribe officials for exit visas or had to attempt to escape over the border without papers at the risk of being turned over to the Austrian and German authorities if caught. Most of the émigrés who waited until the last moment before leaving had adventure-full stories to tell of their perilous journey to freedom. Hermann Broch, for example, was arrested and held prisoner, then released just long enough to enable him to escape. Hochwälder and Weigel slipped over the border illegally into Switzerland, while the majority fled to Prague and from there, via Switzerland, to Paris or Milan. The film by Axel Corti, *An uns glaubt Gott nicht mehr,* provides an excellent portrayal of the hardships and sufferings endured by the exiles. Most of the émigrés eventually made their way to the United States, but a number sought refuge in France, England, Holland, Sweden, and South America as well.[16] Because of the stature of the writers involved, the histo-

---

[16] See Sylvia M. Patsch, *Österreichische Schriftsteller im Exil in Grossbritannien* (Vienna, Munich: Brandstätter, 1985); Hans Würgner, ed., *Österreichische Exilliteratur in den Niederlanden 1934-1940* (Amsterdam: Rodopi, 1986);

ry of Austrian literature in exile represents an important chapter in the overall history of Austrian literature, for it was among the émigrés that the Austrian tradition found its continuity, while the works produced in Austria represented an aberration. The nature of this literature produced between 1938 and 1945 under National Socialism has been virtually ignored up to now and remains to be investigated.

The writers who remained in Austria after the Anschluss had three choices available to them: 1) to endorse the new regime, a course followed by the majority, including such prominent writers as Richard Billinger, Max Mell, Karl Schönherr, Josef Weinheber, and initially by Heimito von Doderer, an early enthusiast of the Nazi party who served in the German army but later repudiated the Nazi movement; 2) to write more or less neutral works to maintain one's integrity while trying to avoid giving offense to the Nazi government, so that one could continue publishing, the course presumably followed by Alexander Lernet-Holenia; 3) or to follow the path of "inner emigration," maintaining public silence while writing manuscripts for later publication, like Otto Basil and Rudolf Kassner, the friend of Hofmannsthal and Rilke, who remained quietly in Vienna throughout the war. Despite his efforts at adopting a low profile, Albert Paris Gütersloh was still branded as a decadent artist because of his painting and forced to work in a war factory. Similarly, Rudolf Henz was fired from his position as head of RAVAG, the radio network, and found it preferable to refrain from writing during the Nazi occupation, devoting himself to restoring stained glass windows.

Lernet-Holenia's situation has brought mixed reactions. Some critics like Hilde Spiel[17] and Hugo Schmidt,[18]rtist feel that he

---

Ulrich Weinzierl, ed., *Österreicher im Exil. Frankreich 1938-1945. Eine Dokumentation* (Vienna: Österreichischer Bundesverlag, 1986); John Spalek und Joseph Strelka, eds., *Deutsche Exilliteratur, Kalifornien*, 2 vols. (Bern, Munich: Francke, 1976).

[17]Hilde Spiel, *Die zeitgenössische Literatur Österreichs*, p. 39.

displayed courageous behavior in defending Austria in such novels as *Beide Sizilien* (1942) and *Mars im Widder,* published in magazine-form in 1941 and then banned until it was published in book-form in 1947. Yet Auernheimer viewed him as an opportunist:

> Lernet Holenia's political attitude always was antidemocratic and profaschist. This is to be read as well from his biography as from his books. The hero of his partly brilliant stories generally is a dashing aristocratic officer whose adventurous life reminds the Anglo-Saxon reader of the "cavaliers" of the English restoration feudalism. There is little hope that this buccaneer of sexual and racial greed ever will change to a decent human being.[19]

Since Auernheimer is known for his personal integrity, this example provides further evidence of the difficulty in assessing individual behavior at that time.

Another example is Weinheber, who is generally regarded as a collaborator, and who committed suicide in 1945 to avoid capture by the Russians. He embraced the National Socialist ideology early and published the journal *Der Augarten* until 1943 to publicize the National Socialist ideology. Yet he also interceded on behalf of his good friend Otto Basil and saved him from imprisonment. Auernheimer feels that extenuating circumstances explain and excuse Weinheber:

> Weinheber followed the tradition of the Austrian nineteenth-century writers who sold themselves to the State for a governmental employment to buy the luxury of independent literary creation; they were lazily busy to become busily idle

---

[18]Hugo Schmidt, "Alexander Lernet-Holenia" in Donald G. Davisu, ed., *Major Figures of Modern Austrian Literature* (Riverside, California: Ariadne Press, 1988), pp. 285-313.

[19]Unpublished report prepared by Raoul Auernheimer in this writer's possession.

> ... Weinheber was generally acknowledged as a genuine poet and artist of language after the publication of his first book of poems: *Adel und Untergang (Nobility and Its End)*. There was a hint in this successful title, which seems to recommend the author more to the fascist Right than to the socially minded Left of an already initiated contemporary readership.... The Nazis would have liked to reclaim this Viennese poet for their godforsaken "ideology," and there is but little doubt that staying in Vienna after "Anschluss" and during the War Weinheber could not help getting along with them in one way or another. Nevertheless, Weinheber may find his way back to human decency, which in fact he never has injured as an artist.... It is hoped that after victory Weinheber will re-establish himself as what he in the pre-Nazi-epoch has been: one of the very best of the contemporary Austrian poets.[20]

A number of provincial writers in Austria such as Rudolf Hans Bartsch, Richard Billinger, Gertrud Fussenegger, Franz Karl Ginzkey, Paula Grogger, Erica Handel-Mazzetti, Mirko Jelusich, Max Mell, Franz Nabl, Hermann Ortner, Heinz Hans Sassmann, Richard von Schaukal, Karl Schönherr, Franz Tumler and Josef Wenter, encouraged by the National Socialist endorsement of *Blut-und-Boden* literature, produced provincial (*völkisch*) works or historical plays, emphasizing Germanic heroes and pre-Christian pagan rituals or glorifying the strength deriving from ties to the soil. Two of these authors, Billinger and Mell, had begun their careers with great promise, drawing the favorable attention of Hofmannsthal, who was enthusiastic about their utilization of religious myths. The latter did not live to see how this initial artistic tendency easily developed in the 1930s into works fitting the National Socialist ideology. All of these writers produced works acceptable to the new regime and grew in reputation beyond the level of their true literary significance because of political sponsorship; after the war they continued for the

---

[20]Ibid.

most part to write without suffering any appreciable public or critical reaction to their earlier opportunism. In contrast to these writers, another close friend of Hofmannsthal, Leopold von Andrian, rejected Nazism and in 1937 before the Anschluss wrote the volume *Österreich im Prisma der Idee, Katechismus der Führenden* to argue against National Socialist ideas. In consequence, he spent the years 1938-1946 in Brazil.

For the writers in exile the first major problem to be faced, after achieving some kind of stability in their personal lives and in their living conditions, was language. Very few émigré writers learned the language of their host country well enough to write in it, with the exception of several writers in England who did actually produce books in English: Vickie Baum, Robert Hans Flesch-Brunnigen, Robert Neumann, Hermynia zur Mühlen, Salke and Berthold Viertel, and Martina Wied. Other writers published autobiographies and factual accounts in English: Ilse Barea, Franz Borkenau, Sir George Franckenstein, Willi Frischauer, Bruno Heitig, Hans Peter Kraus, and Oskar Kokoschka.[21] This situation has created an interesting body of work that now falls between two literary traditions, not counting either as Austrian works or as part of the English literary tradition.

In general, in England as in the United States, the majority of authors wrote their works in their native German and then employed a translator to render them into English. Except for Hermann Broch, who found a dedicated translator in Jean Untermayer, none of the other writers were as fortunate as Thomas Mann, whose works were unusually well translated by the dedicated efforts of Helen Tracy Lowe-Porter. Both Broch and Mann knew enough English to be able to work with their translators in polishing the renditions, but most writers had to find translators wherever they could, usually individuals recruited by the publishing house. The primary prerequisite, then as now, was that they work cheaply, and the results rarely achieved a level above

---

[21]Sylvia Patsch, *Österreichische Schriftsteller im Exil in Grossbritannien.*

adequate, if that. But the quality of the translations was not the main concern to the authors. To be published at all was a major triumph. All of the exiled writers shared a concern about keeping their German style intact, an indication that they all harbored the expectation of being read by German readers again, and usually lived in the hope of returning "home" after the war.

Not only the language-problem and the difficulty of presenting their works in translation handicapped the émigré writers. They also had grown accustomed to writing for a known audience whose shared interests and backgrounds they knew well. Now they faced the difficulty of writing for a totally different audience in a new setting without that shared background. Stefan Zweig, the most translated Austrian author, whose works had appeared regularly in English as well as in many other languages, suffered no loss of reputation and no difficulty or break in the continuity of his production while moving to England, to the United States, and, finally in 1941, to South America. The most cosmopolitan of all Austrian writers, he had made successful lecture-tours both in the United States and in South America, and he was well known on both continents. His series of historical biographies were all well accepted by the public in English, and *Marie Antoinette,* his most popular contribution in this genre, was even included in the abridged-book series of the *Reader's Digest.* Zweig's novella *Brief an eine Unbekannte* was also made into a popular film entitled *Letter to an Unknown Woman,* although Americans do not generally recognize Zweig as the author of the story that served as the basis of the movie.

Major success was also achieved by Ernst Lothar, who produced two novels that became bestsellers and choices of book clubs, *Die Zeugin* (1941, *A Woman is Witness*), and *Unter anderer Sonne* (1943, *Beneath Another Sun*). Other successes included *Der Engel mit der Posaune* (1944, *The Angel with the Trumpet*), *Die Tür geht auf* (1945, *The Door Opens*), *Heldenplatz* (1945, *The Prisoner*), and *Die Rückkehr* (1949, *Return to Vienna*) After a disappointing beginning of his exile in New York, where he attempted to found a German-speaking theater together with Raoul Auernheimer and others, Lothar was successful in obtaining a teaching position at Colorado College in Colorado Springs, where he was able to use his experience as a director both in putting on productions of plays and in teaching Austrian dramatic literature to his students. Lothar was highly influential in creating a favorable image of Austria in the United States through his sphere of influence as a teacher and through his lectures and writings. His wife, Adrienne Gessner, enjoyed a successful career as a prominent actress on the New York stage.

But for every émigré who successfully made the transition to a new country and a new life, there were many others who found the adjustment difficult. Felix Braun supported himself meagerly in England; while in the United States, Raoul Auernheimer, a close friend of Lothar, was assisted financially by his son-in-law and daughter, who had settled in California in the late 1920s. The tragedy of Auernheimer's later years was caused by his inability to produce works that appealed to an American audience. His literary debut in English translation began auspiciously enough, for in 1938, after his release from the concentration camp at Dachau and his arrival in New York, where he was joined by his wife, he sought to emulate his good friend Stefan Zweig by writing a historical novel *Metternich—Statesman and Lover* (1941). This was a favorite genre of émigré writers because it was a more universal form that could appeal to readers in every country. Moreover, the historical setting also allowed inoffensive comments on the contemporary political situation by allusion and analogy. Auernheimer tried to publish a direct account of his imprisonment, but it was rejected by publishers on the ground that the book was not sensational enough and did not describe enough atrocities. When Auernheimer remonstrated that he could not write about anything that he had not personally witnessed, his plea was ignored. He finally found it possible to publish an excerpt in the weekly magazine, *Christian Science Monitor,* but was prevented from presenting Americans with his full text containing the kind of insight that would have been useful in 1939.[22] His full account appeared in print only as part of his autobiography, *Das Wirtshaus zur verlorenen Zeit,* published posthumously in 1948.[23]

Auernheimer's fate is representative of the majority of writers in exile, most of whom were not major writers on the order of Broch or Werfel, but who nevertheless had been well-known authors with a substantial following in Austria. Auernheimer, for example, a cousin of Theodor Herzl, had moved in the best literary circles in Vienna as a friend of Hofmannsthal and Schnitzler[24] and had pursued a successful career as drama critic and feuilletonist for the *Neue Freie Presse,* Austria's most prestigious newspaper, until he resigned in 1933 to protest what he held to be pro-fascist leanings of the newspaper. He was replaced by his former friend and P.E.N. Club nemesis, Felix Salten.

Auernheimer's difficulties in publishing his works in exile reveal another dilemma of exiled authors: what was acceptable for publication? The continuing German-language publishing houses had to be careful to print what they could sell, and American, British, or French publishers were also highly selective for the same economic reasons. Sentiment or former friendships played no role in determining their choices; the market ruled. Propaganda was out, as were accounts of Nazi brutality—until the war broke out, and then they were acceptable. Historical novels were safe, and escape literature, avoiding rather than addressing the political reality, was also a desideratum. Since the publishers had the last word about what they could or would

---

[22]Raoul Auernheimer, "Inside Barbed Wire," *The Christian Science Monitor* (26 September 1942).

[23]Raoul Auernheimer, "Gastspiel in der Hölle," *Das Wirtshaus zur verlorenen Zeit* (Vienna: Amalthea, 1948), pp. 223-272.

[24]Donald G. Daviau and Jorun B. Johns, eds., *The Correspondence of Arthur Schnitzler and Raoul Auernheimer* (Chapel Hill: University of North Carolina Press, 1972).

print, authors struggling for survival had little choice but to cooperate. The history of publishers during the years of exile is an important chapter in itself[25] as is the history of film.[26] A number of writers were recruited by Hollywood—Werfel and Torberg among them—and a few Austrian directors like Billy Wilder, Fritz Lang, Otto Preminger, and George Froeschel achieved major careers. Few of the authors succeeded as well, even those who worked as scriptwriters in Hollywood.

Auernheimer is also representative of another extremely important aspect of life in exile: the attitude of the émigrés toward Austria. Even though he had spent six months in Dachau, Auernheimer harbored no ill feelings toward Austria. On the contrary, he remained a devoted patriot. One of the greatest achievements of the Austrian writers in exile, one of inestimable importance for influencing the Allied treatment of Austria after the war, was the unified, loyal, and patriotic stance of the émigrés. Almost unanimously the writers in exile exculpated Austria from any responsibility for their fate and went to great lengths in their writings and in their public speeches to create an autonomous identity for Austria, carefully separating it from Germany and hence from complicity in German guilt in causing the war.

Auernheimer wrote a number of essays and gave many talks before a variety of American groups on such topics as "Austria—Not in Germany," "Hitler and Napoleon," "There Was a Country Named Austria," "Some Words about Austria," all designed to create in the minds of Americans the fact that Austria

---

[25] Murray G. Hall, *Österreichische Verlagsgeschichte 1918-1938*. 2 vols. (Vienna: Böhlau, 1985); also M.G.H., "Buchhandel und Verlag der dreißiger Jahre im Spiegel von Innen- und Außenpolitik," in Klaus Amann and Albert Berger, eds., *Österreichische Literatur der dreißiger Jahre*, pp. 164-177; and Wulf Koepke "Die Exilschriftsteller und der amerikanische Buchmarkt," in *Deutsche Exilliteratur seit 1933*, vol. 1, *Kalifornien*, edited by John M. Spalek and Joseph Strelka (Bern, Munich: Francke, 1976), pp. 117-134.

[26] See Erna M. Moore, "Exile in Hollywood," in *Deutsche Exilliteratur seit 1933*, vol. I, *Kalifornien*, pp. 21-39.

should be regarded as a separate entity from Germany and that Austrians should not be considered Germans and certainly not Nazis. The exiles generally depicted Austria as the helpless victim of annexation, and they attributed their own fate of being driven into exile to the circumstances caused by the German Nazis and not to their countrymen. This positive image of an Austria occupied against its will prevailed in the minds of the Allies and contributed to the Allied decision to treat Austria differently from Germany after the war. Austrian writers in various parts of the United States, particularly in Los Angeles and New York as well as in England and France, all presented the same message. These individual efforts effectively supplemented the attempts of the émigrés to create larger political groups which could speak with the more powerful voice of unity. An open appeal to President Roosevelt entitled "Für ein freies Österreich" in the French anti-Hitler review *Freies Österreich,* is indicative of the tenor of all these statements:

> And yet there is one motto—a single one—to which the entire nation of Austria subscribes, for which, according to the pledge of impartial and objective observers, Monarchists and Republicans, Christians and Jews, Democrats and Socialists will fight and die. This motto is: "Down with Hitler. For a free, autonomous, independent Austria.[27]

In the United States *The Austro-American Tribune* was founded similarly to create a sense of group spirit among the Austrian exiles.

Another example of the strong feeling for Austria is the case of Friedrich Torberg, whose novel *Auch das war Wien* contributes to the revisionism occurring today about Austria's conduct in the 1930s and particularly at the time of the Anschluss. The work, planned as the first part of a trilogy covering the stages of his flight into exile, was written in 1938-1939 and prepared for

---

[27]*Freies Österreich,* Jg. 3, Heft 1 (May 1940), 4-5.

publication in 1941 while he was in the United States. Yet, although the novel was completed, Torberg refrained from publishing it. His wife released the manuscript after his death in 1984. The novel, which is quite weak— probably one of the reasons Torberg declined to publish it— drew little notice after it appeared, but the film version, *38,* by director Christoph Gluck was nominated for an Academy Award as the best foreign film of 1987. The film has attracted added attention because of its relevance to the current controversial political situation caused by the accusation of complicity in war crimes leveled against the Austrian president, Kurt Waldheim. The film and the novel are contributing to the broad revaluation of the reaction of Austria to the Anschluss and the amount of resistance to it. Since Torberg did not release the novel, it is apparent that beyond his dissatisfaction with it as a work of art he had changed his mind about the contents, which were written in a period of anger and heightened emotions. In the United States he joined those voices attempting to exculpate Austria from war guilt, and, like the vast majority, he lived for the day when he would be allowed to resume his life in Austria. As soon as it was possible, after the war he returned to Vienna to help rebuild and reorganize the literary scene and particularly to combat communist influences.

In essence, then, the literary scene in Austria during the 1930s was a heterogeneous, fragmented period with the major writers attempting to cling to a status quo that had already disappeared in 1918 with the end of the monarchy and the advent of the First Republic, along with a group of writers following political expediency, and a new generation of writers who were still in the initial phases of their careers. There was a tendency among the older writers like Broch, Musil, Roth, and Zweig to continue to perpetuate the Austrian tradition and a general refusal to acknowledge that the age which best suited their temperaments and to which they had attuned their writings was changing before their very eyes. The attempt to preserve a mood of nostalgia created a head-in-the-sand attitude or what Doderer termed "Apperzeptionsverweigerung" toward politics. In consequence, a reality for which they were not prepared and against which they were defenseless simply overtook the writers and changed or took their lives. Whether earlier recognition of the threat of Nazism could have changed the situation in any way is a moot point, but little was done, as most of the leading writers abrogated all responsibility to act as a public conscience and to take an active role in guiding the country on the political level. While this valuable lesson was not lost on the German writers of the postwar period who determined to take a more active role in the political sphere, it played little role in Austria because there was little need to treat the issues raised by the war, since Austria had been absolved of any responsibility by being declared the first victim of Hitler.

The writers who made a concerted effort to control the course of Austrian literature were those enthusiastically predisposed toward National Socialism. in 1936 after establishing the "Bund der deutschen Schriftsteller Österreichs," which developed into an organization analogous to the *Reichschrifttumskammer* in Germany, seventy of the members celebrated this event by contributing to a *Bekenntnisbuch* to pledge their loyalty to Hitler and the aims of National Socialism. The programmatic introductory poem by Max Stebich clearly sets the tone and indicates the aspirations of this group of writers as well as their assistance in preparing the way for Hitler:

> Die führenden nationalen Dichter Österreichs
> schlossen sich
> im Dezember des Jahres 1936
> in der Zeit unerträglichster Verfolgungen und
> Verfernungen des deutschen Menschen ihres Heimatlandes
> zusammen zu einem
> Bund der deutschen Schriftsteller Österreichs
> Unermüdlich und unbeirrbar, mutig und opferbereit
> halfen sie
> durch die Kraft ihrer Persönlichkeit,
> durch ihr dichterisches Werk

> den Weg zur Befreiung ihres Volkes
> bahnen und vollenden.[28]

Most of the contributors were second-rate writers who had played little significant role in the literary history of Austria but who now hoped for greater importance by virtue of controlling literary matters after driving out or silencing the major writers. Each of the contributors attempted to surpass the others in proclaiming the jubilation of Austrian writers at rejoining Germany or in celebrating in the jargon of the time their ecstatic feelings at having returned home to the German Reich. The tone and style, as might be expected, reflected political fanaticism in terms of hyperbole and rhetorical excess. The writers' motivation stemmed from a desire to demonstrate loyalty in order to gain political and economic advantage. But other factors played a role: political conviction, political views on the basis of family background, and political innocence because of the naiveté of the writers concerned.

The *Bekenntnisbuch,* begun in December 1936 and published, ironically, by the Kristall-Verlag in Vienna in 1938, represents the *nadir* of twentieth-century Austrian literature, a wholesale repudiation of the humanistic and humanitarian values that the best of Austrian literature has always represented. The situation proved to be only a temporary one, however, for the true Austrian literary canon remained alive among the exiled writers. The attempt of the scholars and publishers to replace the traditional literature with an ideologically motivated culture proved to be an

---

[28] "The leading national poets of Austria / joined together / in December of the year 1936 / in the time of the most unbearable persecutions and / estrangements of the German people from their homeland / in a / League of German authors of Austria. / Tireless and determined, courageous and self-sacrificing / they helped / through the strength of their character, / through their poetic work / to open and complete / the way to the liberation of their people." *Bekenntnisbuch österreichischer Dichter,* ed. Bund deutscher Schriftsteller Österreichs (Vienna: Krystall-Verlag, 1938), p. 7.

abysmal failure. The interrupted tradition was revived immediately in the postwar period[29] and has continued to develop and flourish to the present day, not only surviving one of the most difficult chapters in Austrian literary history, but ultimately prevailing.

---

[29]Donald G. Daviau, "The Postwar Revival of the Austrian Literary Tradition," in *Deutsche Exilliteratur der Nachkriegszeit* (Frankfurt am Main: Peter Lang, 1981), pp. 73-87.

Austrian Universities and the Anschluss

Walter Höflechner

How and in what way did the universities contribute to the coming of the Anschluss in the years before 1938?[1]

The universities were one of the most important factors in Austria which led to the Anschluss. The main reason that they played such an important role was because they fostered both science and nationalism. As these two, science and nationalism, grew together in an ambivalent process at the end of the nineteenth century, they both gained significant influence. The catalyst in this process was the word "German" (Deutsch).

In the middle of the nineteenth century, when the process began, Austria was nearly fifty years behind the Prussians in science and technology, and Austria tried to solve her problem by importing young scientists, young professors from Prussian and other German universities. Hermann Bonitz, for example, one of the most important reformers, beside Leo von Thun and Franz Exner, had been called from Berlin. In the 1850s and 1860s a large number of enthusiastic young men came to Austrian universities. Their enthusiasm for science won them great influence over their Austrian students, an influence enhanced by the way in which they contrasted with the older professors at the Austrian universities, professors who had been schooled in the Pre-March (*Vormärz*), in the years before 1848. The older Aus-

---

[1]This chapter is based on the author's *Fragment einer neueren Geschichte des Hochschulwesens in Österreich.* Part I of *Die Baumeister des künftigen Glücks. Vom Ausgang des 19. Jahrhunderts bis in das Jahr 1938.* Publikationen aus dem Archiv der Universität Graz, 23 (Graz, 1988).

trian professors were not considered to be true scientists, in the modern sense of the word, either by their younger German colleagues or by their students. In this situation "German scholarship" (*deutsche Wissenschaft*) became a mighty and effective slogan, which soon was beyond question or need of justification.

Three factors intensified the effect of the idea of "German scholarship" and its impact:

The first was the discussion of Darwin's theory of evolution, which brought about the discussion of "free" science and cognition without any assumption of religion or its influence, or any other ideological system, on the one hand, and science in connection with, or under the premise of, religion and faith, on the other hand. German scholarship had been, and was then, non-Catholic, whereas in Austria science, and the whole state, had been dominated by Catholicism. The disciples of German scholarship also became proponents of anticlericalism and anti-Catholicism, and both increased mightily until the beginning of World War I.

The second factor was the feeling of border-consciousness. Like Prussia, Austria originated from a small territory at the eastern border of the Holy Roman Empire. In this regard, Austria's role was interpreted in different manners: in a liberal and positive manner, holding Austria to be a connecting link between two different elements of Europe; in a negative manner, holding Austria to be a frontier territory at the border separating good from bad, superior from inferior. The consequence of the second interpretation was that Austria developed a feeling of mission and self-preservation—and both were bad because they induced an erroneous self-assessment. In a time of growing nationalistic fervor, the people of the German-speaking territories in Austria saw themselves as frontiersmen, especially in science and culture. It takes only a few minutes to collect a page of special *epitheta* characterizing, for example, the University of Graz as a bulwark of occidental culture and, especially, of German science against the storming hordes coming from the East, as an outpost in the heavy and heroic fight at the frontier against the Slavs, and so on. Over and over, one can read about the Huns and Avars, the Mongolians, the Turks and the Slavs attacking poor old Austria. As early as the fourteenth century Austria had been regarded as *cor et clippeus Romani imperii*, as heart and shield of the Holy Roman Empire.

The third factor was the result of the victory of Prussia, of the Germans over the French in 1871, and the foundation of the German Reich at Versailles. Thereafter the international relations of Austrian scientists were focused in Germany, although in former times Austrian scientists—such as Josef Hammer-Purgstall and others—had enjoyed the best of relations with colleagues in nearly all the European countries. Just when a new generation of scientists arose and brought with it a new stage in the development of science, Austrian connections were reduced, not in quantity but in the quality and variety. It is a very important point, a very serious matter, that this change occurred in a period of exciting progress in science, and it would have effects until our own days, for we Austrians are still wanting in our international relations.

Twice during the pre-Anschluss period the United States tried to initiate academic relations with Austria. The first approach occurred during the last years before World War I, when Columbia University in New York City tried to establish connections with the University of Vienna; the second took place in 1910, when the mayor of Washington, D.C. sent a golden key to the rector of the University of Vienna as an invitation for a visit and as a signal for the beginning of scientific cooperation. In fact, George Stuart Fullerton became a visiting professor in Vienna in 1913, and he was even made an honorary professor of the university, but it was too late; the war began in 1914. After the war, the victors punished the vanquished by locking them out of international conferences and international cooperation. The French were the most enthusiastic in that enterprise, the British and Americans to a lesser degree. Then later, after the end of the war, the Americans, after first lending material support, began their next undertaking, one to break the isolation of Austrian (and German) scientists by efforts of the Rockefeller Foundation and, after 1927, even more by the Carnegie Endowment for International Peace. Professors from the University of California, Berkeley, Cornell University, Stanford University, and Columbia University came to Austria; however it was, for the second time, too late—the universities in Austria had already decided the direction that they would take.

Another important force, nationalism, was at work at the Austrian universities in preparing the way for Anschluss. It requires no extended explanations, for it was one of the most significant problems in the history of the Austro-Hungarian Monarchy and is, therefore, well known.

In the last decade of the nineteenth century the process of cultivating distinctions and separations of the nations seeking emancipation was a process that also took place in the universities. It is well known how the young, rising nations demanded their own universities: universities for the Czechs, universities for the Slovenes, for the Ruthenes, for the Poles, and all the rest. In the same spirit, the German-speaking Austrians began to see the universities in their territories of the monarchy as German universities, for the idea of a "German university" corresponded to their own idea of a university.

It may be remembered that the word "Austrian" at that time included all the nations in the Austrian part of the monarchy; it had never been a designation for the German-speaking population alone. Toward the end of the nineteenth century and thereafter, people needed a designation for the German-speakers to differentiate them from the Czechs, Poles, Slovenes, and others. The word they used was "German."

The only people who seemed not to belong to any of the established nations, and who had been excluded when nations began to be defined in a very strict sense, and when the notion of race as a criterion of determination began to gain influence, were the Jews.

In the 1870s and 1880s universities in Austria became the scene of the development of a very rigid and radical German nationalism which was more and more oriented toward Prussia. Austrian students in Vienna, Graz, Innsbruck, and Prague sang "Deutschland, Deutschland über Alles," and the birthday of Bismarck was celebrated by students and professors in a very enthusiastic manner. For such an event, the statue of Franz Josef was taken away from the hall. When Kaiser Wilhelm I died, the German-national students wore black and sent delegations to his funeral.

The universities also became the scene of the struggle between German-national students and Catholic students. The German-nationals did not accept Catholic students' corporations (fraternities) at official university ceremonies because they regarded them as pupils of the reactionary system of Catholicism and as antagonists of free science. One can hardly imagine what this was like—decades of often bloody struggles and hatred, lasting up until 1914.

And the universities also became the arena of an unparalleled anti-Semitism. The name of the eminent surgeon, Theodor Billroth, is connected with the rise of anti-Semitism because he wrote of the "incredible number of poor Jews" coming from Galicia and other eastern parts of the monarchy and wanting to study in the Vienna medical school. It must be said that Billroth was not anti-Semitic. When Hermann Nothnagel founded an association to *oppose* anti-Semitism, Billroth became a member. Billroth's daughter married a Jew. Nevertheless, Billroth's book initiated a new wave of anti-Semitism, mostly at the universities. It was a new and very dangerous kind of anti-Semitism because Billroth defined the Jews as being a separate nation and stated that a Jew never could become a German or a Slav, that he would always be and remain a Jew, even if he spoke German or was a Catholic. It was at this time also that anti-Semitism took on the trappings of scientific knowledge from pseudo-scientific, racist ethnology. In this manner the Jewish people were, once again, being effectively locked out from membership in the German *Volk*.

It was in 1896 that the German-national student corporations in Vienna, and then at other universities too, declared that henceforward they would not "give satisfaction" to a Jewish student in a duel because Jews were "human beings without any kind of gentlemen's honor." With this declaration the German-national students of the university of Vienna at the end of the nineteenth century made a distinction between two kinds of human beings: between the knightly German-Aryans and the "subhuman creature of the brute Jew." So a part, at least, of the Austrian students at the close of the nineteenth century laid what decades later became the basis for Nazi discrimination against the Jews.

In the same period students established national associations at the universities. The most influential association was that of the Germans, and its members regarded themselves as the masters among the students at the German-speaking universities. All others were supposed to have only guest status and could not be native academic citizens of these universities. The number of Jews admitted to the universities should not bring the percentage of Jews there to exceed the percentage of Jews in the general population of the country.

After World War I, when so many people came from the East to Vienna—and again, many of them were Jews—as refugees (about 200,000), many tried to become Austrian citizens, but only those were welcome who were members of the German *Volk* (*Volksdeutsche*). And who could be accounted a member of the German *Volk* by option? He or she who spoke German and was a member of the German "race." In 1921 the Administrative Supreme Court (*Verwaltungsgerichtshof*) in Vienna stated that what should be understood as the essential characteristic of race was: "an inherent, by physical and psychical factors determined, peculiarity of a human being, a permanent characteristic which cannot be deliberately given up or changed." All the non-German nationalities of the Austro-Hungarian Monarchy had new successor states to which they could belong and call home. The only ones who did not belong to a new state, but were considered a foreign people, were the Jews, who, if one accepted the dictum of the Administrative Supreme Court, could be citizens of Austria but could never be Germans.

The German-nationals and the Catholics together formed the Deutsche Studentenschaft, the German Students Association, which became the official representative of all the German-Aryan students at the universities in Austria. The rectors and the academic senates, but not the government, recognized the Deutsche Studentenschaft as a factor in the decision-making process at the universities. That meant that the German Students Association dominated all the other student groups at the universities. They dominated the Jews and the Social Democrats, who avoided the association and fought against the German-nationals. The German Students Association put anti-Semitism in practice at the universities by demanding a decrease in the number of Jewish freshmen. The Austrian universities became "Deutsche Lehr- und Forschungsstätten" by law!

German nationalism increased even further. In 1918, one of the leading spokesmen for the German national students in Vienna declared that a lack of national feeling in the German people of the Reich had been the true reason for the disaster in losing the war. That was because the Germans in the Reich were not real Germans but rather were Bajuvarians, Prussians, and the like; real Germans, in the true sense of the word, were the Austrian Germans alone, for only they could have a true sense of being German from their experience at the eastern border, fighting against the Slavs and Turks for centuries. Therefore, it would be necessary for the Austrians to explain to the "Reichsdeutsche," clearly and unmistakably, what it truly meant to be a German.[2] This would be done, in fact—by Adolf Hitler!

The demands of the German Students Association were accepted by the universities in practice in 1918-1919 and officially adopted in 1924. The Institute of Technology in Vienna became the first university in German-speaking territories which officially stated the *numerus clausus* for Jewish students. In 1927, the Prussian Minister for Education, the famous Carl Heinrich Becker, accused the Austrian German-national students of inciting his students in Prussia, and other territories of the Reich, to anti-Semitism—and he was right. The radical nationalistic and national socialistic tendencies in the German Students Association in the Reich were instigated, in the main, by the students from Austria and from German-speaking areas in Bohemia.

The German Students Association would not have expanded in such a manner and would not have been accepted by the universities, the academic administration, the rectors and deans, if an important part of the professors—not a majority in number, but a majority in activity—had not supported them. The German Students Association did not enlist an overwhelming majority of the students, but it did enlist the active ones. Many of the leading National Socialists came out of the generation of students who matriculated in the first years after World War I at the University of Graz, for example, Ernst Kaltenbrunner and Max de Crinis.

In the last decades of the nineteenth century a great number, even a majority, of the professors at the universities held German-nationalist feelings. But they did not support the radical German-national students in such a way as the professors did after World War I. What was the difference? Before the fall of the monarchy, the goal of the German-national students, the

---

[2]Helge Zoitl, *Kampf um Gleichberechtigung. Die sozialdemokratische Studentenbewegung in Wien 1914-1925* (unpublished dissertation, University of Salzburg, 1976), p. 96.

creation of a single Greater German Empire, including all the German-speaking people, had been a subversive goal. After the war, however, a union of the German and Austrian states had become a very self-evident and natural matter of course for all the political parties in Austria. The goal had become a legal one, then, the single political desire of a majority of the people.

German scholars have always been inspired by the idea that scholars should lead the people in common progress and the supreme goal was the advancement of cognition, of science. As a result of the war and the isolation of the Germans, the German-nationals and other scholars in Austria, in defiance of the victors, saw their supreme goal as the establishment of one unified nation. Science and cognition were seen as a mere intellectual aid in the process of achieving another, superior goal. "Wissenschaft ist national!" (Science is something national!) was one of the common slogans at that time. "International" was a word which was synonymous with "Jewish." Science in Austria, and even in Germany, at that time could not be international or cosmopolitan in the eyes of the German-nationals. Therefore, the German-national professors decided that they should be the leaders and driving force in the Anschluss movement. They initiated activity in this field in 1925-1926, when the interest for Anschluss slowly began to decrease in the general public. The reason that their activities began just at that time was that the state had renounced Anschluss for twenty years in the Geneva Protocol of 1922, and, before 1925, the universities had been involved in internecine problems and struggles. In 1925 some of the inter-university institutions, such as the Austrian rectors' conference and some others, were renewed.

In 1925 and 1926 large German-national congresses were held in Vienna and supported by the universities. In the summer of 1925, the Austrian rectors' conference passed a resolution favoring Anschluss. A very important factor was that, starting in 1923, German professors, in cooperation with Austrian professors, began to work out an adaptation of the Austrian university system to the German system. These activities were started by Catholic politicians, who also tried to bring German students to Austrian universities. Indeed, the number of German students at Austrian universities increased, slowly at first, but by the end of the 1920s the number had grown hugely. The highest concentration of German students at an Austrian university was at Innsbruck University Medical School; in 1932 they amounted to 67 percent of the spring semester's enrollment! Without doubt, this influx of Germans had taken on a Nazi hue by the end of the 1920s.

Austrian scholars also began to participate in the Deutsche Notgemeinschaft der Wissenschaften (German Emergency Society for Sciences) and they founded their own association, the "Deutsch-österreichische Wissenschaftshilfe" (German-Austrian Aid to Science), which fostered a dependency of Austrian scholarship on the Germans. From the middle of the 1920s, all these institutions took on political connotations. At the same time, the most prominent German-national professors at the universities, especially at Vienna, took over the important academic positions: as deans, as rectors, and in the academic senate. In 1927, Rector Hans Molisch at the University of Vienna began to break the strength of resistance and opposition of the Social Democrats at the university. When he drafted the student regulations, which had been demanded by the German Students Association, he outlawed the Social Democrats' associations. The mayor of Vienna, the prominent Social Democrat, Karl Seitz, reacted with a new decree for police procedures, which permitted the police to intervene also in academic territory, i. e., to move onto campus in pursuit of matters of police attention. Until then, the police had not been allowed to enter academic territory unless specifically called to do so by the rector.

There were anti-Semitic and anti-socialist acts of violence in the early 1920s in the Austrian universities, and, beginning in the spring of 1927, a series of acts of brutality and violence started there and continued until 1933. Then, after modest beginnings in

1923, around 1926 and 1927 the small Nazi groups among the students began their substantial and most efficient work. They put a fright into the universities, especially in Vienna, with their "Swastika Terror," the terror of Hitlerism. In 1930 one of those Nazi students wrote: "There was only one course for us, . . . to terrorize the universities until the day on which our Führer would stand at the head of the nation. That we have done, as God and the Jewish press are our witnesses."[3]

From the middle of the 1920s the Nazi students began their activities in the German Students Association, at first under other names. When the National Socialist German Students League (NSDStB, National Sozialistischer Deutscher Studentenbund) was founded in Munich in 1926, there were branches established at Austrian universities also. The most important enemies of the Nazis were the German-nationals! The reasons were twofold: because the German-nationals did not want to be under the sway of a political party and to have to recognize a constitutional political system, and because the Nazis detested the student corporations (fraternities) with all their conservative ceremonies and their duels. In those universities where the German nationals were the most dominant, the Nazis did not gain majorities in elections very quickly. For example, at the University of Graz, where the German-nationals were a force to be reckoned with, the Nazis *never* gained a majority in student elections!

There was some attempt at opposition to the German-national tide that was swelling in the universities. Archbishop, later Cardinal, Theodor Innitzer, when he became rector at the University

---

[3]"Es gab für uns nur einen Weg, . . . die Hochschulen unter Hakenkreuzterror zu stellen bis zu dem Tage, an welchem der Führer an der Spitze der Nation steht. Das haben wir getan, Gott und die Judenpresse sind unsere Zeugen." Michael Gehler, "Die Studentenschaft an der Universität Innsbruck 1918-1938 unter Berücksichtigung der Korporationen und ihrer Verbände. Ein sozial-, wirtschafts- und politikgeschichtlicher Beitrag zur österreichischen Studentengeschichte in der Zwischenkriegszeit" (unpublished dissertation, University of Innsbruck, 1987) pp. 544-545.

of Vienna (1928-1929), and Hermann Beitzke, when he became rector at the University of Graz, were two who would stem that tide, but when Wenzel Gleispach became rector at the University of Vienna in the autumn of 1929, that tide went to flood. It was a turning point and a point of no return in the history of Austrian universities.

On 8 April 1930 Gleispach published the student law at the University of Vienna. It was a signal triumph of the German Students Association because in that "law" their demands were met in full and accepted as official. The Socialists and the Jewish students immediately initiated legal proceedings at the Supreme Court, challenging the validity of this intra-university law of Gleispach. In 1931 the Supreme Court decided that the law of Gleispach was not valid in a formal, legal sense because the university could not enact law on its own; but the Supreme Court kept judicial silence on the intent of the law.[4]

As soon as the Supreme Court pronounced this dictum the assault of the Nazi and the German-national students on the socialist and Jewish students began, and the universities had to be closed within the hour. This also marked the beginning in the universities of opposition to the government, an opposition that would continue until March 1938.

In 1931-1932 the Austrian government took a very important political measure. Dire economic circumstances compelled the government to seek a large, new international loan, which was granted by the Lausanne Protocol. But a condition of the loan was that Austria had to agree, once again, to renounce Anschluss and continue to be an independent, second German state beside, but separate from, Germany. This decision had two consequences for the universities: the goal of the Nazis and the German-nationals became again subversive; and the German-nationals gave in

---

[4]On this question cf. also Brigitte Fenz, "Volksbürgerschaft und Staatsbürgerschaft. Das Studentenrecht in Österreich 1918-1932" (unpublished dissertation, University of Vienna, 1977).

and formed a union with the Nazis in 1932. This act followed the demise of the Greater German Party (*Großdeutsche Partei*), because, thereafter, there was no political party in Austria, other than the Nazis, which stood for the Anschluss.

This signaled the universities' descent into the morass of civil war. At the University of Vienna, the followers of Gleispach, Hans Übersberger and Emil Abel, dropped the last veil of decency and Nazi students, in uniform, were used as security police at the university.

The authoritarian administration of the Austrian government that took the reins in 1933, with its very severe laws subjecting the universities and outlawing the German Students Association, could not bring about a reversal of the trend. Even when, for economic reasons, the number of professors at the universities of Vienna, Graz, and Innsbruck was diminished from 432 to 313 (a reduction of 28%), little changed. Nor did dismissals of professors deemed to be Nazis or Nazi sympathizers, in the years 1933-1934 and following, reverse the trend. A large number of assistants were discharged, an even larger number than the number of professors discharged. There were still Nazi-cells at the universities, and a great portion of the students were Nazis or Nazi sympathizers, despite the opposition of students supported by the authoritarian, Catholic government. The bacillus of Nazism had infected the universities, and there was no remedy against it. The newly formed Catholic opposition against the idea of German nationalism, with its *Ostmärkische Sturmscharen* (They also had an "Arier-Paragraph" and a "Reichsführer," Kurt von Schuschnigg), could not master the situation either. The socialists and Nazis were then working underground, for they had been declared illegal by the Dollfuss government. Socialist students in the medical school would find their banned *Arbeiterzeitungen* hidden in the corpses in the Institute of Anatomy in Vienna. Nazi students organized to applaud provocatively whenever a lecturer mentioned the name of a famous German scholar such as Fichte. In response, any form of applause at the universities was forbidden by law.

No other institutions in Austrian life experienced developments in those years similar to that of the universities or exerted the same kind of influence in the population. It was generally recognized in those years that the universities were the leaders in pro-Anschluss support and of German feeling and thinking, and were so identified by the newspapers of the right. The newspapers of the left identified the universities as schools of racism, hatred, and National Socialism. All the intellectual, political, and economic leaders of Austria had gone through the political tutoring of the Austrian universities. For many decades, the professors—and not just those in history and literature—formed the impressions, the picture of the world (*Weltanschauung*), for generations of students, most of whom were not able to imagine that another, different picture of the world was possible.

In 1930 Hitler said that nothing would give him more confidence in the future of National Socialism than for Nazis to have great success in the universities.[5] That would apply not only to German universities but also, and even to a higher degree, to Austrian universities.

When one recounts these grim and regrettable events, one should also point out that there were many professors, doubtless a majority of them, who did not agree with what was done and said and did not want the outcome. However, only a few demonstrated their opposition by word or deed; most of them kept silent. And, although leaders in the Austrian universities—rectors, the senates—and even whole schools (*Fakultäten*) articulated protests against the government's breaking of the Supreme Court in May of 1933 and against similar activities in those times, one can find no serious discussion about what was happening at the same time in Hitler's Reich, where, in the spring and summer of 1933 the "Gleichschaltung" of the universities

---

[5]Gehler, "Die Studentenschaft", p. 543.

began and so many professors, including all the Jewish professors, were dismissed.

Nearly all the years in the interwar period were years of great economic hardship for all the Austrian people. In the universities in many winters there was not enough coal for heating, and people worked in their heavy coats—and only by daylight hours, for there was no money for electricity. Funds for books and equipment were lacking; many members of the faculty and supporting staff had to be dismissed—and just when Austria suffered under a woefully high rate of unemployment.

The parlous and straitened circumstances of the First Republic weakened the Austrian universities, and the Anschluss, for which the university people themselves helped to prepare the way, further debilitated the Austrian universities to such an extent that not until the 1960s did they recover the number of faculty positions that they had in the spring of 1914! One will never be able to measure or know the value of the losses in those years to the life of the mind and spirit.

Triumph and Neglect: Austrian Hochschulen and the Anschluss

John Haag

Austrian *Hochschulen* were in a state of suspended animation from 1933 to 1938, having been stripped of their autonomy by the Dollfuß regime in the summer and autumn of 1933, a process that was followed by more detailed legislation in 1934 and 1935.[1] While all Austrian institutions of higher learning had long been centers of *deutschnational* radicalism, each school developed in its own unique fashion. At the University of Vienna a significant percentage of Jewish and Social Democratic students served to dramatize the *Überfremdung* that was seen by the anti-Semitic *Deutsche Studentenschaft* as the greatest threat to the integrity of higher education in Austria. Throughout the 1920s and 1930s Jewish student enrollment at the University of Vienna was in percentage far in excess of that of the Austrian Jewish population, which was less than three percent of the nation's total population. Thus, in 1933 at the University of Vienna during the Spring semester 2,246 of the total enrollment of 11,671 students were Jewish. But while Austrian anti-Semitic propagandists never tired of citing such statistics, they rarely mentioned that other *Hochschulen* had far fewer Jewish students. In the same summer semester of 1933, the University of Graz had only forty-seven Jews in a total student body of 2,556, while

---

[1]Hans von Frisch, *Die Gewaltherrschaft in Österreich 1933 bis 1938. Eine staatsrechtliche Untersuchung* (Leipzig and Vienna: Johannes Günther Verlag, 1938), pp. 97-107.

at the University of Innsbruck, at the same time, out of a total enrollment of 2,571 only nineteen students indicated they were of the Jewish faith.[2]

The absence of Jewish students at a *Hochschule* did little to moderate the radicalism of the *Deutsche Studentenschaft* at that institution. If anything, the localization of the "Jewish-Marxist danger" in Vienna served to hasten the radicalization of schools outside the capital city. Thus it was that in 1931 the College of Mining (*Montanistische Hochschule*) at Leoben in Styria could boast 86 percent of its student body as members of one or another National Socialist organization. In Vienna, although it contained virtually no Jewish students, in the same year at the College of Agriculture (*Hochschule für Bodenkultur*) had fully 70 percent of its students enrolled either in the NSDAP or in one of its subsidiary bodies, the SA, SS, or NSDStB (*Nationalsozialistischer Deutscher Studentenbund*).[3]

Throughout his time in power, Chancellor Engelbert Dollfuß was too busy keeping Austrian independence intact to deal with the problem of *Hochschulen* in more than a purely reactive fashion. His goal was simply to establish peace and order in these centers of anti-Austrian agitation, something that was accomplished in the late summer and early autumn of 1933 by introducing police on academic soil on a permanent basis. Dollfuß's successor Kurt Schuschnigg, who continued to retain his portfolio as Minister of Instruction until relieved by Hans Pernter in 1936, saw the problem as one of providing impressionable youth with ideals at least as powerful as those based on the National Socialist *Weltanschauung*. Starting in 1933, Austrian academic youth were strongly impressed—one might say se-

---

[2]Sylvia Maderegger, *Die Juden im österreichischen Ständestaat 1934-1938* (Vienna: Geyer-Edition, 1973), pp. 152-153.

[3]*Verdrängte Geschichte? Die Hochschule für Bodenkultur im Austrofaschismus und Nationalsozialismus* (Vienna: Österreichische Hochschülerschaft an der Universität für Bodenkultur, n.d.), p. 11.

duced—by events (and perceptions of events) taking place in the new-born Third Reich.

It was Schuschnigg's hope that the Austrian state and its educational apparatus could win over disloyal young men and women by convincing them in their early years that the very best aspects of the German spirit were to be found embodied not in Nazi Germany but in the Austria of the Vaterländische Front. This German-Austrian spirit was to be brought to pupils and students in the form of "patriotic instruction" (*vaterländische Erziehung*).[4] On the *Hochschule* level, required courses of two hours per week for two semesters on the "Ideal and Historical Foundations of the Austrian State" were a feature introduced into the curriculum of all institutions of higher education during the winter semester of 1935-1936.[5] That these lectures were less than successful in molding a new Austrian consciousness can be gathered from the fact that one of the faculty members entrusted with presenting them at the University of Vienna, the historian Heinrich Kretschmayr, was during these years an *Illegaler*—a secret Nazi.[6]

Talk as they might about competing *Weltanschauungen*, Schuschnigg and his Nazi foes were dealing with a concrete situation in which very real social and economic problems pressed down on the great majority of academic youth. Massive unemployment and poor career prospects were universal themes during the 1930s throughout Europe, but the situation in Austria may well have been uniquely grim. By global standards Austria was, to

---

[4]Kurt von Schuschnigg, "Vaterländische Erziehung," in Josef Alois Tzöbl, *Vaterländische Erziehung* (2nd ed., Vienna: Österreichische Volksschriften, 1933), pp. 6-7

[5]"Staatssekretär Pernter über die Hochschulerziehung," *Neue Freie Presse*, June 6, 1935, a.m.

[6]Friedrich Heer, *Der Kampf um die österreichische Identität* (Vienna: Hermann Böhlaus Nachf., 1981), p. 380; "Akademie der bildenden Künste feiert den Anschluß," *Völkischer Beobachter*, (Vienna ed., March 22, 1938).

quote the University of Vienna's Professor Ferdinand Degenfeld-Schonburg, a country full of *Hochschule* graduates ("ein Land der Akademiker.")[7] Already in the late Habsburg era Austria led the world in the risky business of producing too many individuals with advanced degrees. During the winter semester of 1910-1911, Austria managed to produce 14.7 *Hochschule* students per ten thousand of its population, slightly ahead of the German Reich with 13.9, and France with 11.3. Despite the greatly reduced need for individuals with advanced degrees after 1918, the overproduction of graduates continued and indeed accelerated. Thus, while France in 1933 maintained 20.9 *Hochschüler* per ten thousand of her population, and the German Reich found itself burdened in that year of catastrophic depression with 16.2 students for the same segment of the population, Austria found herself in a unique situation by producing unwanted *Akademiker* on the level of 38.3 redundant degree-holders per ten thousand of population. Throughout the 1920s, and even more so in the 1930s, only a small fraction of these *Hochschule* graduates could realistically look forward to finding jobs appropriate to their training, or indeed any position at all, upon receiving their degrees. A number of jobs created by the regime in 1933 in libraries, the Federal Statistics Office, and other public agencies resulted in a modest number of posts paying from 40 to 60 cents a day![8] In addition to these miserable prospects facing all graduates, one must also take account of the years of deep privation endured by students who could expect little or no support from their impoverished bourgeois families. One such student, proba-

---

[7]Ferdinand Graf Degenfeld-Schonburg, "Gegenwart und Zukunft unserer Akademiker," *Monatsschrift für Kultur und Politik*, I, 4 (April, 1936), 308; Ferdinand Degenfeld-Schonburg, *Geist und Wirtschaft. Betrachtungen über die Aussichten der deutschen Akademiker* (Tübingen: J.C.B. Mohr, 1927), p. 27.

[8]Walter M. Kotschnig, *Unemployment in the Learned Professions. An International Study of Occupational and Educational Planning* (London: Oxford University Press, 1937), p. 216.

bly quite representative of thousands of others in similar circumstances, studied for his law degree in the mid-1930s on a monthly income of ten Schillings. Living in a room provided by the University of Vienna's *Asylverein* in the Porzellangasse, he subsisted on polenta seven days a week, seasoning his meager fare with salt from Monday to Saturday, and with sugar on Sundays. To maintain even this basic-survival standard of life, the young man earned desperately needed Groschen carrying coal, cleaning windows, shoveling snow, and tutoring. After good results in an examination, he could look forward to a substantial (and free) meal at the *Professorentisch*—a traditional reward for talented but needy students. More out of prudence than from deep inner conviction, this student joined the *Vaterländische Front*, an insurance policy many young professionals signed up for during the pre-Anschluss years. This representative student's name? Dr. Rudolf Kirchschläger.[9]

Austrian Nazi students had a long tradition of surviving official disapproval and harassment. They had survived the eclipse of Hitler in 1923 after the failure of his Munich *Putsch*. By the mid-1920s, in the person of a rabid racist named Robert Körber, Vienna's Nazi students found an aggressive *Führer*. Körber wrote countless articles in the *völkisch* press, was always on hand to give anti-Semitic speeches in academic circles, and appeared always to be in charge of the violent *Krawalle* that convulsed the university, his own *Hochschule für Welthandel*, and other Viennese *Hochschulen*.[10] Körber's militant leadership created a positive environment for the creation of an official Nazi student organization in the last months of 1926. By the time the Nazi Student League (*Nationalsozialistischer Deutscher*

---

[9]Borys Jaminskyi, *Der Weg in die Hofburg: Dr. Rudolf Kirchshläger* (Vienna: Verlag Dkfm. Willi Schlager, 1975), pp. 23-24.

[10]Körber has been describedf as the Austrian version of Julius Streicher. See Michael Siegert,"Numerus Juden raus," *Neues Forum*, XXI, 241-242 (January/-February 1974), 37.

Studentenbund: NSDStB) took its first census in November 1926, the Vienna NSDStB was by far the largest grouping in the organization with Berlin in second place with thirty-six members.[11]

But it was not impressive growth of membership alone that accounts for the survival of the Nazi Student League in Vienna. Tenacity and iron will enabled these young men and women (female students had their own organization, the *Arbeitsgemeinschaft nationalsozialistischer Studentinnen:* ANSt) to win out over their numerous rivals and survive official disapproval. The Vienna NSDStB survived the rectorship of Theodor Innitzer in the academic year 1928-1929, when—as an exception to the prevailing tolerance of the administration toward student violence—a major crackdown resulted in significant disciplinary measures being taken against Nazi student rowdies. The NSDStB survived the collapse of the *Deutsche Studentenschaft* in December 1932, when the powerful Catholic *Cartellverband* (CV) fraternities withdrew from that coalition of anti-Semitic, anti-Marxist student groups. They survived the ban of the Austrian Nazi Party and the NSDStB in June and of the *Deutsche Studentschaft* in August 1933.[12] And they even survived the traumatic events of July 1934, when the Austrian Nazi movement was thrown into profound crisis after the failure of the *Putsch* of July 25.

Despite all these setbacks, few if any Nazi students lost their faith in the Third Reich. Many of them enjoyed the thrill of engaging in conspiratorial activites for what they regarded as a noble cause. Within weeks of the outlawing of the NSDStB, in July 1933, its leaders organized a month-long training camp at Reifnitz on the Wörthersee in Carinthia. Just to show their supreme confidence, the Nazi student leaders daily swam and dived

---

[11] Bundesarchiv Koblenz, Sammlung Schumacher, 279/I/37.

[12] "Preventivmaßnahmen an den Hochschulen," *Wiener Zeitung,* August 31, 1933; "Ordnungmachen an den Hochschulen," *Reichspost,* August 31, 1933.

into the lake with their vacationing neighbor, Minister of Instruction Kurt Schuschnigg. They even went so far as to take photographs of themselves on the diving board with the totally unsuspecting Minister of Instruction.[13] The excitement of conspiracy, and the firm belief that they were in the right, inspired Nazi students in Vienna, Graz, Innsbruck and Leoben to prepare for long-term adversity. Indeed, Austrian National Socialism was essentially a youthful phenomenon, and it has been estimated that at least three-quarters of the active Nazis on the eve of Anschluss were youngsters.[14] Many of these young men were willing to take risks and pay the price for turning their convictions into deeds. A glance at the statistics for individuals interned in May 1934 at the Wöllersdorf detention camp is suggestive: of forty-four internees from the free professions and the academic community, twenty-eight were members of the NSDAP, fourteen were Social Democrats, and two were Communists. Of the twenty-two students in this group, fully twenty were Nazis, with only one each from the Social Democratic and Communist camps.[15]

The growing strength of Nazi Germany, and the obvious inability of the regime of the *Vaterländische Front* to mobilize the loyalty of all sectors of the Austrian population, but particularly the intellectual classes, are a fundamental aspect of the Austro-German Agreement of July 11, 1936. One of the most perceptive political observers at the time, Ernst Karl Winter, recognized the failure of the government to win the loyalty of Austria's youth. Writing in the preface to his 1936 biography of

---

[13]Helmut Triska, "Das deutsche Studententum der Ostmark in den fünf Verbotsjahren," *Deutschtum im Ausland*, XXI, 5 (May 1938), 230.

[14]Evan Burr Bukey, *Hitler's Hometown: Linz, Austria 1908-1945* (Bloomington: Indiana University Press, 1986), p. 165.

[15]Gerhard Jagschitz, "Die Anhaltelager in Österreich," in Ludwig Jedlicka and Rudolf Neck, eds., *Vom Justizpalast zum Heldenplatz. Studien und Dokumentationen 1927 bis 1938* (Vienna: Druck und Verlag der Österreichischen Staatsdruckerei, 1975), p. 150.

Rudolf IV, Winter noted that "the universities on Austrian soil, which notoriously have not been Austrian for a long time, must become Austrian again if this state, a free and independent Austria, is to exist.[16] The full extent of the failure to transform allegiance at Austrian *Hochschulen* can be gathered from the report of the Trustee (*Sachwalter*) of the government-controlled *Österreichische Hochschülerschaft*, which concluded that only eighteen percent of the student body could be considered *staatstreu* in their loyalties.[17] It is doubtless significant that the Trustee of the University of Vienna student body, the law student Heinrich Drimmel, believed that the only reason his institution was spared major acts of violence during the years 1934-1938 was the fact that friendships—some dating back to childhood—with Nazi student leaders made it possible for him to work out peaceful compromises behind the scenes with the illegal but powerful Nazi student organization at the university.[18]

The agreement of July 11, 1936 dismayed those elements loyal to the idea of an independent Austria; in the academic world, the general political amnesty that accompanied this *Ausgleich* not only released Nazi students from incarceration but gave unmistakable signals to *betont national* elements that their activities would henceforth be granted much greater latitude than before. Starting in 1936, Nazi students, both Austrians and citi-

---

[16]"Die Hochschulen auf österreichischem Staatsboden, die notorischerweise seit langem nicht mehr österreichische Universitäten waren, müssen es wieder werden, wenn dieser Staat ein freies und unabhängiges Österreich bestehen will." Ernst Karl Winter, *Rudolph IV, von Österreich* (2 vols., Vienna, 1936), II, XI-XII, cited in Ernst Hoor, "Wandlungen der österreichischen Staatsidee. Vom Heiligen Römischen Reich zur österreichischen Nation," in Georg Wagner. ed., *Österreich. Von der Staatsidee zum Nationalbewusstsein* (Vienna: Verlag der Österreichischen Staatsdruckerei, 1982), pp. 453 and 459.

[17]Walter Goldinger, *Geschichte der Republik Österreich* (Vienna: Verlag für Geschichte und Politik, 1962), p. 295.

[18]Heinrich Drimmel, *Die Häuser meines Lebens. Erinnerungen eines Engagierten* (Vienna: Amalthea, 1975), p. 180.

zens of the German Reich studying in Austria, began to increase the amount and intensity of propaganda and agitation aimed at discrediting the Schuschnigg government. As early as the winter semester of 1933-1934, an organization of Reich German students headquartered in Vienna, the *Wirtschaftsstelle reichsdeutscher Hochschüler in Österreich,* began to function as a Nazi fifth column infiltrating and subverting Austrian student groups to serve the interests in foreign policy of the Third Reich. Most of the German students associated with this body were carefully screened National Socialist militants chosen for their potential for proselytizing the specifically German nuances of the Hitlerite *Weltanschauung.*[19] Buoyed up by the belief that the forces of history were on their side, Austrian Nazi Students and faculty were further encouraged by a circular letter dated July 15, 1936, from *Deutsche Studentenschaft* headquarters in Berlin. This secret directive indicated the tasks ahead in the area of *Weltanschauung* struggles, noting that one of the main tasks would be to win over the entire Austrian teaching profession to Nazi ideology and the concept of a Greater Germany. Other areas of ideological struggle outlined in the document included not only increased militancy against the Jews but also a "struggle for German unity against political Catholicism in every form." The *Deutsche Studentenschaft* leadership in Berlin regarded their agenda for propaganda in essentially military terms, speaking of "shock troops in the Austrian universities [preparing] the way for broadcasting it through the people."[20] Not only in Vienna but in

---

[19] Gerhard Fliess, "Deutsche Studentenschaft (DSt) 1919-1936," in Dieter Fricke et al., eds. *Die bürgerlichen Parteien in Deutschland. Handbuch der Geschichte der bürgerlichen Parteien und anderer bürgerlichen Interessengruppen vom Vormärz bis zum Jahre 1945* (2 vols.) Berlin (DDR): Das europäische Buch, 1968, 1970), I, 601; Michael Stephen Steinberg,"Sabres, Books and Brown Shirts: The Radicalization of the German Student, 1918-35" (2 vols., Ph.D. Dissertation, The Johns Hopkins University, 1971), II, 705-706.

[20] Martin Fuchs, *A Pact with Hitler: The Death of Austria,* transl. Charles Hope Lumley (London: Gollancz, 1939), pp. 56-58.

the provinces as well the new student militancy soon erupted into acts of defiance. At the University of Graz, a number of prestigious *Burschenschaften* had snubbed the government by boycotting the celebrations of that institution's three-hundred-and-fiftieth anniversary in 1936, an action that served to underline the continued hostility of a high percentage of academic youth to the regime.[21]

The years 1936 and 1937 saw informed public opinion less and less confident about Schuschnigg's ability to lead the Austrian state. Former Minister of Instruction Emmerich Czermak confided his misgivings to his diary on February 13, 1937, noting that there was "generally no longer any trust" in the Chancellor's political instincts.[22] In the academic world the growing power-vacuum was noted by the Catholic National intellectuals who had since the early 1930s been concentrated at the University of Vienna. Led by Professor Othmar Spann, whose 1921 book *Der wahre Staat* was regarded as Holy Writ by the circle of romantic dreamers and schemers who congregated in his seminars, the Catholic Nationals also included such eminent scholars as the legal historian Karl Gottfried Hugelmann, the literary historian Josef Nadler, the geographers Fritz Machatschek and Hugo Hassinger, the prehistorian Oswald Menghin and mediaevalist Hans Hirsch, as well as the philosopher Hans Eibl. Coming from a *deutschfreiheitlich* background, but increasingly allied with the Catholic Nationals, was the theorist of a *gesamtdeutsch* historical ideology, Heinrich Ritter von Srbik.[23] Above all else,

---

[21]"Eine wohlverdiente Strafe," *Österreichische Akademischen Blätter*, I, 8 (June 20, 1936), 123-124.

[22]Diary entry of February 13, 1937, cited in Ludwig Jedlicka, ed., "Aus dem politischen Tagebuch des Unterrichtsministers a.D. Dr. Emmerich Czermak 1937-1948," *Österreich in Geschichte und Literatur*, VIII, (1964), 271.

[23]Klaus Breuning, *Die Vision des Reiches. Deutscher Katholizismus zwischen Demokratie und Diktatur (1929-1934)* (Munich: Max Hueber Verlag, 1969), pp. 255-256; Adam Wandruszka, "Heinrich Ritter von Srbik—Leben und Werk," *Anzeiger der phil. hist. Klasse der Österreichischen Akademie der Wis-*

what united these Catholic National intellectuals ideologically and emotionally was their passionate belief in the *Reich*. This new, authoritarian state and society would take the German *Volk* far beyond the travails of the Western democratic civilization that had brought Europe to the brink of destruction. On the ruins of a selfishly individualistic capitalism and a menacing Marxism a new and uniquely German culture would be created, and they, as learned men pure in spirit, would clearly play a leading role in this noble reconstruction of the Central European social order. Deeply committed to these ideals, the scholarship of these men was permeated by the romantic belief that the superior German *Kultur* amd its profound *Geist* could only be properly interpreted by a select elite of intellectuals like themselves.

Spann and the other Catholic National intellectuals were able to convince themselves and the circles they moved in that despite its reliance on violence and lack of intellectually convincing ideological arguments, National Socialism contained many potentially positive elements and could in fact—if properly guided—be made to evolve into a healthy organic entity. These men made such arguments not only in their own lectures and books but also in the pages of the Viennese Catholic journal *Schönere Zukunft*.[24] As the leader of a well-entrenched *Kreis* of young intellectuals uncritically loyal to himself, Othmar Spann used his own journal *Ständisches Leben* as a forum to argue for the possibility of transforming National Socialism into an authentically conservative movement cleansed of its violent, deceitful elements and its "un-German" materialistic racism as defined by Alfred Rosen-

---

senschaften, CXV, 21 (1979), 355, which notes Srbik's membership in the *Burschenschaft Gothia* and his student experiences during the turbulent Badeni crisis of 1897.

[24]Peter Eppel, *Zwischen Kreuz und Hakenkreuz. Die Haltung der Zeitschrift "Schönere Zukunft" zum Nationalsozialismus in Deutschland 1934-1938* (Vienna: Hermann Böhlaus Nachf., 1980), pp. 13, 81, 277-279 and 323-331. See also Peter Broucek, *Katholisch-Nationale Persönlichkeiten* (Vienna: Wiener Katholische Akademie, 1979) [Wiener Katholische Akademie, Miscellanea LXII].

berg. Spann and his disciples clearly envisaged themselves as the only individuals fitted for this great task of building a genuinely idealistic Third Reich, a "true state."

Spann's delusions were shared by most of his Catholic National colleagues at the University of Vienna. One of them, Heinrich Ritter von Srbik, had clearly thought long and hard about the true essence of National Socialism, but his conclusions reveal his dreams about what the true Germany should be like rather than what it in reality had become. Writing to fellow historian Oswald Redlich a few days before the signing of the July 1936 Austro-German Agreement, Srbik noted with satisfaction his own role in preparing that accord, as well as his rejection of an offer of the Vice-Chancellorship by Schuschnigg. In an admiring tone Srbik went on to describe Hitler as "an unusual man in whom millions have a blind trust," adding that he regarded the bloody events of June 30 and July 25, 1934, as "ghastly" but also pointing out that the Röhm purge needed to be seen in terms of its victims, who after all had been "truly highly unworthy human beings." As for the failed *Putsch* of July 25, 1934, Srbik regarded this as "one of the blackest days of recent German history" but also believed it to be the work of "irresponsible elements."[25] Without citing evidence to argue his point, Srbik ignored his historical training by simply asserting that neither Hitler nor the German government had known anything about these violent deeds. Along with all the other Catholic Nationals, Srbik could not bring himself to the point of coming to grips with the notion that the German state could have been taken over by a group of criminal nihilists; the true Germany represented profoundly spiritual forces, and any regime that governed the

---

[25]Klaus-Jörg Siegfried, *Universalismus und Faschismus. Das Gesellschaftsbild Othmar Spanns* (Vienna: Europaverlag, 1974), and Martin Schneller, *Zwischen Romantik und Faschismus. Der Beitrag Othmar Spanns zum Konservatismus der Weimarer Republik* (Stuttgart: Ernst Klett Verlag, 1970).

German state had thus to be at least redeemable for these same pure energies.

As far as he could analyze the picture, Srbik regarded Alfred Rosenberg's racial radicalism as the major problem confronting National Socialism, for Hitler himself clearly had shown himself to be a moderate who recognized the complementary natures of German nationalism, National Socialism and Christian values. Finally, looking at the situation as an Austrian, Srbik felt confident in predicting the desirable nature of a policy of reconciliation with the Third Reich. Austria could only benefit from such a rapprochement, because it was clear that a totally Nazified Austria would always remain "an impossibility for us."[26]

Working with individuals who harbored such illusions about the true nature of National Socialism's ideology and goals made it easy for Austrian Nazis and their directors in Munich and Berlin to manipulate individuals who needed little if any persuasion to lend intellectual and social respectability to the brown cause. Kurt Skalnik has recently described such well-educated and well-intentioned individuals as "Salonnazis,"[27] Grossly overestimating their own significance, and ignoring the fierce anti-intellectualism of the Nazi movement since its inception, they made National Socialism *salonfähig* but rarely if ever got their hands dirty.

Enjoying their newly found status, the Catholic National intellectuals moved to center stage of the turbulent political environment. They were even able to obtain funding for their own journal, *Die Warte,* which appeared from January 1936 until the publication of a self-congratulatory final issue after the An-

---

[26] Jürgen Kämmerer, ed., *Heinrich Ritter von Srbik. Die wissenschaftliche Korrespondenz des Historikers 1912-1945* (Boppard am Rhein: Harald Boldt Verlag, 1988), pp. 458-459

[27] Kurt Skalnik, "Ein 'Salonnazi' im Selbstporträt," *Die Furche,* no. 50 (December 11, 1987), 22. This is a review of Reinhard Spitzy, *So haben Wir das Reich verspielt* (Munich: Langen Müller Verlag, 1986).

schluss, in August 1938.[28] *Die Warte* was dominated by three of the most prestigous Catholic National faculty members of the University of Vienna, Professors Eibl, Nadler and Srbik, and the leitmotif of this journal aimed at the Austrian intelligentsia was the idea that a union of Austria and the German Reich was a natural union that would result in a renewal of Germanic hegemony in Central Europe. Perhaps the politically most active member of the circle of intellectuals involved with *Die Warte* was Professor Oswald Menghin, Rector of the University of Vienna during the academic year 1936-1937. Menghin was a prominent *Brückenbauer*, one of the influential Austrians who had convinced themselves that the gaps between conservative Catholic ideology and the more moderate elements of National Socialism could in fact be bridged. The respected prehistorian Menghin was a member of the Committee of Seven (*Siebener-Ausschuss*), the "first serious attempt to obtain legal status for the NSDAP under the guise of a cover organization."[29] Another instance in which the *Brückenbauer* elite lent their considerable prestige to a major scheme to infiltrate the weakened Austrian body politic was the 1937 plan to create a "Deutsch-sozialer Volksbund," which was inaugurated in a Linz newspaper in February of that year. The petition calling for the founding of this crypto-Nazi body was signed by 493 prominent Nationals including such academic luminaries as Menghin, Spann, Srbik, Eibl and the Nobel Prize laureate Julius von Wagner-Jauregg.[30]

Deceased as well as living faculty members continued to play a role in the highly politicized atmosphere of academic Vienna

---

[28] See the programmatic article by Hans Eibl, "Christlich und Deutsch," *Die Warte*, I, 1 (January 1936), 1, which speaks rhapsodically of the "zukunftsträchtiges Zauberwort: Das Reich, das Reich, das ewige Reich."

[29] Radomír Luža, *Austro-German Relations in the Anschluss Era* (Princeton: Princeton University Press, 1975), p. 39.

[30] Walter Wiltschegg, *Die Heimwehr. Eine unwiderstehliche Volksbewegung?* (Vienna: R. Oldenberg, 1985), pp. 99-100.

in the last months before the Anschluss. Thus it was that the funeral of the Marxist philosopher Max Adler in June 1937 became an occasion for not only his students and former colleagues to pay their last respects but to voice their deepest feelings about the anti-Marxist regime. Adler's funeral thus was transformed into Vienna's last major anti-fascist demonstration before the Anschluss.[31] Not to be outdone, Nazi students and faculty transformed the December 1937 funeral of the noted plant physiologist Hans Molisch into a major gesture of united opposition to the Schuschnigg government. Hans Berner, an alumnus of the *Landsmannschaft Balthia,* gave an address so vehemently critical of the regime that he was arrested and *Balthia* was banned.[32] The growing perception that time was running out for the Austrian *Christlicher Ständestaat* brought on a sea-change in the mentality of the academic classes. Dr. Herbert Elias, a Jewish professor in Vienna's medical school, noted how, starting in 1936, "everything became politicized and corrupted."[33] Significant numbers of Nazi students ceased to study for their degrees, keeping in mind what had happened in Nazi Germany in 1933, where students who had distinguished themselvles as *Alte Kämpfer* were richly rewarded by being granted diplomas despite the fact that they had not completed the normal course of study or passed their examinations. Even pro-Nazi faculty members despaired over the rapid decline in academic standards, but they too could offer only token resistance when confronted with

---

[31] Alfred Pfabigan, *Max Adler. Eine politische Biographie* (Frankfurt am Main: Campus Verlag, 1982), p. 272.

[32] Hans Berner, *Der Weg geht weiter. Eine Sammlung von Aufsätzen aus den Jahren 1935-1938* (Vienna: Verlag Wilhelm Frick, 1939), pp. 70-71; Karl Wache, "Die österreichischen Landsmannschaften im Aufbruch der Ostmark," *Landsmannschafter-Zeitung,* LII, (1938), 38.

[33] Herbert Elias,"Erinnerungen eines österreichischen Arztes 1885-1938" (unpublished ms, Handschriftensammlung des Instituts für Geschichte der Medizin der Universität Wien), pp. C3 and D1.

an insidious form of blackmail.[34] Those faculty members who regarded the Third Reich as a veritable German Renaissance had not counted on an academic environment in which students intimidated teachers. In the real world of Austria in 1936 and 1937, Nazi student activists flourished in an agitated atmosphere that destroyed the peace and quiet essential for successful scholarship and research.[35]

Personal relationships were increasingly perverted by political pressures as the regime lost its grip on events and individuals scrambled to make good impressions on those they felt would soon wield power. One medical school professor, determined to take out an insurance policy for the future by joining the Nazi cell in his faculty, quickly discovered the high price of membership. The professor had to approve the *Habilitation* of a Nazi physician even though that individual was generally regarded as being unqualified to teach. The drastically changed mood at the medical school affected the relationship between the Jewish professor Herbert Elias and his students. At the conclusion of his popular lectures, Elias continued to receive the applause of his students, but unlike before, when his students would greet him on the street, now young people who had been friendly only minutes before simply "did not recognize" their teacher on the street.[36]

Throughout 1937, student activism was on the increase throughout Austria and particularly in Vienna. Marxist students, whose political parties had been banned in 1933 and 1934, had been organized since February 1935 in a United Red Student Union (*Geeinter Roter Studentenverband*) and had kept their cells busy distributing pamphlets, flyers, and illegal posters.

---

[34]G.E.R. Gedye, *Fallen Bastions: The Central European Tragedy* (London: Victor Gollancz, 1939), p. 78.

[35]Daniel Horn, "The Hitler Youth and Educational Decline in the Third Reich," *History of Education Quarterly*, XVI, 4 (Winter 1976), 425-447.

[36]Elias, "Erinnerungen . . ."

Their burning hatred of fascism and belief that, despite its protestations of peace, Nazi Germany would soon act aggressively against Austria kept their organization intact and enthusiastic.[37] Even Jewish nationalist students, who had generally withdrawn from the political limelight since the destruction of the Social Democratic party in February 1934, now developed a new militancy as anti-Semitism increased not only in Nazi Germany, but in semi-fascist states like Poland, Hungary and Romania.[38] To protest academic anti-Semitism in these countries, and implicitly in Germany and Austria as well, the small but militant Austrian Zionist student organization called for a twenty-four-hour fast in March 1937 at Vienna's Jewish student *Mensa*. The fast was deemed 100 percent successful as hungry students sat before their plates but refrained from ordering their lunches as a sign of solidarity with their persecuted brethren.[39]

The full depth of student discontent was revealed by the strike of medical students that took place in November 1937. The immediate cause of the upheaval was the government's plan to lengthen the period of medical study by one year as well as the imposition of a fee of ten Schillings monthly to subsidize the costs of hospital internship. Genuine economic grievances over these measures quickly took on a political coloration. The strike was highly effective, receiving wide publicity and closing down the university. While the majority of students involved had Nazi sympathies, they were joined by Marxist and Jewish students

---

[37] Marie Tidl, *Die Roten Studenten, Dokumente und Erinnerungen 1938-1945* (Vienna: Europa Verlag, 1976), pp. 5-13; Walter Göhring, "Der illegale Kommunistische Jugendverband" (unpublished Ph.D. dissertation, University of Vienna, 1971), pp. 219-222.

[38] Nathaniel Katzburg, *Hungary and the Jews. Policy and Legislation, 1920-1943* (Ramat-Gan: Bar-Ilan University Press, 1981), pp. 60-79; Celia S. Heller, *On the Edge of Destruction: Jews of Poland Between the Two World Wars* (New York: Columbia University Press, 1977), pp. 119-125.

[39] Josef Fränkel, "Der Hungerstreik der jüdischen Hochschüler Wiens," *Selbstwehr* (Prague), XXXI, 16 (April 9, 1937), 3 and 4.

who regarded the situation as an opportunity to mount an offensive against the regime, which revealed its weakness by making major concessions on the disputed issues.[40]

Alarmed by the increasingly agitated atmosphere of his institution, Rector Ernst Späth of the University of Vienna announced on September 12, 1937, a prohibition of all assemblies, speeches, singing of songs, and similar public activities in lecture halls, corridors, stairs, and courtyards.[41] These bans had little effect, at least in part because many of the *betont national* faculty were now openly egging on their students with provocative statements. One of the most beloved teachers for Nazi and Rightist students, Othmar Spann—who had been a secret member of the Nazi party ever since May 1933—received tumultuous applause whenever he characterized the Austrian corporative constitution of 1934 as a "carnival prank" (*Fastnachtscherz*).[42]

As the winter semester of 1937-1938 drew to a close, many students increasingly neglected their studies in the belief that great events were soon to transpire. Many of the Nazi students had a thoroughly militarized frame of mind, being active members of the SA or SS. Those in the SS were organized as *SS-Standarten* 11 and 89 of the *Allgemeine SS*. While idealism and a sense of being on the side of historical inevitability often was a major element in the motivation of individuals, more mundane factors also played a role. The Austrian government, once it decided that its *Hochschulen* could not play a decisive role in

---

[40] *Reichspost,* November 23, 1937; "Ein Erfolg der Roten Studenten," *Arbeiter-Zeitung* (Paris), January 4, 1938; Tidl, *Die Roten Studenten,* pp. 12-18.

[41] Albert Massiczek, "Die Situation an der Universität Wien März-April 1938" in *Wien 1938* (Vienna: Verein für Geschichte der Stadt Wien, 1978) [Forschungen und Beiträge zur Wiener Stadtgeschichte, 2], p. 218.

[42] Ibid., Berlin Document Center,, *Personalakte* Othmar Spann; Spann first criticized the Dollfuss constitution of May 1934 as "einen unheimlichen Fastnachtscherz" in his book *Kampfende Wissenschaft. Gesammelte Abhandlungen zur Volkswirtschaftslehre, Gesellschaftslehre und Philosophie* (Jena: Verlag von Gustav Fischer, 1934), p. 246.

leading the opposition, simply ignored them while keeping them under control with a minimum of police supervision. The *Vaterländische Front* organization in the *Hochschulen* was weak and poorly funded. The NSDAP, on the other hand, recognized the importance of winning over the academic youth, many of whom were already sympathetic to the dynamism of the Third Reich. To reinforce these positive feelings, the Austrian Nazis offered students who joined them free meal tickets, clothing subsidies, and a monthly stipend of 100 Schillings.[43]

Many of the Nazi students in Vienna spent the last months before the Anschluss under strict military discipline. They spent much of their time not studying, but discussing current events and drilling in the fraternity houses of *Burschenschaften* that had for several years been closely allied with the Nazi student league.[44] The eagerness of many Viennese *Burschenschaften* to enter into alliances with the NSDStB revealed an amazing lack of political realism, given the fact that by 1935 the overall organization of all students dueling fraternities in the Reich, the *Deutsche Burschenschaft,* had been forced to dissolve itself.[45] Nazi students also spent these last months quartered in the homes of a number of pro-Nazi professors (Hans Eppinger, Wilhelm Falta, Hans Spitzy), because they were in close proximity to the university.[46] Many of these young men visualized a dramatic and bloody *Machtergreifung* in which they would play a major role. Often, the most militant Nazi students were the sons of fathers whose support of National Socialism did not go beyond

---

[43] Irmgard Bärnthaler, *Die Vaterländische Front. Geschichte und Organisation* (Vienna: Europa Verlag, 1971), p. 50.

[44] Erich Witzmann, "Der Anteil der Wiener waffenstudentischen Verbindungen an der völkischen und politischen Entwicklung 1938," (Inagural-Dissertation, University of Vienna, 1940), pp. 163-164.

[45] "Die Auflösung der Studentenschaften," *Neue Freie Presse,* October 30, 1935, a.m.

[46] Massiczek, "Die Situation an der Universität Wien," p. 219.

verbal approval. The sons of Professors Othmar Spann, Hans Übersberger, Othenio Abel and Karl Gottfried Hugelmann were all militant Nazis who were often involved in illegal activities against an Austrian state they regarded as corrupt and in the clutches of the enemies of *Deutschtum*.[47] These young men ardently hoped for a situation in which their deeds went far beyond their fathers' mere words.

After the Berchtesgaden meeting of Hitler and Schuschnigg on February 12, 1938, and the naming of Arthur Seyss-Inquart as Minister of the Interior, the Nazi wave swept all of Austria's *Hochschulen*. The announcement on February 16 of a sweeping amnesty for political prisoners was followed the next day by a directive from Minister of Instruction Hans Pernter that extended the amnesty for political infractions committed by secondary school and *Hochschule* students.[48] At the University of Vienna, Rector Späth continued to struggle against the Nazi student offensive, banning on February 24 any display of flags in black, white and red colors—the colors of Nazi Germany.[49] During a March 5 speech in Linz, Seyss-Irquart approved the wearing of swastikas by individuals and the "nondemonstrative" use of "Heil Hitler" as a public greeting, noting that all public offices and schools were expressly excluded from this new policy.[50]

With the government virtually paralyzed, the dam had now been breached on academic soil, and students throughout Vienna, not to mention Graz, Innsbruck and Leoben, now brazenly displayed their *Hahenkreuz* pins and armbands, enthusiastically

---

[47]"Das Strafverfahren gegen Dr. [Adalbert] Spann eingestellt," *Neue Freie Presse*, November 21, 1934, a.m.; Berlin Document Center, *Personalakte* Othenio Abel, Karl Gottfried Hugelmann und Hans Übersberger.

[48]Wladimir von Hartlieb, *Parole: Das Reich. Eine historische Darstellung der politischen Entwicklung in Österreich von März 1933 bis März 1938* (Vienna: Adolf Luser Verlag, 1939), pp. 478-480.

[49]Massiczek, "Die Situation an der Universität Wien," p. 220.

[50]*Neue Freie Presse*, March 6, 1938, a.m.

"Heil Hitlering!" each other. On March 8, the Trustee of the *Hochschülerschaft* asked Rector Späth for assistance from the University Police (*Hochschulwache*), exasperated as he was by the almost universal disregard for the ban on display of swastikas. In this seemingly inevitable Nazi sweep of Austrian higher education, a few feeble signs of resistance could be discerned. One was the attempt on the morning of March 9 by a representative of the illegal Social Democratic intellectuals' organization to establish ties with the *Hochschule* branch of the Vienna Fatherland Front organization. While it was doubtless sincerely intended, this was but a futile gesture, one that was too little and too late in terms of realistic actions that might still be organized against the Nazi tide.[51] Instruction Minister Pernter, only a few days before his arrest and three years' incarceration in Dachau, received soothing assurances from Police President Michael Skubl (who was soon to serve in the Seyss-Inquart Anschluss cabinet as *Staatssekretär* for security affairs) that he would support the *Hochschulwache* in its attempt to enforce the ban on Nazi insignia.[52]

The situation remained extremely tense as Chancellor Schuschnigg made his dramatic call for a plebiscite. On March 11, Rector Späth announced to his faculty and staff the plebiscite scheduled for the next Sunday. Also announced on this occasion was the start of the Easter vacation on Monday, March 14—scheduled earlier than usual in all likelihood because of the troubled political climate.[53] That same Friday morning, in the Florianigasse in Vienna's Josefstadt district, bloody clashes took place between about thirty members of the *CV-Verbindung Austria* (Kurt Schuschnigg's own fraternity) and ten or so SA men

---

[51]Heinrich Drimmel, "Die katholischen Intellektuellen," in Erika Weinzierl et al., eds. *Kirche in Österreich 1918-1965* (2 vols., Vienna: Verlag Herold. 1966, 1967), I, 343.

[52]Massiczek, "Die Situation an der Universität Wien," p. 221.

[53]Archiv der Universität Wien, SZ 662 1937/38.

from the Nazi *Bund Oberland.* The Catholic students had been busy painting the *Kruckenkreuz* of the Fatherland Front on the walls of buildings when the two groups encountered one another. The bloody brawl that took place resulted in fifteen casualties among the two groups, several of them serious.[54] Perhaps the most dramatic event of March 11 was the march down the Ringstrasse by a heterogeneous group of student supporters of the Schuschnigg plan for plebiscite. Assembling at the university, students from the Socialist, Communist and Catholic conservative-monarchist *Lager* chanted "Freiheit für Österreich!," giving passionate vocal evidence of the rapidly waning hope that Anschluss with Nazi Germany could still be prevented at this late moment.[55]

The next day, March 12, witnessed the de facto takeover of all Austrian *Hochschulen* by Nazi students and faculty. As early as March 11, the University of Innsbruck was occupied by students in SS uniforms who demanded that the current rector be replaced by a scholar fully sympathetic to National Socialism, the historian Harald Steinacker. At Vienna's *Hochschule für Bodenkultur,* the local head of the NSBO (Nazi Industrial Cell Organization) took the initiative in deposing the rector, replacing him with a mere *Privatdozent,* an individual who while doubtless a fanatical Nazi was soon replaced owing to his quirky and capricious behavior.[56] At the University of Vienna, the transi-

---

[54]Karl Itzinger, *Tagebuch vom 10. Februar bis 13. März 1938. Ein Überblick über die letzten Tage des Kampfes und die ersten Tage des Sieges* (Linz: Zeitgeschichte-Verlag Ernst Seidl, 1938), p. 61; "Blutiger Zusammenstoß in der Florianigasse," *Neue Freie Presse,* March 11, 1938, p.m.

[55]Tidl, *Die Roten Studenten,* pp. 23-24.

[56]Willi Weinert, "Die Maßnahmen der reichsdeutschen Hochschulverwaltung im Bereich des österreichischen Hochschulwesens nach der Annexion 1938," in Helmut Konrad and Wolfgang Neugebaur, eds., *Arbeiterbewegung—Faschismus —Nationalbewußtsein. Festschrift zum 10jährigen Bestand des Dokumentationsarchivs des österreichischen Widerstandes und zum 60. Geburtstag von Herbert Steiner* (Vienna: Europaverlag, 1983), p. 130.

tion was effortless in view of the fact that for a number of days governmental control at that institution had been nominal at best. Rector Späth—by birth a Sudeten German who was by no means anti-Nazi in his sympathies—lost no time in sending a letter to Chancellor Seyss-Inquart assuring him of the total loyalty of the *Alma Mater Rudolphina* to the new, Nazi government.[57]

The University of Vienna was represented in the Seyss-Inquart cabinet by Professor Oswald Menghin, appointed to the post of Minister of Instruction. Menghin and his ministry were very busy in mid-March 1938, purging all Austrian *Hochschulen* of rectors and deans loyal to the Fatherland Front regime. The new, pro-Nazi *kommissarische Rektoren* and Deans of Faculties were loyal to National Socialism to varying degrees, but all had been essentially frozen out of power from 1933 to 1938. At the University of Vienna, Rector Späth was replaced as rector by the botanist Fritz Knoll, and all faculty deans stepped down in favor of individuals who at the very least were not anti-Nazis. Some, like the Dean of the Medical Faculty, Eduard Pernkopf, were enthusiastic supporters of Hitlerite doctrines, supporting the Third Reich to the bitter end. Pernkopf, who was inaugurated as the second (and last) Nazi rector of the University of Vienna in May 1943, saw his institution descend into physical and moral ruin by the spring of 1945.[58]

While personal careers moved ahead by leaps and bounds in March 1938, entire institutions came back to life, if only briefly. One such instance was the *Deutsche Studentenschaft*, illegal

---

[57] *Neues Wiener Tagblatt,* March 13, 1938, quoted in Christine Klusacek et al., eds., *Dokumentation zur österreichischen Zeitgeschichte 1938-1945* (Munich: Jugend und Volk, 1971), p. 28.

[58] Berlin Document Center, *Personalakte* Eduard Pernkopf, "Personalfragebogen für die Anlegung der SA-Personalakte," Vienna, March 17, 1940), which notes that Pernkopf joined the NSDAP on April 17, 1933.

since August 1933 and now legally restored to existence.[59] But these were illusory rebirths, since the thirst for monopolistic power of the Nazi Student League remained a constant element in Austrian student life; the *Deutsche Studentenschaft* flourished briefly and shared the limelight with the NSDStB, but after the plebiscite of April 10, 1938, it was abolished. The same fate awaited the various *Burschenschaften Corps* and *Landsmannschaften* that had long allied themselves with the Nazis. These "reactionary" organizations were permitted to celebrate the Anschluss and help propagandize the populace for the April 10 plebiscite. But by late spring 1938, all these bodies had been absorbed by the NSDStB.[60]

Given the high degree of Nazification of Austrian *Hochschulen* prior to the Anschluss, they played a surprisingly minor role in that event itself. Nazi doctrine was fiercely anti-intellectual, and Adolf Hitler himself had little but contempt for people with academic backgrounds, a negative bias that was given concrete form by Hitler's obvious snub of the university in March, 1938—of numerous cultural centers he visited in Vienna during those days of triumph, the university was not included. Only in a brief "audience" in the Hotel Imperial on March 17 did Hitler take notice of "the oldest university in the Greater German Reich."[61]

Gleichschaltung of Austrian higher education began on March

---

[59]"Grosse Kundgebung der ostmärkischen Studentenschaft in Wien," *Deutsche Akademiker-Zeitung* [Vienna], XXX, 7 (April 1, 1938), 9.

[60]The fraternities comprising the *Waffenstudententum* of Vienna were officially absorbed by the NSDStB in a ceremony at the Großer Konzerthaussaal on June 8, 1938. See Franz Gall, *Alma Mater Rudolphina 1365-1965. Die Wiener Universität und Ihre Studenten* (3rd ed., Vienna: Verlag Austria Press, 1965), p. 191.

[61]Gall, *Alma Mater Rudolphina*, p. 31; the university itself was visited by Gauleiter Josef Bürckel that same day, which was briefly noted in the press: "Bürckel sprach zu den Studenten," "Bilder vom Tage," *Völkischer Beobachter*, Vienna ed., March 18, 1938.

17, with the swearing-in of all state officials, an action authorized by Hitler through a document signed on March 15. Excluded from the ceremony were *Volljuden* and Jewish *Mischlinge*, defined as individuals with three Jewish grandparents.[62] By late March, lists of faculty and staff members to be purged were being prepared for Oswald Menghin's Ministry of Instruction by the newly created National Socialist *Dozentenbund* at each institution. Some of the names on these lists had added to them in parentheses the word *Schutzhaft*—a recommendation of "protective custody" in a concentration camp. Anti-Semitic and antidemocratic prejudices long before 1938 had seen to it that two institutions, the College of Veterinary Medicine in Vienna and the Mining Academy in Leoben, had achieved faculties and staffs so racially and ideologically orthodox by Nazi standards that not a single name could be submitted to the ministry.[63]

Measures designed to deal with the Jewish *Überfremdung* of Austrian *Hochschulen* were announced on March 19. Any further registration of Jews for courses was banned, while those already enrolled were now defined as being in a "limited" category, which meant that they could from this point on be expelled at any time with or without a reason being given. On April 20, a *numerus clausus* restricting the enrollment of Jewish students to two percent was announced, it being noted that even this limited number might not be permitted if the presence of Jews in any way infringed on the rights of Aryans to sign up for certain courses. On May 2, Jews were informed that they could enter the University of Vienna only with a special permit. By the start of the 1938-1939 winter semester in October 1938 the Jewish student quota had been lowered to one percent and even the most

---

[62]Brigitte Lichtenberger-Fenz, "Österreichs Universitäten unter dem nationalsozialistischen Regime," in Steirische Gesellschaft für Kulturpolitik, *Grenzfeste Deutscher Wissenschaft. Über Faschismus und Vergangenheitsbewältigung an der Universität Graz* (Vienna: Verlag für Gesellschaftskritik, 1985), pp. 5-6.

[63]Weinert, "Maßnahmen der reichsdeutschen Hochschulverwaltung," p. 130.

sanguine observer could see the approaching end of all opportunities for higher education not only for Jews but for all other national groups deemed inferior and undesirable by Nazi racial doctrines. On October 1, Jews lost the right to audit courses, while Jewish *Mischlinge* retained the right to attend lectures.[64]

With the events of *Kristallnacht* in November 1938, Jewish students throughout the Reich, including the Ostmark, were forbidden to enter all institutions of higher learning. As a follow-up to this in Austria, on November 29, 1938, Jewish students and former faculty members were banned from entering the libraries of all *Hochschulen*. In December, even special permission could no longer be granted for Jews to carry out research in a private capacity in any academic institute or institute library. By May 1940 not only Jews but Jewish *Mischlinge* and Czechs were banned from entering all Austrian *Hochschulen*. A radical implementation of the concept of Aryan *Reinrassigkeit* (racial purity) had then been achieved.[65]

What was the impact of the Anschluss on Austrian universities and other *Hochschulen*? First of all, Nazi *Gleichschaltung* purged these institutions of a large number of faculty members, often those whose achievements had won them world-wide reputations. At the University of Graz, three Nobel Prize winners—Viktor Hess, Otto Loewi and Erwin Schrödinger— lost their professorships, while at the University of Vienna the medical faculty in particular found itself essentially decapitated owing to the massive loss of its many highly talented Jewish members. Of 197 active medical faculty on the eve of Anschluss, fully 153 lost their positions as a result of the Nazi takeover.[66] Whether

---

[64]Lichtenberger-Fenz, "Österreichs Universitäten, pp. 6-7.

[65]Ibid., "Verweisung der letzten Juden aus den Hochschulinstituten," *Völkischer Beobachter,* Vienna ed., December 23, 1938.

[66]Judith Merinsky, "Die Auswirkungen der Annexion Österreichs durch das Deutsche Reich auf die medizinische Fakultät der Universität Wien im Jahre 1938. Biographien entlassener Professoren und Dozenten," Ph.D. Dissertation,

they were removed from their posts for racial or political reasons, a high percentage of Austria's intellectual elite were removed from their posts in the space of a few weeks. These individuals disappeared not only from Austrian academic life, but from that of the international world of research as well, for many of them were too old to begin new careers in foreign countries that were often indifferent or even hostile. Some idea of the devastation caused by the Anschluss in Austrian higher education can be gathered from the following statistics: the University of Vienna in academic year 1937-1938 had 186 full professors and 91 associate professors; the next year the numbers had plummeted to 64 and 27 respectively.[67]

Not only emigration and exile faced the victimized faculty of 1938. For some, death was the only remaining exit for their tragic, insoluble hardships. Incomplete research findings indicate the suicides of eleven faculty members of the University of Vienna, and one at the University of Innsbruck. All but one of these suicides took place in 1938. The 1938 suicides included medical faculty professors Gabor Nobl and Wilhelm Knöpfelmacher, eminent physicians who chose to end their lives by their own hands at advanced ages rather than continue to endure the daily humiliations of life in Nazi Austria. The otologist Rudolf Leidler committed suicide in August 1938, aged fifty-eight, convinced that he could not continue his distinguished academic career as an exile. And while Professor Otto von Fürth died of natural causes soon after the Anschluss, his aged widow, son and daughter and even his ninety-two-year-old mother-in-law were rounded up as Jews and deported to disappear "in the East."[68]

University of Vienna, 1980), p. XIX.

[67]*Statistisches Jahrbuch der Stadt Wien,* new ser., V (1938), 177; *Statistisches Jahrbuch der Stadt Wien 1939-1942,* new ser., VI (Vienna 1946), p. 373.

[68]Professor Edgar Lederer, Paris, personal communication; Herbert Rosenkranz, *Verfolgung und Selbstbehauptung. Die Juden in Österreich 1938-1945* (Vienna: Verlag Herold, 1978), pp. 34-35 and 37-39; Merinsky, "Die Auswirkun-

The death-camps which consumed the lives of millions became the final destinations of a number of Austrian faculty members. As early as August 1938, the Catholic Monarchist Professor Zessner-Spitzenberg of Vienna's *Hochschule für Bodenkultur* was killed at Konzentrationslager (KZ) Dachau. At least eight University of Vienna faculty members met death in the extermination camps. Most of these ended their lives in KZ Theresienstadt. They included the biologist Hans Przibram, the neurologist Alexander Spitzer, the law professors Josef Hupka and Stephan Brassloff, and Elise Richter, the first woman to receive a Ph.D. from an Austrian university and the first woman to achieve (in 1921) professorial rank in an Austrian university.[69] Ironically the first camp commandant of Theresienstadt also had close ties to the University of Vienna. Dr. Siegfried Seidl, born in Vienna in 1911, had joined the NSDAP while a law student at the university.[70]

Perhaps the most disillusioned after the euphoria of the Anschluss was but a memory were the Catholic National intellectuals whose dream of a glorious Reich had been a beacon of hope during harsh years of economic depression and national frustration. Othmar Spann, who had greeted the Anschluss with champagne while calling it the greatest day of his life, found the Gestapo at his door a few days later.[71] Spann survived several months at Dachau, but until his death in 1950 never showed any understanding of how his own anti-democratic theory of universalism had predisposed many conservative Austrian intellectuals

---

gen der Annexion," pp. 139-140.

[69]Hans Helmut Christmann, *Frau und "Judin" an der Universität. Die Romanistin Elise Richter (Wien 1865-Thereisienstadt 1943)* (Wiesbaden: Franz Steiner Verlag, 1980).

[70]Zdenek Lederer, *Ghetto Theresienstadt* (New York: Howard Fertig, 1983), p. 74.

[71]Ernst von Salomon, *Fragebogen [The Questionnaire]*, transl. Constantine FitzGibbons (Garden City, N.Y.: Doubleday, 1955), p. 102.

to an uncritical acceptance of National Socialism.

Another Catholic National, Minister of Instruction Oswald Menghin, quickly discovered that the notion harbored by many *Brückenbauer* intellectuals, that at least the essence of Austrian culture, including its conservative Christian values, could flourish under Nazi rule, was no more than an illusion. Celebrating the Anschluss in the Ministry of Instruction's *Verordnungsblatt*, Menghin even went so far as to quote Andreas Hofer's statement that ultimately all human achievements were dependent on God: "Nit i, nit ös, der da oben."[72] In May 1938, the naive Menghin fell victim to the ruthless *Gauleiter* Josef Bürckel, who ordered his staff to demand Menghin's resignation and along with this also liquidated the Ministry of Instruction.[73] Menghin's fall from influence had already been evident by late April 1938, when he lost the status of a member of the Seyss-Inquart cabinet.[74]

The case of Heinrich Ritter von Srbik raises fundamental questions about the political maturity of leading members of the Austrian academic intelligentsia. Laden with numerous honors by the Nazi regime even before the Anschluss, including the Mozart

---

[72]*Verordnungsblatt für den Dienstbereich des Bundesministeriums für Unterricht*, April 1, 1938, cited in Helmut Engelbrecht, *Lehrervereine im Kampf um Status und Einfluß. Zur Geschichte der Standesorganisationen der Sekundarschullehrer in Österreich* (Vienna: Österreichischer Bundesverlag für Unterricht, Wissenschaft und Kunst, 1978), p. 104.

[73]Luža, *Austro-German Relations*, p. 87.

[74]See the letter from Menghin to Seyss-Inquart, April 28, 1938, Allgemeines Verwaltungsarchiv, Vienna, Amt des Reichsstatthalters in Österreich, Rst. 1, 4779/1938, cited in Richard S. Geehr, "Oswald Menghin, ein Vertreter der katholischen Nationalen," in *Geistiges Leben im Österreich der Ersten Republik. Auswahl der bei den Symposien in Wien vom 11. bis 13. November 1980 und am 27. und 28. Oktober 1982 gehaltenen Referate* (Vienna: Verlag für Geschichte und Politik, 1986), pp. 12-13.

Prize,[75] and membership in the Nazi-controlled *Reichsinstitut für Geschichte des neuen Deutschlands*,[76] after the Anschluss Srbik was laden with further honors, including a seat in the *Grossdeutscher Reichstag* and the presidency of the Academy of Sciences in Vienna. While lending his considerable prestige to the Nazis, Srbik tirelessly intervened with various Nazi agencies on behalf of his Jewish students and colleagues, hoping thus to ameliorate their lot.[77] In another such instance of Srbik's blindness toward the true nature of Nazism, he wrote a letter to Rome after the Anschluss to his younger colleague Friedrich Engel-Janosi, of Catholic faith but Jewish ancestry, that he should consider returning to Vienna because he (Srbik) and others would "fight like lions" to secure a position for a scholar as deserving as he.[78]

Even faculty members generally able to adapt to the Nazi regime often seemed unable to fathom its essentially diabolical nature. Thus it was that *SS-Hauptsturmführer* Professor Viktor Christian, Dean of the University Philosophy Faculty, felt enough human compassion in 1941 to attempt to halt the deportation of a colleague's Jewish mother-in-law.[79] Often the personnel policies of the Nazi *Dozentenbund* were simply ignored by strong-willed faculty members. In 1942 an exasperated Nazi

---

[75]Ernst Holzmann, "Kulturbrief aus Deutsch-Österreich," *Bremer Nachrichten*, August 1, 1937.

[76]Helmut Heiber, *Walter Frank und sein Reichsinstitut für Geschichte des neuen Deutschlands* (Stuttgart: Deutsche Verlags-Anstalt, 1966), pp. 577-579.

[77]Professor George B. Wolfe, Caldwell, Idaho, personal communication: Archiv der Universität Wien, *Rektoratsakten*, Z. 261, 1938/39, which documents Srbik's efforts on behalf of Professor Emil Reich, a nearly blind Jewish faculty member threatened with expulsion from his apartment.

[78]Friedrich Engel-Janosi, . . .*aber ein stolzer Bettler. Erinnerungen aus einer verlorenen Generation* (Graz: Verlag Styria, 1974), p. 155.

[79]Michael H. Kater, *Das "Ahnenerbe" der SS 1935-1945. Ein Beitrag zur Kulturpolitik des Dritten Reiches* (Stuttgart: Deutsche Verlagls-Anhalt, 1974, p. 274; Berlin Document Center, *Personalakte* Viktor Christian.

official described the unsatisfactory situation at the Vienna medical faculty, where Dean Leopold Schönbauer "commands an authoritarian regime and allows no other opinions but his own, even if all the party . . . offices have clearly spoken against it."[80] The essentially individualistic nature of academic life was incompatible with the totalitarian demands of the National Socialist ideology, and even faculty members sympathetic to Nazism often took amazing liberties few members of other professions would have dared to attempt. On one such occasion, soon after the Anschluss, the University of Vienna's professor of pediatrics, Dr. Franz Hamburger, refused to remove a picture of Christ from the lecture hall of the Children's Clinic, and did so only when pressured by Nazi officialdom. Hamburger had long been sympathetic to Nazism, and had demonstratively refused to join the Fatherland Front organization at the University of Vienna, but when the Third Reich came to Austria it was obvious that his picture of the new Germany was a naively idealistic one, omitting the actual Third Reich's essential elements of fear and terror.[81]

Why were so many otherwise intelligent and essentially decent human beings so profoundly deceived by Nazism? Why had they given so little thought to the consequences of Anschluss? One must keep in mind the immense impact of romanticism on German intellectual life to grasp how powerful concepts like the idea of the *Reich*, of Aryan racial and cultural superiority, and the mission of an educated elite could create mentalities easily manipulated by the nihilistic Nazi leaders. Central European intellectuals had pitifully little experience in the real world of

---

[80]Reece C. Kelly, "National Socialism and German University Teachers: The NSDAP's Efforts to Create a National Socialist Professoriate and Scholarship," (Ph.D. Dissertation, University of Washington, 1973), pp. 350-351.

[81]Berlin Documenet Center, *Personalakte* Franz Hamburger, 8452-8453, Minister für innere und kulturelle Angelegenheiten, Abt. IV: Erziehung, Kultus und Volksbildung, Vienna, May 4, 1939.

power and politics. Modern professional training had turned many faculty members into *Fachidioten*, brilliantly knowledgeable in small areas of knowledge but almost totally ignorant in many others, particularly in the complex, shifting and morally ambiguous arena of public life.[82] In his posthumously published memoirs, Edmund Glaise von Horstenau speaks of "Professoren [die] bis zur Dummheit weltfremd sind,"[83] and it is perhaps this element of *Weltfremdheit* that must be singled out as the major causal factor in the tragic origins and consequences of Anschluss for higher education in Austria.

---

[82] Erwin Chargaff, *Heraclitean Fire: Sketches from a Life before Nature* (New York: The Rockefeller University Press, 1978), p. 33. Chargaff was a chemistry student at the University of Vienna in the 1920s and counted Professor Ernst Späth among his teachers.

[83] Peter Broucek, ed., *Ein General im Zwielicht. Die Erinnerungen Edmund Glaises von Horstenau,* Band 2: *Minister im Ständestaat und General im OKW* (Vienna: Hermann Böhlaus Nachf., 1983), p. 152.

Between Stalingrad and the Night of the Generals: Popular Opinion in the "Danubian and Alpine Regions"

Evan B. Bukey

It is now generally recognized that, despite deep roots in the Middle Ages, modern Austrian nationalism developed only in the Second World War, primarily as a negation of the Nazi Anschluss. It grew out of the disparate efforts of a tiny minority of Austrians—mostly monarchists and Communists—who refused to accept Hitler's annexation of their country in 1938 and who, through various forms of underground propaganda and resistance, kept alive the idea of Austrian independence. While the overwhelming majority of the population endorsed the Anschluss and, in many cases, supported Nazi policies, the hardships of war eventually gave rise to second thoughts. In 1943 Hitler's defeat at Stalingrad—in which thousands of Austrian soldiers lost their lives—combined with an intensification of Gestapo terror, growing casualty lists, the beginning of Allied aerial bombardment, food shortages, resentment of German administrative control of Vienna, and, above all, fear of foreign conquest began to produce widespread disenchantment, nervousness, and defeatism. When, near the end of the year, the Allied Moscow Declaration unexpectedly promised a restoration of independence, the cherished goal of resistance-fighters and traditional elites at last became a viable option for other Austrians, including substantial numbers of Nazis who were either disillusioned with Hitler's rule or seeking shelter from retribution. The result was the formation of a consensus for the reestablishment of a constitutional order based on Austrian patriotism and liberal democracy. When the Second Republic arose from the ashes of Hitler's Reich, it was thus able to draw on the support of the Austrian people, united in a sense of common purpose, though sharing fragile, complex, and often contradictory views of what it meant to be Austrian.[1]

Fifty years after the Anschluss, the ambiguous and brittle nature of Austrian national identity has been all too clearly revealed in the statements of a head of state who claims to love his country and to profess the "deepest respect" for the martyrs and heroes of the Austrian Resistance but who stubbornly defends his wartime service in the uniform of the Greater German Reich.[2] In light of the official view that the Alpine Republic was "the first country to fall victim to Hitlerite aggression,"[3] both the Waldheim affair and public reaction to it have reopened questions

---

[1] Karl Stadler, *Österreich 1938-1945 im Spiegel der NS-Akten* (Vienna and Munich: Herold Verlag, 1966); Radomír Luža, *Austro-German Relations in the Anschluss Era* (Princeton: Princeton University Press, 1975); Félix Kreissler, *Der Österreicher und seine Nation. Ein Lernprozess mit Hindernissen* (Vienna: Böhlau Verlag, 1884); Gerhard Botz, "Eine deutsche Geschichte 1938 bis 1945? Österreichische Geschichte zwischen Exil, Widerstand und Verstrickung," *Zeitgeschichte*, vol. 14, 1986), 1, pp. 19-38. Other significant studies of Austrian nationalism include: Peter J. Katzenstein, *Disjoined Partners: Austria and Germany Since 1945* (Berkeley, University of California Press, 1976); William J. Bluhm, *Building An Austrian Nation* (New Haven: Yale University Press, 1973); Friedrich Heer, *Der Kampf um die österreichische Identität* (Vienna: Böhlau Verlag, 1881); Heinrich Lutz and Helmut Rumpler, eds., *Österreich und die deutsche Frage im 19. und 20. Jahrhundert* (Munich: Oldenbourg, 1982); Ernst Bruckmüller, *Nation Österreich* (Vienna: Böhlau Verlag, 1984); George Wagner, ed., *Österreich. Von der Staatsidee zum Nationalbewusstsein* (Vienna: Österreichische Staatsdruckerei, 1982); and Erwin Ringel, *Die österreichische Seele* (Vienna: Böhlau Verlag, 1984).

[2] Statement of Kurt Waldheim, 15 February 1988. *Der Österreich-Bericht*, 16 February 1988.

[3] The words of the Moscow Declaration of 1 November 1943. For background and analysis see Robert H. Keyserlingk, *Austria in World War II: An Anglo-American Dilemma* (Kingston and Montreal: McGill-Queens University Press, 1988).

about popular attitudes in Austria under German occupation.

The purpose of this essay is to examine public opinion in what the Nazis called the "Danubian and Alpine Regions" during the eighteen months following the German surrender at Stalingrad and to determine to what extent, if any, Austrians responded to the call of the Allied Moscow Declaration to contribute to their own liberation by engaging in resistance and sabotage, to what extent they continued to support the war effort, and to what extent they remained committed to the Nazi system. It will pay particular attention to reaction to the German generals' plot to overthrow Hitler on 20 July 1944, both as a means of measuring general attitudes toward the Anschluss and as a specific test of the consensus of Austrian historians that the conspirators' "attempt to enroll democratic Austrian politicians as collaborators failed because the once controversial belief in the political and national viability of Austria by then prevailed everywhere in Austria."[4]

Any attempt to gauge the mood in Hitler's Reich must invariably rely on the secret surveys of opinion of the Security Service (SD), which, beginning in 1938, were distilled for the leadership of the regime and have recently been published in the multi-volume collection *Meldungen aus dem Reich*.[5] As specific information on Austria appearing in the series is, with notable exceptions, homogenous or impressionistic, it is necessary for a more textured and accurate assessment to consult the original situation-reports of local authorities.[6] Many of these documents

---

[4]Christine Klusacek, ed., *Dokumentation zur österreichischen Zeitgeschichte 1938-1945* (Munich and Vienna: Jugend und Volk, 1971), p. 365.

[5]Heinz Boberach, ed., *Meldungen aus dem Reich. Die geheimen Lageberichte des Sicherheitsdienstes der SS 1938-1945* (17 vols.) (Herrsching: Pawlak Verlag, 1984).

[6]The only analyses of Austrian situation reports published to date are in Harry Slapnicka, *Oberösterreich als es "Oberdonau" hiess (1938-1945)* Linz: Österreichisches Landesverlag, 1978), pp. 279-284 and Evan B. Bukey, "Popular Opinion in Vienna after the Anschluss," in: F. Parkinson ed., *Conquering the*

have been lost, destroyed, or remain to be found in provincial archives, but a significant collection of surveys of opinion from Lower and Upper Austria has survived nearly intact.[7] For the middle period of World War II there are also scattered surveys from other provinces and Vienna, some judicial records, village police diaries, and a handful of eyewitness accounts by neutral foreign correspondents, Allied agents, and members of the Austrian Resistance. Despite real gaps in the data—especially for Tirol, Styria and Carinthia—it is possible to combine the

---

Past: Austrian Nazism Yesterday and Today (Detroit: Wayne State University Press, 1989), pp. 151-164.

[7] A fairly complete collection of *Landrat* situation reports for Lower Austria is available at the Niederösterreichisches Landesarchiv (NÖLA) Vienna, under the signature NÖLA/ZR/Ia-10 and the Dokumentationsarchiv des österreichischen Widerstandes (DÖW), Vienna: doc. E 19.284. For Upper Austria see National Archives (NA), Washington, D.C., Microcopy T 81, Rolls 6-7; Oberösterreichisches Landesarchiv Linz (OÖLA), Linz, Politische Akten, 1933-1945; Slapnicka, *Oberdonau*, pp. 279-284, and Evan Burr Bukey, *Hitler's Hometown: Linz, Austria, 1908-1945* (Bloomington: Indiana University Press, 1986), pp. 207-213. For Vienna the Allgemeines Verwaltungsarchiv (AVA), in Vienna contains incomplete files of SD situation reports for 1939-1940 in the collection of the Reichskommissar für die Wiedervereiningung Österreichs mit dem Deutschen Reich (Rk), Ordner 312-314, 322, also available in NA, T 84, R 13-14. For the years 1942-1943 there are SD opinion surveys from Tirol and Voralberg in the AVA's Schirach (RStH) files. On Styria and Carinthia documentary material for the period after 1938 remains classified in provincial archives. The director of the Steiermärkisches Landesarchiv, Graz, assures me, however, that the records of the Gau administration were largely lost or destroyed in 1945; according to the director of the Kärntner Landesarchiv, Klagenfurt, there are no opinion surveys of any kind in his archive. DÖW, *Widerstand und Verfolgung in Tirol 1934-1945: Eine Dokumentation* (WVT) (Vienna and Munich: Österreichische Bundesverlag, 1984), vol. 2, p. 386; Stefan Karner, *Die Steiermark im Dritten Reich 1934-1945 Aspekte ihrer politischen wirtschaftlichsozialen und kulturellen Entwicklung* (Graz and Vienna: Leykam Verlag, 1986); Letters to the author of G. Pferschy, Director, Steiermärkisches Landesarchiv, Graz, 25 May 1985 and Alfred Ogris, Director, Kärntner Landesarchiv, Klagenfurt, 3 July 1985. For Salzburg see Ernst Hanisch, *Nationalsozialistische Herrschaft in der Provinz: Salzburg im Dritten Reich* (Salzburg: Landespressebüro, 1983), pp. 260-279.

contemporary sources with the works of scholars such as Karl Stadler, Radomír Luža, Harry Slapnicka, Ernst Hanisch, and Stefan Karner[8] to reconstruct certain main currents of opinion. In the absence of evidence on occupation and class, it is less easy to discern the attitudes of specific social groups, though it may be assumed, as has been suggested elsewhere, that approval of the regime was strongest among those sections of society most overrepresented in the Austrian Nazi party—officials and the aspiring new middle class of employees and managers—and that disapproval was greatest among those groups most overrepresented in resistance movements—skilled workers and middle-class intellectuals.[9] Given Austria's extraordinary geographical diversity, it may also be assumed that pro-Anschluss sentiment was most prevalent in traditional strongholds of German Nationalism—Salzburg, Styria, and Carinthia–and weakest in Vienna and rural Tirol.[10]

Scrutiny of popular opinion in the "Danubian and Alpine Regions" of Greater Germany after the battle of Stalingrad reveals a multifaceted panorama of diffuse and conflicting attitudes, marked by social and geographical contrasts and shaped by nearly half a decade of Nazi rule and war. For Vienna the most vivid glimpses of prevailing conditions can be found both

---

[8] As cited in fns. 1, 6, and 7.

[9] Gerhard Botz, *Wien vom "Anschluss" zum Krieg. Nationalsozialistische Machtübernahme und politisch-soziale Umgestaltung am Beispiel der Stadt Wien 1938-1939* (Vienna and Munich: Jugend und Volk,1978), p. 220; idem, "The Changing Pattern of Social Support for Austrian National Socialism (1918-1945)," in: Stein Ugelvik Larsen, et al., *Who Were the Fascists? Social Roots of European Fascism* (Bergen: Universitetsforlaget, 1980), pp. 202-225; and Radomír Luža, *The Resistance in Austria 1938-1945* (Minneapolis: University of Minnesota Press, 1984), p. 315. See also Katzenstein, *Disjoined Partners,* p. 185 and DÖW, *Widerstand und Verfolgung in Niederösterreich 1934-1945* (WVNÖ) (Vienna: Österreichischer Bundesverlag, 1987), vol. 3, p. 599.

[10] Resistance was strongest in Vienna, the Tirol, and Styria. Luža, *Resistance,* pp. 298-300.

in the recollection of a Swedish correspondent, Arvid Fredborg, who visited the city in February 1943, and in a series of reports compiled several months later by the American embassy in Stockholm from the testimony of Allied agents, Austrian exiles, and informants (including a Nazi engineer and two members of the Vienna Philharmonic Orchestra).[11]

Fredborg, who was no stranger to Vienna, described it as an enormous complex of military hospitals, overrun by foreign workers, and experiencing a deterioration of public services: "The trains were even more worn and creaking, the taxis were more rattling, and the railway stations even dirtier than last time."[12] On the other hand, he also observed that shops offered more than Berlin and most restaurants—including the Sacher—still served top quality cuisine to their guests. What astonished Fredborg was not so much the changes in urban life wrought by the war as the bitter and open animosity of the Viennese toward the Germans, a hostility, he wrote, "that extends through Austrian society from top to bottom." Provoked by the arrogant behavior of Reich German officials and personnel, anti-German resentment was so widespread that it had spawned a strong sense of solidarity, a "renaissance of Austrian patriotism," and even a resistance movement already engaged in acts of sabotage. Fredborg took pains to emphasize that most Austrians disliked German dominance more than Nazi ideology and that few actually sought a return to the First Republic. Nonetheless, he was emphatic in claiming that a majority of the population had broken forever with the Anschluss.[13]

Fredborg's portrait of a Vienna seething with discontent is

---

[11] Arvid Fredborg, *Behind the Steel Wall: A Swedish Journalist in Berlin, 1941-43* (New York: Viking, 1944) and NA, Microcopy (M) 1209, Roll (R) 29, Frames (F) 63-260; *Records of the Department of State Relating to Internal Affairs of Austria, 1930-1944*, Decimal File 863.

[12] Fredborg, *Behind the Steel Wall*, p. 180.

[13] Ibid., pp. 179-187, 247-249.

largely substantiated by a number of reports prepared for Allied diplomats in Stockholm. According to the accounts, disenchantment with German rule was widespread among the middle classes, including large numbers of Viennese Nazis—particularly the *alte Kämpfer* who bitterly resented losing administrative posts to Reich Germans in the *Gau-,* municipal-, and party-bureaucracies. Within the business community, there was a similar sense of discrimination accompanied by general dissatisfaction with the heavy burden of wartime taxation and, in the case of small producers and merchants, indignation at the closing of small-scale firms in compliance with Goebbels' total war measures of mobilization. According to one observer, one of those measures, the (irregular) conscription of women into the workforce, also aroused the ire of the upper and upper-middle classes, "as they often see their wives or sisters working at jobs which they ordinarily would consider a disgrace."[14] As a whole, the Viennese bourgeoisie had become fed up with German rule, but were unwilling to resist it. As one observer put it, "one cannot yet speak of any resistance on the part of the middle classes . . . In March 1938 they all ran over to Nazism as soon as Austria was annexed. In 1943 they began to withdraw from it, since Nazism had disappointed them. It meant war, want, distress, and great losses in human lives as well as what is called by some 'brown Communism.'"[15]

Among the putative beneficiaries of "brown Communism," blue-collar workers, feelings of resentment and opposition prevailed as well. Unlike their employers, most Viennese workers

---

[14] NA, M 1209, R 29, F 93-94, "The Feelings of the Austrian Population," Istanbul, 13 April 1943 and F 155-156, "What People Think about in Austria," 2 August 1943.

[15] NA, M 1209, R 29, F 113, "News from Austria," Stockholm, 31 May 1943. For a similar impression see the handwritten report of the Austrian resistance fighter Josef Meisel after his harrowing escape from Auschwitz, at DÖW, doc. 841, "Bericht uber die Situation in Österreich 1943."

remained both ideologically opposed to National Socialism and loyal to traditions of trade unions. Nearly all yearned for a more pluralistic system. Forced, however, to work long hours under constant surveillance for frozen wages, they refrained from acts of resistance, including the distribution of illegal fliers and leaflets. Further, despite Fredborg's impressions, many remained loyal to the Anschluss, fearing a return of unemployment and even preferring the Nazi term "Ostmark" to Austria—a name they associated with the hated Dollfuß-Schuschnigg dictatorship.[16]

Cutting across class lines, most witnesses concurred in characterizing the Viennese mood in 1943 as one of sagging morale, war weariness, and apathy. With the loss of so many Austrian soldiers at Stalingrad, thousands of grief-stricken families began tuning in Radio Moscow for word of relatives or loved-ones who might have been taken prisoner. Their sense of gloom and foreboding was reinforced by the sight of innumerable hospitals and invalids in the city. Defeat at Stalingrad also unleashed a torrent of criticism of Nazi leaders ranging from Göring (*ein aufgefressenes Schwein*) to local party bosses, though not extending to Hitler who, as elsewhere in Greater Germany, was viewed as a solitary father-figure engulfed by tragedy. Needless to say, anti-Nazi sentiment was accompanied by a renewed wave of anti-German feeling that now included disdain for Reich German refugees from bombed-out cities of the Rhineland and North Germany. There was also unhappiness with continued shortages of fats and vegetables, though general agreement that supplies of rationed food were ample.[17]

---

[16] NA, M 1209, R 29, F 107-108, 112, 123, "News from Austria," Stockholm, 31 May 1943.

[17] Ibid., F 107-130; F 93-94, "The Feelings of the Austrian People"; and F 155-156, "What People Think about in Austria," Istanbul, 12 August 1943. For opinion in the Old Reich see Marlis G. Steinert, *Hitler's War and the Germans: Public Mood and Attitude during the Second World War* (Athens: Ohio University Press, 1977).

Whether the Viennese (and other Austrians) had been "cured of their love for the German Reich" by 1943, as the Socialist politician Adolf Schärf claimed early in the summer,[18] is difficult to say with certainty. While Fredborg remained adamant that the "vast majority of Austrians desire separation from the rest of Germany and above all North Germany,"[19] the testimony of others is more ambivalent, suggesting particularistic disgruntlement with Hitler's policy of keeping Vienna under Reich German control rather than seeking an actual break with the system.[20] As for the Nazi authorities, they took no chances as the Gestapo stepped up sweeps of working-class neighborhoods and intensified its campaign of visible terror against dissenters and resistance-fighters. While the Viennese public prosecutor reported no perceptible rise in subversive activities for the first half of 1943,[21] the People's Court continued to mete out hundreds of death sentences. According to one writer,

> In Josefsstadt there are daily executions of from ten to fifteen anti-Nazis. Those executed are buried near the IIIrd gate of the Central Cemetery . . . .The bodies and chopped off heads . . . are thrown into a large box and carted by lorry . . . to an open mass grave. There the front part of the lorry is lifted in the way used for unloading sand, and the heads and corpses of the murdered persons topple or slither all together into the grave. Then the grave is filled in with chlorine and earth, and the funeral is over.[22]

Outside Vienna, popular attitudes had been molded not only

---

[18] Adolf Schärf, *Österreichs Erneuerung 1945-1955* (Vienna, 1955), p. 25 as quoted by Luža, *Austro-German Relations,* p. 332.

[19] NA, M 1209, R 29, F 93, Johnson (Stockholm) to State Department, 27 July 1943.

[20] Luža, *Austro-German Relations,* p. 288.

[21] DÖW, Film 97, Generalstaatsanwalt, Wien, to Thierack, 1 July 1943.

[22] NA, M 1209, R 29, F 124, "News from Austria."

by Hitler's system and his war but also by specific social, economic, and geographical circumstances. Resentment of the German element, for example, was less pervasive in the provinces, primarily because top administrative posts usually remained in the hands of indigenous Austrian Nazis, who, through the local party apparatus, controlled most aspects of grassroots public life. While a number of Reich German officials did occupy positions of authority as District Presidents (*Landräte*) or Deputy *Kreisleiter*, they normally answered to Austrian party leaders and in some cases enjoyed greater public respect than traditional Viennese bureaucrats.[23] On the other hand, anti-German sentiment was clearly on the rise as a reaction to the arrival of large numbers of evacuees from bombed-out cities of the Ruhr, partly because of the German habit of ridiculing provincial Austrian ways while purchasing food at black market prices, partly because of the refusal of German women to share the burdens of rural life.[24]

In the countryside, the response of the farming population to Nazi regulations and wartime hardships resembled that in neighboring Bavaria. Grassroots opinion in strongly Catholic regions of Upper and Lower Danube, Salzburg, and the Tirol, for example, bitterly opposed the regime's anti-clerical policies including the removal of crucifixes from schools, the use of church bells as scrap metal, the expropriation of clerical property, and the imprisonment of clergymen. There was also hostility to restrictions on the production, distribution, and marketing of whole milk, fats, and livestock. With the conscription of much of the male population by the armed forces during the Russian

---

[23]Hanish, *Nationalsozialistische Herrschaft in der Provinz*, pp. 214-218; Bukey, *Hitler's Hometown*, pp. 170-177, 183-185; and Karner, *Steiermark*, pp. 104-105. On the other hand, Reich German party functionaries were widely resented, at least in Styria. Karner, *Steiermark*, p. 108.

[24]For example, NÖLA/ZR/Ia-10/14/43: *Landrat*, Gänserndorf to Jury, 7 July 1943. See also Luža, *Austro-German Relations*, p. 310.

campaign, serious strains developed both as a consequence of the mounting loss of life, especially by late 1942, and of the massive labor shortage in the countryside. The attempt of the regime to make up at least part of the difference through the use of prisoners of war and foreign laborers only added to the cares of the peasant families who frequently found it difficult to adhere to Nazi regulations forbidding normal social and sexual relations with "non-Aryans."[25]

On the other hand, opposition to Nazi policies was hardly uniform. Once Hitler moderated his assault on the Church in 1941, for example, there was a willingness to support the anti-Bolshevik crusade on the Eastern Front, especially when it was endorsed by Church dignitaries like the bishop of Linz, Josef Calasanctius Fliesser, who both approved of it in countless sermons and sponsored a number of receptions for troops that, in the view of one bewildered *Landser*, equaled those of Göring.[26] In other parts of the rural "Ostmark" popular reaction to Nazi rule was by no means unenthusiastic. In Styria where eleven percent of the population had left the Church since 1938 and in Protestant towns and villages of Carinthia, for example, there appears to have been genuine support of both Hitler's anti-Catholic measures and his war against Yugoslavia. Further, in Styria, Carinthia, and mountainous regions of other provinces a number of peasants expressed appreciation of Nazi agricultural policies that had put an end to foreclosures on farms and consolidated

---

[25] Ian Kershaw, *Popular Opinion and Political Dissent in the Third Reich: Bavaria, 1933-1945* (Oxford: Oxford University Press, 1983), pp. 281-357; Luža, *Austro-German Relations*, pp. 182-191ff; idem, "Nazi Control of the Austrian Catholic Church, 1939-1941," *The Catholic Historical Review*, 63 (1977), 537-571; Slapnicka, *Oberdonau*, pp. 194-224, 252-294; Bukey, *Hitler's Hometown* pp. 191-196, 207-213; DÖW, *Widerstand und Verfolgung in Oberösterreich 1934-1945. Eine Dokumentation*, WVOÖ (Vienna: Österreicher Bundesverlag, 1982) vol. 2, pp. 403-418; WVNÖ, vol. 3, pp. 11-268; Hanisch, *Nationalsozialistische Herrschaft in der Provinz,* pp. 98-104, 150-151, 166-172, 260-273; and WVT, II.

[26] NA, T 81, R 6, F 130-158, SD Abschnitt, Linz, 26 May 1943.

marginal plots into larger holdings. As late as November 1943, the provincial court of appeals in Graz reported general support among farmers in Styria for the Reich Entailed Farm Law, a measure widely resented elsewhere.[27]

In industrial areas, working-class attitudes generally paralleled those in Vienna, though initial enthusiasm for the Anschluss may have been greater in provincial towns and cities than in the second largest city of the Reich. By 1943, Nazi benefits such as the end of unemployment and the introduction of significant welfare measures including health insurance, child and family support, and cheap company housing had been largely offset by a fifteen percent decline in real wages, deteriorating living conditions, restrictions on job mobility, and tightening labor discipline. Although blue-collar unrest remained insubstantial in the massive new industrial plants in Linz and St. Valentin, opposition was strong among wage earners in transportation, mining, and older smokestack industries, especially in Steyr, St. Pölten, Bruck a.d. Mur, and Leoben. According to Gestapo records, industrial sabotage was more widespread in Austria than in the Old Reich, though by late 1942 the back of the Communist resistance had been broken and most Austrian workers, like their German counterparts, had fallen back on a wait-and-see attitude, marked by occasional work-stoppages, absenteeism, and, in at least one case, a wildcat strike.[28]

---

[27]Karner, *Steiermark*, pp. 118-122, 281-285; DÖW, docs. 8351: Unveröffentlichte Manuskripte für das Bundesregierung herausgegebene rot/weiß/rot Buch: Bericht verschiedener Gendarmeriepostenkommandos in Kärnten: Arriach/Villach, 29 May 1946, Drobollach/Villach, 26 May 1946, Rattendorf/Hermagor, 28 May 1946; and 17.858: Kärnten, Gendarmeriechroniken, Althofen, 1940-1941 and Gallizien, 1938-1942. Also DÖW, Film 97, Oberlandesgerichtspräsident, Graz to Thierack, 27 November, 1943.

[28]Luža, *Austro-German Relations*, pp. 152-155 and *passim; idem, Resistance*, pp. 79-155, especially p. 129; Stadler, *Österreich*, pp. 153-239; Karner, *Steiermark*, pp. 293-365; Hanisch, *Nationalsozialistische Herrschaft*, pp. 161-164; Slapnicka, *Oberdonau*, pp. 158-176, 282; and Bukey, *Hitler's Hometown*, p. 208.

Overall, the climate of opinion in the "Danubian and Alpine Regions"—with the arguable exception of Vienna—did not differ substantially from that prevailing elsewhere in Greater Germany. As in the Old Reich, the response of the population to Hitler's defeat at Stalingrad was one of shock and disbelief, followed by waves of despondency, cynicism, fear for the fate of relatives at the front, and wishful thinking.[29] In both Upper and Lower Danube the security organs reported astonishment "that the Führer has allowed *Ostmärker* of all people to be driven to their deaths."[30] The collapse in morale was accompanied by a sharp rise in church attendance and intense discussion about the war's duration, especially in the countryside where the conflict was scarcely comprehended and widely resented. Among blue-collar workers the reaction was one of cynical detachment, marked by general belief that conditions under Bolshevism could not be worse than under the existing system.[31] The Stalingrad debacle also opened up an ever-widening gap between the Nazi party and the general population. Though the SD in St. Pölten reported excellent attendance at ceremonies honoring the tenth anniversary of Hitler's rise to power,[32] authorities in Linz, Grieskirchen, Ried, Feldkirchen, and elsewhere recorded instances of bitter

---

For numerous examples of working-class unrest, dissent, sabotage, and resistance see DÖW, *Widerstand und Verfolgung in Wien 1934-1945. Eine Dokumentation*, (WVW) (Vienna: Österreich Verlag, 1975) vol. 2; *Widerstand und Verfolgung in Burgenland 1934-1945. Eine Dokumentation* (WVB) (Vienna: Österreich Verlag, 1979), pp 166-241; WVT, II, 123-208; WVNÖ, vol. 2, pp. 9-390; and WVOÖ vol. 1, pp. 183-343.

[29] Steinert, *Hitler's War*, pp. 184-257; Dietrich Orlow, *The History of the Nazi Party: 1933-1945* (Pittsburgh: University of Pittsburgh Press, 1973), pp. 411-420; Stadler, *Österreich*, pp. 293-313ff; and Boberach, *Meldungen*, XIV, 5403-5407.

[30] Stadler, *Österreich*, p. 296.

[31] For example, NA, T 81, R 6, F 13343, SD Abschnitt, Linz, 20 February 1943.

[32] NÖLA/ZR/Ia-10/14/43: Polizeidirektor, St. Pölten, 4 February 1943.

criticism and even personal abuse of party functionaries. In Grieskirchen, for example, the grief-stricken mother of a fallen soldier slapped a local group leader for delivering a message of condolence;[33] in Böheim an uncle attacked a cell leader on a similar errand with the words, "You with the party badges are to blame for this shitty war!"[34]

But whatever the disenchantment with the party, the emotional bond to its leader remained intact. As in most parts of Greater Germany, Austrians generally exempted Hitler from criticism of military reverses or unpopular restrictions such as the compulsory closing of small shops and firms. Trust in his leadership remained unshaken. Indeed, after a rare public appearance in Linz on a Sunday in April 1943, morale soared. "If the Führer has time to visit Linz," people said, "things can no longer be so bad."[35]

Throughout 1943 fluctuations in the public mood continued to parallel those in the Old Reich, though Hitler's popularity may have remained stronger in Austria than in parts of Greater Germany, especially those under aerial bombardment.[36] When the front stabilized in early spring, there was a temporary return of confidence, reinforced by optimistic reports of front-line

---

[33] Stadler, *Österreich*, p. 285.

[34] WVNÖ, vol. 3, pp. 552-553.

[35] NA, T 81, R 6, F 13411, SD Abschnitt, Linz, 7 April 1943. On the Führer myth see Ian Kershaw, *The 'Hitler Myth' Image and Reality in the Third Reich* (Oxford: Oxford University Press, (1987). On the persistence of the cult in Austria see Ernst Hanlisch, "Ein Versuch den Nationalsozialismus zu verstehen" in: Anton Pelinka and Erika Weinzierl eds., *Das grosse Tabu: Österreichs Umgang mit seiner Vergangenheit* (Vienna: Verlag der österreichischen Staatsdruckerei, 1987), pp. 157-158.

[36] Steinert, *Hitler's War*, p. 191; NA, T 81, R 6, F 13183, SD Abschnitt, Linz, 5 May 1943; and Hanisch, "Versuch," pp. 157-158. At the Minneapolis symposium, Fritz Molden suggested that local officials may have exaggerated Hitler's popularity as a means of presenting growing disenchantment with Nazi rule in the best possible light. While this may indeed have been the case, the testimony of neutral observers also stresses the persistence of the *Führer* cult—at least throughout 1943. See fn. 17.

soldiers home on leave. The loss of Tunisia in May, however, produced a downward slide in morale, leading to pessimism, apathy, and serious doubts about the outcome of the war. As elsewhere in the Reich, the general stupor was accompanied by perceptible changes in social and sexual behavior, including a sharp increase in the purchase of birth-control devices, the breakup of innumerable marriages, and growing "sexual license" between lonely women and prisoners of war or foreign workers.[37] Among the young, there was also a sense of alienation from the regime, or at least from the Nazi party and its associations. As in the cities of western and northern Germany, the security service reported both a rise in juvenile crime and—in Vienna and in Hollabrunn—a growing number of scuffles between teenage gangs and the Hitler Youth.[38] Throughout society as a whole instances of ordinary crime remained low, but as the year progressed, despite an upsurge of death sentences by the People's Court, the number of political offenses for subversion, defeatism, listening to foreign radio broadcasts, and black marketeering accelerated rapidly.[39]

Meanwhile, word of Mussolini's overthrow coupled with the first American air raids in Austria (on Wiener Neustadt, 13

---

[37] Steinert, *Hitler's War*, pp. 219-215, 230-232; NA, T 81, R 6, F 13058, SD Abschnitt, Linz, 26 May 1943; DÖW, Film 97, Oberlandesgericht, Graz to Thierack, 29 March 1943; Stadler, *Österreich*, pp. 303-304.

[38] WVNÖ, vol. 3, pp. 572-573. On the upsurge of juvenile protest see Christian Gerbel, Alexander Mejstrik, and Reinhard Siedler, "Die 'Schlurfs': Verweigerung und Opposition von Wiener Arbeiterjugendlichen im 'Dritten Reich,'" in: Emmerich Tálos, Ernst Hanisch, and Wolfgang Neugebauer, eds., *NS-Herrschaft in Österreich 1938-1945* (Vienna: Verlag für Gesellschaftskritik, 1988), pp. 243-268. For the Old Reich see Detlev J.K. Peukert, *Inside Nazi Germany: Conformity, Opposition, and Racism in Everyday Life* (New Haven: Yale University Press, 1987), p. 160 and *passim*.

[39] For example see Slapnicka, *Oberdonau*, pp. 290-291 and DÖW, Film 97, Generalstaatsanwalt, Vienna to Thierack, 1 July 1943. On the other hand, for evidence of a *decline* of subversive activities see WVNÖ, vol. 3, p. 598.

August, and Klagenfurt, 9 September) sent morale plummeting to new depths. According to opinion-surveys in Lower Danube, people expressed bitter despair at the loss of an ally but also anger with those whom they indiscriminately blamed for the "betrayal"—most of the Italian population. Although Otto Skorzeny's dramatic rescue of the *Duce* and a subsequent radio address by Hitler briefly raised public spirits in late September, the authorities reported from numerous localities that "faith in a victorious end to the war has largely disappeared in nearly all layers of the populace."[40] Particularly demoralizing were the growing streams of Allied bombers in the skies and a gradual awareness of the insufficiency of anti-aircraft guns and fighter interceptors to provide protection for Austrian cities. Indeed, the first attack on Wiener Neustadt unleashed a general panic that sent hundreds of foreign workers fleeing into the countryside and thereafter led to a general exodus of city dwellers to outlying areas.[41]

By the end of the year, word of major setbacks in Russia, realization that local casualties were exceeding those of World War I, and a sharp deterioration of middle-class living standards all produced something approaching universal discontent, defeatism, and despair. While trust in Hitler persisted and most of the population still stood behind his war in the East, many people began turning psychologically against what was more and more regarded as foreign rule. As the district president in NeuNkirchen delicately reported, "It must be stated with deep regret that the Greater Germany idea, the idea of the unity of all tribes of the German people, was much stronger and keener in

---

[40] NÖLA/ZR/Ia-10/14/1943: Der Landrat des Kreises Neunkirchen an den Reichsstaathalter in Niederdonau, 10 October 1943. See also the district presidential reports for October 1943 from Baden, Eisenstadt, Wiener Neustadt, Gänserndorf, Hollabrunn, and Amstetten.

[41] NÖLA/ZR/Ia-10/14/1943, *Landrat,* St. Pölten, 8 September 1943 and *Polizeidirector,* Wiener Neustadt, 7 September 1943.

the years before the Anschluss than today."[42]

What distinguished popular opinion in the "Danubian and Alpine Regions" of Greater Germany in 1943 was a recrudescence of a sense of being Austrian. It is true that a sense of regional identity had remained strong among Catholic villagers and farmers, especially in the Tirol, that genuine patriotism had motivated disparate groups of monarchist and Communist resistance-fighters from the outset, and that anti-German feeling had prevailed among the grouchy and grumbling Viennese ever since 1940, if not earlier. Nonetheless, Hitler's defeat at Stalingrad gave rise to popular thought of restoring the state that until just a few years before nobody wanted. At first, people approached the problem from the perspective of wishful thinking, hoping that relatives captured by the Russians would receive better treatment than Reich Germans. Rumors circulated that Austrians usually surrendered wearing distinctive badges and armbands, that Austrian prisoners of war in England already enjoyed better food and warmer blankets than "Prussians," and that Churchill intended to unite Austria and Bavaria into a postwar state ruled by Otto von Habsburg. Among middle-class circles, word had it that the Allies were deliberately sparing Austrian cities from aerial bombardment.[43] Besides wishful thinking, there was also

---

[42]NÖLA/ZR/Ia-10/14/1943, *Landrat*, Neunkirchen, 10 October 1943. See also the district presidential reports from November and December in the same collection; Slapnicka, *Oberdonau*, pp. 291-292; OÖLA, Pol. Akten, O Ö 12/36, SD Abschnitt, Linz, 2 November 1943; and Boberach, *Meldungen*, vol. 15, p. 5894.

[43]Luža, *Austro-German Relations*, pp. 330-332; Stadler, *Österreich*, pp. 294-303; NA, T 81, R 6, F 13319-13343, 75-75, SD Abschnitt, Linz, 8 and 19 February, 8 March 1943. The Resistance Fighter Fritz Molden recalls a meeting with his parents in early summer 1943 on the Bavarian Chiemsee in which his father "thought the war could not last more than a year at the outside. Various straws in the wind had led him to believe that the Allies would restore Austrian independence." Fritz Molden, *Exploding Star: A Young Austrian against Hitler* (New York: William Morrow and Company, 1979), p. 131.

a good deal of self-pity, characterized by an intensification of anti-German feeling. Even in Graz, the longtime stronghold of Austrian Nazism, it became common to hear people saying "Berlin does not understand Austrians. They regard us as enemies, and they make no effort to treat us as friends."[44] Elsewhere, the security organs reported an upsurge of anti-Nazi graffiti and, here and there, shouts of "Hail Austria!"[45]

On the basis of the existing evidence it is difficult to determine to what extent the new sense of Austrian identity was based on daydreams, discontent, anti-German sentiment, rejection of Nazi ideology, opportunism, or genuine patriotism. Even so, the conclusion seems inescapable that it was little more than a reaction-formation or a natural tendency to fall back on regional loyalties in times of crisis, as, for example, was the case after the collapse of the Habsburg monarchy. Given the welter of overlapping, often contradictory attitudes—including the continued popularity of Hitler—grassroots commitment to a resurrected Austrian state was obviously much weaker and more tenuous than has generally been acknowledged by contemporary Austrian historians, although in all fairness, it should be emphasized that most of them agree that the development of national feeing was a slow, gradual process that began in 1938 with a handful of dissenters and resistance-fighters, was endorsed in 1943 by surviving elites of the First Republic, and thereafter extended well into the postwar period.[46] Recognizing the fluctuating, contradictory, and ambivalent nature of mass opinion, it now remains to see whether a common sense of Austrian identity was stimulated either by the Moscow Declaration of 1 November

---

[44]NA, M 1209, R 29, "Styria—the Land of Sorrow," *Allehanda*, 16 January 1944.

[45]For examples of pro-Austrian outbursts see WVNÖ, vol. 3, pp. 568-577; WVT, vol. 1, pp. 282, 300; and Slapnicka, *Oberdonau*, p. 292.

[46]The consensus view is argued most forcefully perhaps by Kreissler in *Der Österreicher und seine Nation*.

1943, in which the Allies promised independence after the war while urging Austrians to contribute to their own liberation, or by the attempt of the German generals on 10 July 1944 to overthrow Hitler and end his war.

According to a comprehensive report prepared by the Security Service for Berlin, word of the Moscow Declaration touched off widespread discussion throughout the "Danubian and Alpine Regions":

> The fact that an independent Austrian state is supposed to be set up again has aroused "old memories" among people. Tied to this is the hope in Vienna, for example, that the city will be spared enemy air attacks, since according to the Moscow interpretation, "Austria" is an occupied country. The impact of the publication "We Austrian Balkanese" in the *Oberdonauer Zeitung* of 6 November has been propitious in that it has made clear to readers that only [we in] the Ostmark itself can put an end to the enemy's notion of a restored "Austria."[47]

Despite the real concern of the authorities, there is little evidence in the records that the Moscow Declaration significantly stimulated either widespread Austrian patriotism or indigenous opposition, though it undeniably gave heart to those already engaged in active resistance.[48] What the Allied proclamation did accomplish was to lend brief credence to the prevailing view that Austria might somehow escape the ravages of war, especially an intensification of Anglo-American bombing raids. During the winter of 1943-1944 what appeared to be a suspension of air attacks was accompanied by an upsurge of anti-Nazi propaganda, emanating from both the Allies and native resistance-groups. In the studios of Radio Moscow, for example, the station "Radio

---

[47] Boberach, *Meldungen* (8 November 1943), vol. 15, p. 5996.

[48] Cf. NÖLA/ZR/Ia-10/23/1943 and 1944: District presidential reports, November 1943-August 1944 and Kreissler, *Österreicher,* pp. 299-301 and Luža, *Resistance,* p. 197.

Austria" announced the formation of the Austrian Freedom Front (ÖFF), a new version of the Popular Front, which called for armed insurrection and was later able to distribute a great many fliers throughout Vienna and other industrial areas demanding a "Free Austria." At the opposite political extreme, the Gestapo in Vienna, Graz, and Salzburg began picking up copies of *Alpenland,* a paper identifying itself as the "organ of the government of Austria" and promising a new postwar democratic state to include the "tribe-related provinces of Bavaria, Württemberg, Baden, the Rhineland-Palatinate, and South Tirol." By spring, virtually everywhere thousands of pamphlets addressed "To the Austrian People!" were raining down from Allied aircraft.[49]

The response of the Austrian population to the flood of new propaganda appears to have been one of indifference. Most people showed little inclination to follow the Communist lead and, in fact, usually approved the execution of Communist "traitors" by Nazi courts;[50] there was also widespread hostility to partisan bands beginning to operate on the borderlands of Carinthia and Styria, though one participant recalled after the war that attitudes actually ranged from "passive to denunciatory."[51] Nor was there much positive response to the appeals of monarchists or conservatives, for although expressions of sympathy for Otto von Habsburg were reported here and there, the continued support of the Church for Hitler's war on the Eastern Front helped keep the anti-communist faithful from breaking with the regime. It does seem that some segments of the population placed a degree of stock in Western Allied appeals "To the Austrian people," but the intensification of the bombing war in late spring

---

[49] Kreissler, *Österreicher,* pp. 299-301 and Luža, *Resistance,* p. 197.

[50] For example, see WVNÖ, vol. 2, pp. 81-82 and vol. 3, pp. 576-577.

[51] Kreissler, *Österreicher,* p. 302.

1944 dashed their hopes and aroused deep anger.[52] As the public prosecutor in Linz put it in his report on 5 June 1944:

> Overall, it can be stated that enemy propaganda has either abated or must have less attraction to certain circles of the populace at the moment than earlier. Defeatist outbursts have become much rarer. There are, unfortunately, still German people in the district who must be cited and prosecuted for the stupid shouting of Hail Austria, but they are few. The terrorist air attacks have been a cleansing thunderstorm for "Austrian-infected minds." Despite all the pamphlets, the stupid-minded talk that the Ostmark will receive preferential treatment by the enemies of the German people is believed by no one anymore.[53]

As in other parts of the Reich, the extension of Allied bombing-raids to Austria in 1943-1944 enabled the Nazi dictatorship to divert attention from criticism of the regime to hopes of revenge and retaliation. Despite separatist sentiment, popular attitudes thus continued to parallel those in the Old Reich. By the spring of 1944, the security organs in Tulln, Gänserndorf, Lilienfeld, Wiener Neustadt, Baden, and Linz were reporting that the "burning desire for retribution" was so great that news of retaliatory raids over Britain, no matter how small, was greeted with considerable satisfaction. The popular mood remained "depressed," "apathetic," or "calm and earnest," but, overall, morale was indisputably higher than the year before. Despite fear of invasion from across the Alps and real concern for Russia's frightening power, a good many people anticipated the summer with hope that secret weapons and determined resistance might

---

[52] WVNÖ, vol. 2, p. 569; Slapnicka, *Oberdonau*, p. 292; and NÖLA/ZR/Ia-10/23/1944; Scheibbs, 5 June 1944, Neunkirchen, 17 June 1944, and Oberpullendorf, 15 July 1944.

[53] OÖLA, Pol. Akten, Sch 80, Generalstaatsanwalt, Linz to Thierack, 5 June 1944.

at last bring a favorable end to the war.[54]

Word of the Anglo-American landings in Normandy on D-day, 6 June 1944, thus produced a sense of relief in many quarters that the moment of decision had finally arrived. Indeed, announcement ten days later of the first V-1 attacks on London elevated the mood to a level unparalleled in years. Throughout the towns and villages of both Upper and Lower Danube there was a return of confidence, a feeling that the "leadership has done the right thing."[55] As the district president in St. Pölten noted,

> The use of reprisal weapons has fulfilled a long-desired wish. All people are hoping that with these engagements a decisive stage of the war has been reached and that they can count on a speedy conclusion to it.[56]

On the other hand, not everyone was so sanguine. In Vienna and Wiener Neustadt, where air raids were becoming more frequent, people remained "anxious and nervous." In Mistelbach, Gänserndorf, and Scheibbs there was fear of the awesome material superiority of the enemy forces.[57] In Eisenstadt, the District President wrote:

---

[54] Steinert, *Hitler's War*, pp. 234-237; NÖLA/ZR/Ia-10/23/1943: Tulln, 14 February, Gänserndorf, 7 February, Lilienfeld, 7 March, Wiener Neustadt, 7 March, and Baden, 16 February; and OÖLA, Pol. Akten, Sch. 80, Generalstaatsanwalt, Linz to Thierack, 5 June 1944. On the other hand, the district president in Mistelbach wrote that "the majority of the farming population places little stock in a successful end to the war. . . .Our Luftwaffe's raids on London and other English cities are not regarded as retribution but as the logical consequence of Anglo-American air attacks, hardly decisive to the outcome of the war." NÖLA/ZR/Ia-10/23/1944: Mistelbach, 28 June 1944.

[55] Boberach, *Meldungen*, vol. 15, pp. 6596-6598.

[56] NÖLA/ZR/Ia-10/23/1944; St. Pölten, 8 July 1944.

[57] NA, T 77, R 1037, F 6509660, Wehrkreiskommando, XVII, Vienna to OKW, 21 July 1944; NÖLA/ZR/Ia-10/23/1944; St. Pölten, 8 July, Wiener Neustadt, 6 July 1944, Mistelbach, 28 June, Gänserndorf, 10 July and Scheibbs, 7 July. See also Boberach, *Meldungen*, vol. 15, pp. 6631-6634.

> The populace is behaving quietly and earnestly, but is quite depressed. The great mass of the people is dissatisfied with developments surrounding the invasion in France. Typical are comments such as: "If we didn't succeed in throwing the enemy forces into the sea where they conquered so little land, how will it be possible when they have pushed further inland?" Continued retreat in the East has also contributed to the lukewarm mood. People are caught up in daily cares and sorrows, and have become quite indifferent to good and bad news. The deployment of V-1 reprisal weapons has not had the anticipated response and has contributed little to any improvement.[58]

The nervous, fluctuating mood in the weeks after D-day was accompanied by deteriorating material conditions and growing physical exhaustion. In the countryside, a good many farmers found themselves in the anomalous position of suddenly having enough cash to pay off long-standing mortgages but unable to keep up cultivation owing to shortages of labor, motor fuels, lubricating oils, and agricultural implements, including scythes and sickles.[59] While rationed food supplies remained generally adequate, some wage earners began to show signs of malnutrition. From Lilienfeld, near St. Pölten, the district president reported, for example, that workers in heavy industry were approaching the point of exhaustion, especially since the introduction of the twelve-hour working day.[60] In Wiener Neustadt collective stress was so great "that it takes only the slightest incident for men as well as women to lose their nerve [. . . and] burst into tears."[61] Adding to the atmosphere of worry and fear was news of the loss of Cherbourg and the collapse of Army Group Center in the Ukraine. By mid-July, public spirits had tumbled to a new low. There were few signs, however, that the

---

[58]NÖLA/ZR/Ia-10/23/1944: Eisenstadt, 11 July 1944.

[59]NÖLA/ZR/Ia-10/23/1944: Oberpullendorf, 14 July and Melk, 29 July 1944.

[60]NÖLA,/ZR/Ia-10/23/1944: Lilienfeld, 9 August 1944.

[61]NÖLA/ZR/Ia-10/23/1944: Wiener Neustadt, 9 August 1944.

long-suffering, silent majority of the Austrian people had yet broken with the Nazi regime. Nor was there evidence of a "solidarity of opposition"[62] nor a sense "that the political and military events of 1943 and 1944 . . . had awakened a new national consciousness among a great number of Austrians."[63] Indeed, popular reaction to the brief "liberation" of Vienna in the wake of Count Stauffenberg's unsuccessful attempt to assassinate Hitler on 20 July 1944 would reveal that, despite great unhappiness and dissatisfaction, most Austrians remained loyal to Greater Germany.

The story of 20 July 1944 in Austria is well known and need be retold here only briefly. As in Paris, officers in the headquarters of the 17th Military District in Vienna carried out Stauffenberg's orders with little hesitation or difficulty, taking into custody the chiefs of the Viennese Gestapo and SS as well as major functionaries of the NSDAP in both Vienna and Lower Danube. By 8:00 pm, troops of the Vienna Guard Battalion were in position on the Schubertring and most key potential adversaries were under arrest. Shortly thereafter, teleprinter orders arrived appointing the former Austrian politicians Karl Seitz and Josef Reither political representatives and Colonel Rudolf Count von Marogna-Redwitz military liaison officer. Telephone calls to Berlin requesting clarification then led to gradual realization of the revolt's failure and around 11:00 pm to a release of prisoners. Meanwhile, in Salzburg, officers on duty at the headquarters of the 18th Military District simply ignored Stauffenberg's orders and placed no troops on alert. The next morning the Gestapo began the arrest and detention of both the (largely unwitting) Viennese *Putsch* participants and hundreds of suspected opponents, including former members of parliament, party leaders,

---

[62] As claimed by Ludwig Jedlicka, *Der 20. Juli 1944 in Österreich* (Vienna: Herold Verlag, 1965), p. 12.

[63] Kreissler, *Österreicher,* p. 315.

ministers, mayors, and civil servants of the First Republic.[64]

As elsewhere in Greater Germany, most people in the "Danubian and Alpine Regions" reacted to news of the attempt at assassination with shock, anger, and dismay. Among all classes of society in Lower Danube there was a feeling of initial horror followed by an outpouring of relief and joy at the *Führer's* "miraculous" escape.[65] In Vienna, a young army officer arriving at the *Westbahnhof* was struck by both the sultry weather and the sense of emotional loyalty to Hitler. "There was much complaining in Vienna," he recalled, "but the belief in the omnipotence, genius and foresight of the *Führer* was still at hand."[66] As details of the plot became better known, people expressed bewilderment, outrage, and indignation at the betrayal of so many high army officers at a time of military crisis in both West and East. The public prosecutor in Linz, for example, wrote that "the perpetrators elicited not the slightest sympathy and were everywhere detested. Remarks that might have approved the assassination-attempt are absolutely unknown to me."[67] In Vienna, the prosecutor later noted "the populace expressed its horror at the crimes of 20 July. Until now, citations for approving these events have been issued only rarely."[68]

Generally speaking, the July bomb plot, like the Allied landings in Normandy, had the effect of briefly solidifying public

---

[64]Jedlicka, *20. Juli*, pp. 50-92 and Peter Hoffmann, *The History of the German Resistance 1933-1945* (Cambridge: Massachusetts Institute of Technology Press, 1977), pp. 457-459, 465-470).

[65]NÖLA/ZR/Ia-10/23/1944: District presidential reports for August 1944 from Wiener Neustadt, Oberpullendorf, Neubistritz, Lilienfeld, Krems, Korneuburg, Horn, Gmünd, Eisenstadt, Bruck a.d. Leitha, Wiener Neustadt (Police Director), Waidhofen a.d. Thaya, Gänserndorf, Hollabrunn, Mistelbach, Melk, and Zwettl.

[66]Ralf Roland Ringler, *Illusion einer Jugend. Lieder, Fahnen und das bittere Ende: Hitler Jugend in Österreich: Ein Erlebnisbericht* (St. Pölten, 1977), p. 121.

[67]DÖW, Film 97, Generalstaatsanwalt, Linz to Thierack, 7 August 1944.

[68]DÖW, Film 97, Generalstaatsanwalt, Vienna to Thierack, 1 October 1944.

opinion behind the Nazi regime. On 22 July, some forty thousand Upper Austrians crowded onto the main square in Linz to demonstrate their loyalty to Hitler; in neighboring Salzburg the turnout was estimated at twenty thousand. There were also mass rallies on the Schwarzenbergplatz in Vienna and in Gmünd, Amstetten, Oberpullendorf, Melk, and countless other towns. According to surviving records, attendance was heavy in all cases.[69]

On the other hand, morale remained low. With the introduction of the seventy-two-hour work week, the extension of Gestapo terror, the acceleration of Allied bombing, and the ominous approach of the Red Army, there was little talk of victory or resistance. As the District President in Eisenstadt noted in an insightful report worth quoting at length:

> In speaking about the mood and bearing of the populace, that of convinced National Socialists—who comprise 1-2 percent of the population at most—will be excluded. News of the attempt on the *Führer* and his deliverance was received here with general excitement and relief, particularly as people fear chaos in the event of his death or removal. Only a small group from laboring circles refrained from condemning the hideous crime. It must be stated, however, that people's faith in the superiority of the highest military and diplomatic leadership has vanished or been seriously damaged. Most people no longer dare believe in complete victory. A few still hope in the impact of new, unknown weapons. In general, only negative impulses such as fear of disorder and of Bolshevism are holding people together. Nonetheless, work goes on, even if it is losing momentum from exhaustion and anxiety for the future.[70]

Although the events of 20 July 1944 appear to have had little

---

[69]Bukey, *Hitler's Hometown*, p. 213; Hanisch, *Nationalsozialistische Herrschaft in der Provinz*, p. 234; and NÖLA/ZR/Ia-10/23/1944: District presidential reports for August from Gmünd, Oberpullendorf, Amstetten, and Melk.

[70]NÖLA/ZR/Ia-10/23/1944: *Landrat*, Eisenstadt, 15 August 1944.

impact in awakening a sense of Austrian patriotism among ordinary people in the "Danubian and Alpine Regions," the Reich leadership was so alarmed by reports of deteriorating morale that SS Security Chief Ernst Kaltenbrunner undertook a special inspection trip in early September to Vienna, Lower and Upper Danube, and Salzburg. In Vienna he found the mood extremely dejected and "the bearing of nearly every level of the populace in need of immediate attention." The defeatist attitude in the city, he reported, was "susceptible to all the news from the Southeast, to all kinds of propaganda about atrocities, to certain 'Austrian tendencies,' and to every type of Communist propaganda. Personal impressions in working-class and suburban districts, especially at the beginning of work, during shift changes, and at first aid stations and similar places are exceedingly unfriendly."[71]

To restore morale Kaltenbrunner recommended ending Reich German control of the metropolis and entrusting its administration to the Viennese NSDAP, a group that had been deliberately excluded from power since 1938 and whose discontent was responsible for much of the prevailing anti-German sentiment. He found the mood much better in Lower Danube, though easily "infected" by Vienna, and "a fresh, positive breeze" blowing in Upper Danube. Best of all was the situation in Salzburg.[72]

Stunned by Kaltenbrunner's account, Hitler's deputy, Martin Bormann, sent an aide, Helmut Friedrichs, to see for himself. After conferring with Viennese functionaries and the *Gauleiter* of Lower Danube, Hugo Jury, Friedrichs reported that Kaltenbrunner's fears were exaggerated. According to Jury, the mood was "typically Viennese," mirroring the city's diverse population and 140,000 foreign workers. While admitting a certain danger from Slavic elements, he emphasized that the general reaction to recent bombing raids indicated that the population stood behind the party. To the extent that dissatisfaction existed, he attributed it to

---

[71]Jedlicka, *20. Juli*, pp. 96-97.
[72]Ibid., pp. 95-98.

the outcome of the program of aryanization that had left too many Austrians without spoils. Overall, the *Gauleiter* argued, the Viennese would hold up as other Germans, "especially if the front should draw near to Vienna from the South." In that event, "the Viennese, workers as well as middle-class, will show their full strength . . . against Bolshevik troops."[73]

In reviewing this survey of popular attitudes in the "Danubian and Alpine Regions" between Stalingrad and the Night of the Generals, the question arises as to why Austrian patriotism scarcely developed beyond the embryonic stage during a period of rising distress, xenophobic discontent, and significant underground opposition. Considering the intensity of anti-German sentiment and the comparatively high level of active resistance, why did the Moscow Declaration fail to appeal to a common sense of purpose and national resolution? Why wasn't Austrian national feeling stronger? Leaving aside the obvious fact that people do not normally intellectualize about national identity, especially in times of crisis and stress, at least three answers come to mind:

First, few Austrians thought of themselves as anything other than German. It is true that before 1938 some Viennese and a handful of Habsburg loyalists elsewhere had lived in an environment that the resistance-fighter Fritz Molden evocatively called "a kind of prolongation of the Austro-Hungarian monarchy,"[74] but they were the exception. The truth was that after 1918 the overwhelming majority of Austrians regarded themselves as Germans trapped in a state nobody wanted, viewing union with the Reich as the only way out of their difficulties. Of the three political camps, only the Christian Socials tried to develop a sense of national pride, but it was predicated on the dubious notion of Austro-German superiority to the Reich. In 1938 with the endorsement of Hitler's Anschluss by both the former Social

---

[73]Ibid., p. 100.

[74]Molden, *Exploding Star*, p. 49.

Democratic chancellor, Karl Renner, and the Austrian episcopate, the issue of nationality seemed settled once and for all. Indeed, of those few Austrians who later joined the plot against Hitler on 20 July 1944, nearly all regarded themselves as German patriots seeking a return to the rule of law within the framework of Greater Germany. In this regard, it should also be mentioned that for many Social Democrats, otherwise bitter opponents of Nazism, the idea of being part of the German nation persisted until the end of World War II—and beyond. Several days after proclaiming the Second Republic, for example, Karl Renner defended his support of the Anschluss to the Viennese civil service, regretting only the course it had taken and ruefully adding that "for us nothing remains than to give up the idea of the Anschluss [though] for many that may be difficult."[75]

Second, while many Austrians came to reject both the Anschluss and the Nazi party, they remained emotionally bound to Hitler. As in the Old Reich, the *Führer's* popularity did not erode significantly until the last winter of the war. Further, a substantial number of people continued to derive benefits from National Socialism, including not only the 693,000 members of the NSDAP (and their families) who held important posts in the power structure, administration, and police apparatus of the system, but also countless others who profited from Hitler's program of secularization and technocratic modernization. Among the latter were the new *Mittelstand* of employees, technicians, and younger managers who found productive careers in thriving new industrial enterprises. Also included were many blue-collar workers who both enjoyed new social welfare benefits and dreaded the return of unemployment in a restored Austrian state.

Third, those Austrians seeking independence and espousing a positive national identity were themselves unpopular. On the right, monarchists and Catholic conservatives had been the first

---

[75]Ernst Schmieder, "Juden möchten rasch reich werden," *Profil*, 29 February 1988, p. 29.

to fight Hitler, it is true, but they were also the stalwarts of the Christian corporative dictatorship, the regime that had crushed organized labor in 1934 and thereafter had pursued policies so short-sighted and selfish that at least two-thirds of the population felt alienated to the point of welcoming the Anschluss in 1938. For most people, in other words, 1934 remained a more painful memory than 1938. On the left, the Communists were regarded as a radical fringe group. Despite their heroic activities on behalf of Austrian independence, they were seen, even by other Austrian patriots, as taking orders from Moscow. The Communists also had to endure the animosity of the Church, the one body to retain a modicum of institutional autonomy but which supported Hitler's war against Bolshevism to the bitter end. Despite its spiritual resistance to Nazism, the Church was more a supporter of the Greater German Reich than a proponent of Austrian independence.

Ultimately, it would be left to the postwar generation to build an Austrian nation. That they succeeded was owing partly to a consensus that there was no other choice, partly to a horrific memory of the Nazi past, and partly to the extraordinary efforts of the fathers of the Second Republic, who by accepting the "victim myth" of the Moscow Declaration cleverly detached their country from the fate of defeated Germany and through tenacious diplomacy eventually brought the Allies to sign the State Treaty in 1955. From today's perspective, it was this achievement that awakened popular national feeling and should be regarded as the real foundation of contemporary Austrian identity and pride.

Conscience and Obedience

Gordon C. Zahn

It may be appropriate to introduce this essay, which is presented in the company of such impressive scholarship, with the remark: "And now for something completely different." These words are written from a socio-theological perspective (a term calculated to infuriate members of the sociological and theological fraternities, both of whom insist that the twain must never meet) and are intended to serve the dual function of focusing on personal responsibility and, at the same time, broadening the implications of the issue beyond any specific place (such as Austria) or event (such as the Anschluss).

Dealing with resistance to any political regime, but especially one which possesses total power and is willing to exercise it as brutally as Hitler's Third Reich did, is a matter to be approached with caution. It is one thing to praise the few heroes who did resist; quite another to judge those who knew what was happening but remained silent or, most difficult of all, those who knew but closed their eyes, unwilling to admit even to themselves the need to resist. To praise and honor the first is easy enough. The second deserves criticism, but that criticism should be tempered by circumspection and compassion. It is the third category which is of greatest concern because, if one is honest with himself, this is where most people are likely to be counted.

Those who knowingly and intentionally support the evil will have earned the censure, even punishment, that may be their lot, but at least they deserve credit for knowing a choice had to be made and for having made it. That, after all, is what the question of resistance is about: the obligation to make responsible moral choices and, once that is done, to recognize an order of priority among the choices made.

Much of what is written here may be out of fashion with the mechanistic, even deterministic, views of human behavior which still rule the social sciences. Advances in behavioral modification and subliminal manipulation have demonstrated their empirical validity and utility—and give even more frightening glimpses of *potential* uses. For a sociologist to insist upon a role for moral considerations and individual responsibility is to risk being charged with academic heresy.

Be that as it may, the approach of this essay rejects theories which would reduce individuals' actions to programmed responses to situational or physical stimuli. It is undeniable that a greater part of our actions are, or can be, subject to external controls and conditioning. It is even possible by means of chemical and psychological processes, or both used together, to reduce individuals, conceivably entire populations, to a state of total dependency and unquestioning acquiescence. But I would insist that such successes, if we dare to call them that, are achieved at too great a cost: the *dehumanization* of the subjects involved.

To be human is to have the power to choose, the freedom to choose, and, no less important, *the obligation* to choose. Take these away and the nature and dignity of the human person is destroyed. Whether one speaks of the traditional philosophical categories of "intellect" and "will," or accepts more contemporary sophisticated conceptualizations of the person as a complex of individualized capacities and needs, makes little difference. Lives and human experiences are not determined by some external and irreversible constellation of natural forces. Instead they are the product of the sequence of choices—great or small, right or wrong—that one makes and has made. Even when personal or social catastrophe strikes, how one chooses to relate to it will have as much to do with its impact and duration as the event itself and its immediate consequences. Often enough, the catastrophe itself will be the product of choices one made or failed to make.

Considered in this context of choices to be made, the concept of resistance assumes a meaning somewhat broader than its general usage. It includes active confrontational modes, of course, such as public demonstrations or covert underground, even revolutionary, actions; but resistance takes less dramatic forms as well. Simply saying no, thereby setting oneself apart from the silent conformity which, we have learned too well, is all that is needed for evil to prevail, can be truly heroic resistance in a totalitarian order—or even, at times, in a society of consensus. After all, merely saying no is both the beginning and the essence of resistance.

The resistance of "individual witness" has always been a subject of special interest for this writer. About twenty-five years ago an article entitled "The Private Conscience and Legitimate Authority"[1] caused something of a stir in Catholic circles—and, to a lesser degree, non-Catholic circles as well. The controversy focused on a call for a reassessment of the traditional theological formulations of the Christian's obligation to render obedience to legitimate authority, especially in time of war. Noting what was the obvious fact that modern nations are no longer governed by "the Christian prince" so dear to Scholastic tradition (and suggesting, as an aside, that they never were) the article argued that it was no longer permissible for the individual citizen who was also a believer to grant "the presumption of justice" to the secular ruler.

In developing that thesis the article drew upon the tragic past of the Nazi experience and the horrors of World War II. Without rejecting the theological truism that all authority comes from God, the article urged that, having learned how easily authority as exercised by human beings can be abused and how disastrous the effects of that abuse can be, we need a moral theology which

---

[1] *Commonweal,* March 30, 1962, p. 3.

would require that every exercise of this authority be exposed to the test of the enlightened moral conscience of the individual subject to it. To many this sounded like an open invitation to anarchy; to many it still does.

That thesis and, even more, the reaction to it have direct relevance to the subject of this book. Not only is the old standard of unquestioning obedience—"theirs not to reason why; theirs but to do and die"—still with us, but it seems to be enjoying a resurgence of popularity. That it is essentially incompatible with the sense of personal dignity and responsibility which should govern the thoughts and behavior of the mature and spiritually enlightened individual is often ignored if not, in fact, denied. It was given its classic expression by Adolf Eichmann at his trial: "My guilt lies in my obedience," he declared. On that foundation he pleaded his case. "Obedience is praised as a virtue, and I would therefore request that my having obeyed be the sole fact that is taken into account." The sole fact! That defense failed to save Eichmann, but the spirit it expressed found explicit echo in Colonel Oliver North's assurance, not long ago, that, if so ordered by his commander, he was ready to stand on his head in the corner and salute. The favorable reception given North's televised testimony revealed the disposition on the part of the viewing public to accept that affirmation of total obedience to his superiors as justification for a host of dishonest and illegal activities on his part.

The article mentioned above had a rather modest objective. It sought to establish the legitimacy of conscientious objection for Catholics and members of other mainstream churches, a rather radical position at the time. That need is now no longer as urgent as it was. Official ecclesiastical pronouncements have since affirmed the right—indeed the *duty*—to obey one's conscience even, or especially, in time of war.

If now we know—or should know—that the believer need not always obey, a much more troubling question presents itself: When are we called to resistance? Under what circumstances could there be a moral obligation to *disobey?* The issue finds striking illustration in the contrasting choices made by two Austrians called to service in Hitler's armed forces in what few would deny was an unjust war when measured by any of the traditional theological standards.

We are all familiar with the controversy surrounding the election of Kurt Waldheim. The choice he made was obedience. Not necessarily the all-justifying obedience demonstrated by Eichmann, certainly. Indeed, if we take Waldheim at his word, it was simply a surrender to the inevitable. He went to war and did his duty because, as he still insists, there was no alternative.

Once in uniform, it is clear he conducted himself according to the principle affirmed by Oliver North, namely, that to obey superiors is always the part of the subordinate. Not surprisingly, for Waldheim this also proved to be the path of advancement. To the extent that he has allowed his record to become known, his military service was that of a model junior officer, marked at every stage by a combination of efficiency and opportunism. The same combination, it is reasonable to assume, can be applied to any ambitious junior officer thirsting after promotion regardless of what uniform he wears. In Waldheim's case the formula worked quite well. Doing what he was ordered to do—and doing it efficiently—led to assignments of greater significance and responsibility.

The orders he initialed, the information he passed on to those above him in the military hierarchy, may be causing him difficulty and personal inconvenience and anguish today, but there is nothing to suggest that they troubled him at the time. That some of those orders were part of a pattern that, after the war, led to the execution, on charges of war crimes, of the most senior officer in his command was not, he now protests, within his range of responsibility to decide and, therefore, can carry no implication of shared guilt on his part.

Waldheim's postwar career was more of the same as he made his way onward and upward. He knew the right paths to follow, the right contacts to make, and the right strings to pull. In the process he prudently closed the book as far as his military background was concerned and, when embarrassing questions were raised, he was not above fudging the record by convenient lapses of memory or outright denials. Today, as we know, after serving with honor and some distinction as General Secretary of the United Nations, he became president of Austria.

The other man was a simple peasant from an isolated and obscure village, a married man and father of three young daughters. Like Waldheim he had previously performed his required military training in the Austrian army. In 1938 when Austria was invaded and became, with a considerable display of enthusiasm, part of the Third Reich, he openly voiced his strong opposition and, at the time of the Anschluss plebiscite, was the only one in his village to cast a negative vote. Later, after being called back for a brief period of refresher reserve training, he made it clear to his family and friends that he would never go again. Just putting on the Nazi uniform, he explained, made him feel dirty. Ordered to active service in March 1943, he reported six days late and then only to declare his refusal to take part in what he considered an unjust war being waged by an immoral regime. Six months later, on August 9, 1943, he was beheaded in Berlin.[2]

Kurt Waldheim describes himself as a "devout Catholic," a term which certainly applies to Franz Jägerstätter. Indeed, so devout was the peasant's Catholicism that he had been selected by the pastor to serve as sacristan for the village church. Even today, those who knew him as friend and neighbor still speak of him as *too extreme* in the intensity of his devotion. Many go so far as to explain his refusal, and its inevitable outcome, as the

---

[2] For a detailed account of Franz Jägerstätter see Gordon C. Zahn, *In Solitary Witness: The Life and Death of Franz Jaegerstaetter* (New York: Holt, Reinhardt & Winston, 1964).

thoroughly tragic result of a mind unsettled by religious fanaticism!

For Jägerstätter it was something vastly different; it was the ultimate choice between obeying God or obeying man. For him, too, there was no alternative. Young Waldheim, if we take him at his word, again made his more pragmatic assessment of the situation and chose the course of prudent conformity to Nazi authority. If today he makes much of the fact that he came from an anti-Nazi family background, that had not deterred him from taking the military oath swearing unconditional obedience to Adolf Hitler by name. Nor does having done so cause him any personal regret today. Certainly there is no credible evidence that he has ever bothered to consider the duty he so willingly accepted (and, as time went on, the higher duties he sought) in the *moral* context that brought the peasant to the executioner's block.

To be fair, the fault is not entirely Waldheim's. The formation of devout Catholics did not put much emphasis on the values for which Jägerstätter was willing to sacrifice his life. Quite the contrary was true. In his search for spiritual advice and support from priests—and even from his bishop!— the peasant met with stern reminders of his responsibility for his family's welfare and his obligation as a citizen to render obedience to legitimate authority. He would have received the same responses from American priests and bishops too, for such notions were entirely in keeping with the theology of the day.

This is where the circumspection and compassion recommended earlier come in. One need not agree with those who hold that Waldheim was to be treated as a pariah, unworthy of being received by Popes or being permitted to enter the United States. Indeed, in the absence of more evidence than has been produced until now, which would establish a direct link to criminal activity, his "Watch List" designation is unjust and a departure from the presumption-of-innocence-principle of jurisprudence in which we rightfully take much pride. As far as John Paul II is concerned, it was his prerogative to decide whom he should receive. One could be far more scandalized by other political leaders he has welcomed—some of them, one regrets to say, American.

As citizens of a nation which has waged (and supported others in waging) wars of unrestrained cruelty, Americans are not privileged to cast any stones, much less the first. Remember those fifty-square-mile blankets of napalm in Vietnam? The routine search and destroy missions with the orders to "shoot anything that moves"? Or, for that matter, the atrocities that were committed by our surrogates in Central America, Angola, and who knows where else? Nor does the part our forces played in helping Klaus Barbie, and other truly *major* war criminals, escape leave much justification for putting up barriers against someone whose crime consisted of initialing and passing on orders and reports.

We are not the only residents in this particular glass house. One finds it difficult to reconcile the vehemence with which so many individuals and organizations prominent in the support of Israel pursue this peripheral malefactor while remaining silent, if not openly supportive, of deliberate reprisal-bombing raids against refugee camps and lethal response to stone-throwing rebels protesting alien occupation forces—and, more recently, Israeli military assaults on peaceful villages in order to send other villages a message. Are Palestinian guerrillas really that much different from Yugoslav partisans of World War II?

One of the more distressing aspects of the Waldheim controversy is the drumfire of criticism unleashed against the Austrian people and nation as a result of his election. Long acknowledged as the first victim of Nazi aggression, they suddenly find themselves cast in the unpopular role of unreconstructed ally of Nazi Germany, and collaborator. This, too, is unjust. It would be naive to deny the long and tragic history of anti-Semitism on the Austrian scene or to assume it has vanished completely. In the same vein, it is probably true that there are individuals, even groups, with nostalgic longing for the dubious glories of the Nazi past. One can be quite certain, however, that these are not the factors accounting for the election of Waldheim. A far better explanation lies in the predictable reaction to attacks of outsiders on the candidate for doing what he (and most of the voters) regarded as his duty. In a very real sense those attacks involve by implication all veterans of the war, their families, and, indeed, everyone who gave them support.

Circumspection and compassion, yes; exoneration, no. Lt. Waldheim's guilt *did* lie in his obedience, and that guilt *was* shared by all who wore the uniform or participated in the unjust war waged by an immoral regime. Until President Waldheim and all the others are willing to accept the fact of such guilt, they will not have come to terms with the failures of their personal and national history. This is not, one hastens to add, a reversion to the infamous theory of the responsibility of peoples that motivated the Morganthau Plan and similarly vindictive policies proposed at the war's end. It asks nothing more than a belated assessment of the validity of those individual choices favoring obedience over resistance. It goes without saying that Americans might do well to make a similar assessment of their own past.

Austria can boast of a laudable record of resistance and individual heroism, and it would be tragic were that fact to be overlooked or ignored as a result of the Waldheim controversy. One of the more gratifying results of the accidental discovery of the Jägerstätter story is the renewed attention being given those (in Germany as well as in Austria) who paid with their lives for refusing to perform what the government defined as their duty. (A 1986 review of conscientious objection in the Third Reich mentions no fewer than twenty Austrians of diverse religious and political persuasions!)[3] It is unfortunately true that most such

---

[3] Albrecht and Heidi Hartmann, *Kriegsdienstverweigerung im Dritten Reich* (Frankfurt: Haag und Herchen Verlag, 1986) includes a bibliography of other recent titles on the subject. Another account of Austrian martyrs is Ernst

stories are lost to history, but every effort should be made to devote serious scholarship to the task of saving as much of that inspiring record as possible so that the most correct balance may yet be struck.

More than the historical record is at stake, of course. It is crucial that the story be told so that it may serve as an example for future generations and a preparation for the even greater challenges that may lie ahead. Among these challenges would be the one posed by the Catholic bishops of the United States in their 1983 pastoral letter defined as "the challenge of peace." Although tensions among the great powers have abated, in this nuclear age the choices all of us make, and may yet be called upon to make, could represent, in a very real sense, the *ultimate* choice as to whether or not the world and its inhabitants are to endure. To Thomas Merton, the well-known Trappist contemplative with a firm grasp on what was going on in the world outside the monastery's walls, nuclear war would be nothing short of global suicide, freely chosen, a moral evil second only to the Crucifixion.

If this challenge is to be met, all the institutions of society must make a serious reassessment of their responsibilities in the formation of consciences. The patterns of thought and value of the past have lost their relevance. To cling to them is a luxury we can no longer afford. Political leaders may no longer indulge in chauvinistic platitudes and rituals that indiscriminately confer the status of hero upon all who fought in the nation's wars, quite irrespective of the justice or injustice of the cause for which they fought and died. We can no longer tolerate the indecently exploitive practice of making memorials of past carnage the occasion—or, even worse, the justification!—for promoting the nationalism which, already between the two World Wars, was identified as the characteristic heresy of our day.

T. Mader and Jakob Knab, *Das Lächeln des Esels* (Bloektach: Verlag an der Säge, 1987).

Organized religion, too, must atone for the uncritical support it has all too willingly given princes and principalities in the past. If the most obvious scandals—the blessing of cannons and battle flags, the *Gott mit uns* belt buckles, the lavish ecclesiastical celebrations of military victories, and the like—are no longer as common as they were, much remains to be done. The German bishops' call for loyal service to folk and fatherland in World War II—as a Christian duty!—is a blasphemy that must never again be repeated by any clergymen, in any nation. So, too, with the pious cliché on which Eichmann based his plea. It must be replaced by the formal recognition that though obedience *can be* a virtue, *unquestioning or blind obedience*, even in an objectively good cause, is *always* a vice. The individual's obligation to make a responsible moral choice is never to be betrayed or denied.

Artists and the custodians of popular culture must not abuse or demean their talents or position to contribute to the glorification of war or the romanticization of the grim sacrifices war demands. Educators, from the earliest grades upward, have an especially crucial role to play. Their teaching of history and promotion of civic virtue must give due emphasis to the futility of war and its tragic human costs and not concentrate, as they are prone to do, on the glamour and excitement of the battle. And a point of special concern: high schools, colleges, and universities which have compromised their academic integrity by including military training in their curricula should replace these programs with concentrations on peace studies and institutes.

The avoidance of the threat of ultimate war is everyone's responsibility. To cite Thomas Merton again, we must "wake up to the fact that our own minds are just as filled with dangerous power today as the nuclear bombs themselves . . . This problem," he went on, "is going to be solved in our thoughts, in our spirit or not at all. It is because the minds of men have become what they have become that the world is poised on the brink of total disaster."[4]

And it will remain as long as we perpetuate attitudes and values which over the centuries have produced multitudes of Waldheims and only occasionally a Jägerstätter. The military credo of unquestioning obedience, so openly professed by North (and so faithfully practiced by Waldheim), is no longer acceptable in the nuclear age. It must be made clear to all that it is never the part of *any* subordinate knowingly to cooperate or to comply with orders of even doubtful morality. Merton's answer is, instead, a call to protest and resistance: "It is no longer reasonable or right to leave all decisions to a largely anonymous power elite that is driving us all, in our passivity, towards ruin."

Every citizen, then, must be ready to say no, to protest, in short, to resist. And, yes, be ready to disobey. If the day ever comes when that ultimate choice is to be made, the last remaining hope for the survival of the human race, the last safeguard against that "moral evil second only to the Crucifixion," may be the conscience of some disobedient soldier who refuses to press the button or turn the key.

---

[4]*Thomas Merton on Peace.*

Tirol and the Austrian Resistance in the Last Years of the War

Radomír Luža

Since the collapse of the Habsburg monarchy, the Anschluss attitude remained popular in the Tirol. The idea that Vienna was force-keeping-us-from-the-way-we-want-to-be had taken hold. The National Socialist successes in the Reich helped the Austrian National Socialist Party to come out of nowhere in the municipal elections on March 7, 1933. The Nazi Party (*Nationalsozialistische deutsche Arbeiterpartei* [NSDAP] or Nazis) became the strongest party in Innsbruck, winning 41.2 percent of the votes.[1] In the wake of the Anschluss, 14.6 percent (48,149 persons) of the Tirolean population joined the party, by far the highest percentage in any Austrian province.[2] The liquidation of the concept of Austrian statehood and the coming of the war in 1939 threatened seriously to undermine the conditions of the Austro-German partnership.[3] The German Reich had become a reposi-

---

[1] Johann Holzner, *Untersuchungen zur Überwindung des Nationalsozialismus in Österreich* (Ph.D. Dissertation, University of Innsbruck, 1971), pp. 31-32. The NSDAP gained 202 votes in 1929, 1196 votes (41 percent) in 1931, and 15,001 votes (41.2 percent) in 1933.

[2] The second highest percentage of NSDAP membership was in Salzburg with 10.9 percent. Österreichische Bundeskanzlei in Military Government Austria, *Report of the U.S. High Commissioner,* November 1947, p. 187.

[3] The number of active NSDAP members in the Reichsgau Tirol-Vorarlberg went down. February 1941 = 58,300; February 1942 = 54,590. The Reichsgaue Niederdonau, Salzburg and Vienna also had declining curves. Bundesarchiv Koblenz (BA), *Sammlung Schumacher,* 3031/376.

tory of evil-doing for those who questioned whether Tirol's place was in Hitler's camp.[4] The idea of the Anschluss began to evaporate and the *Land* found itself once again a part of the Austrian homeland.

The tenacity with which some Austrians clung to their moral and political convictions, as well as to their traditions, provided the basis for the resistance. By nature an elite movement, the resistance aimed at the more morally and politically self-conscious segments of Tirolean society, those who became convinced, because of national, moral, or ideological motivations, that the National Socialist regime had to be brought down. In the Tirol, as elsewhere in Austria and Europe, resistance to German National Socialism was the exception and accommodation was the rule. The nature of the Austrian resistance differed from that of the underground in other Nazi-occupied European countries. The Austrian movement for liberation lacked the organizational framework and central leadership of the Polish or French underground. Austrian society formed itself within the institutional hinterland left over by the republic or set up by the newly arrived Germans. There was no need for the underground to form a complex clandestine establishment because there was no social vacuum for it to fill. The resisters were often opposed by their fellow citizens who spoke the same language and belonged to the same ethnic community. The National Socialist occupation did not bring such radical ethnic, political, and social changes as, for instance, was the case in Poland or Yugoslavia. Moreover, the existence of a strong native National Socialist Party and a military conscription limited the depth of popular solidarity and made

---

[4]The number of peasants who joined the NSDAP in the Tirol was relatively small. According to the 1947 NS figures on registration, those who worked in agriculture and forestry in the Tirol formed the third largest group, while they formed the second largest group in Carinthia, Styria (the British zone), and Lower Austria, Burgenland and the Soviet occupied Upper Austria (the Soviet zone). [U.S. Department of State] Military Government Austria. *Report of the United States Commissioner,* March 1947, p. 211.

the task of the authorities much easier. In Poland and in the Czech lands, resistance was based on a wide-ranging feeling of anti-German and anti-Nazi national consensus and transcended the boundaries between the resisters and those who remained outside of its networks. With a much restricted popular constituency, the Austrian underground formed a more loosely structured and narrower political movement which existed, in the main, apart from the majority of the population. The Moscow Declaration of November 1, 1943, called the Austrian people to contribute to their own liberation and had a strong resonance among the scattered underground groups. Yet the scale of political resistance was still modest. Without the existence of a political center in exile, there were few contacts with the Allies and little assistance from abroad until late 1944. Only toward the end of the war, as part of Allied strategy, did the Austrian resisters manage to establish direct contacts with the Allies, receive their first supplies, and make use of their intelligence activities. Owing to its proximity to the approaching American armies, Tirol became the center of the movement for liberation.

In 1944, there existed a cluster of dispersed and independent clandestine circles in the Tirol. Whatever their individual ideological inclinations, they all proclaimed their ultimate goal to be Austria's independence. In almost every larger community the self-contained local groups brought together activists who were generally reluctant to act beyond their local boundaries and thus reinforced the isolation.[5] The informal character of the circles, with their limited membership, with the absence of any systematic activity, and with the lack of a unified chain of command made it easier for the underground to avoid detection and ensure its survival. The belief that the fall of the regime was imminent led them to be fully prepared for it. The dedicated people who worked in the Tirolean underground became the leaders of an

---

[5]Karl Gruber, *Ein politisches Leben, Österreichs Weg zwischen den Diktaturen* (Vienna: Molden, 1976), p. 33; Holzner, *Untersuchungen*. pp. 52-88.

uprising that would rock the Tirol. They were eager to break out of their isolation. They put aside their political dissensions and personal differences and forged more effective lines of communication with the Allied armed forces. The Allies, in turn, could not be expected to commit supplies to some disparate and fragmented groups with no organizational and political base.

All of this changed when the Fritz Molden mission set the clandestine activities into a completely new context. Molden, whose father was a prominent liberal journalist and whose mother was a well-known writer, was closely associated with the Viennese resistance. He escaped to Switzerland from his *Wehrmacht* unit stationed in North Italy in the summer of 1944. After he gained the full confidence of the Swiss and United States authorities, the young Austrian helped to set up clandestine contacts with the allied powers, to develop an effective intelligence network in the country, and to promote the constitution of a resistance center in Vienna. He realized that the process of centralizing the underground should parallel American-run operations. For his twelve clandestine journeys from Switzerland via Northern Italy to Austria in 1944-1945, he was provided with the uniform and false papers of a non-commissioned *Wehrmacht* officer. In the course of his trips, he created a group in Innsbruck and organized the contacts between the underground in Vienna and the United States Office of Strategic Services (OSS) in Bern. He built a number of escape routes, courier lines, contacts and reception-parties for the OSS scout-liaison missions, which arrived in the Innsbruck area in February of 1945. A new political center in Vienna, called the Provisional Austrian National Committee (POEN), with its regional headquarters in Salzburg and Innsbruck, was to coordinate the clandestine work and to represent the country in its contacts with the United States, Great

Britain, France, and the Soviet Union.⁶ The destruction of the POEN by the Gestapo on March 7, 1945, greatly enhanced the importance of the Tirolean network which had been set up in the fall of 1944 under the guise of the POEN's predecessor, the clandestine organization known as the O 5.⁷

As the fronts closed in on Austria, the Tirol, next to Vienna, became the epicenter of the Austrian liberation-movement. Those working outside of the Tirolean resistance became the leaders of the efforts to form a unified command. A native Tirolean, Dr. Karl Gruber, developed a good relationship with some of the leaders of the resistance who worked toward the unification of the dispersed underground. he emerged as the crucial figure in the Tirol. Gruber remained in touch with the clandestine groups in Germany, Vienna and the Tirol from his Berlin residence and also cooperated with the American authorities in Switzerland. He arrived in Innsbruck on March 14, 1945, to resume his talks with the local groups. Gruber sensed that the overwhelming majority desired a central command. Gruber's objective was an armed uprising launched at the proper moment, in conjunction with the advancing United States troops. He realized that a direct blow rocking the Nazi rule would go a long way toward demonstrating the credibility of the Austrian claim to independence.⁸ In the

---

⁶For the O 5, set up in Vienna in 1941-1942 as the clearing house of the resistance by Dr. Hans Becker, see Radomír Luža, *The Resistance in Austria, 1938-1945* (Minneapolis: University of Minnesota Press, 1984), pp. 160-164. For Fritz Molden's achievements, see his *Fepolinski und Waschlapski auf dem berstenden Stern. Bericht einer unruhigen Jugend* (Vienna: Molden, 1976). The book was published in the American translation under the title *Exploding Star. A Young Austrian Against Hitler* (New York: William Morrow & Co., 1979). Helmut Heuberger stated that still in the fall of 1944 "die einzelnen Gruppen damals gewitzigt durch grauenhafte Erfahrungen, jede grössere Vereinigung scheuten, sich nach außen mit äußerster Vorsicht abschossen." Privatarchiv Otto Molden (OM), *Bericht Helmut Heuberger,* Mappe II.

⁷See Luža, *The Resistance,* pp. 212-215, and 249..

⁸Gruber, *Leben,* p. 33.

following weeks, Gruber involved the military and civilian activists in his preparations for the final blow. Gruber's leadership gradually absorbed the main groups in the Tirol.[9] The process of unifying the underground was completed by fusing his network with the O 5 organization.[10] His military chiefs, largely active members of the *Wehrmacht* units stationed in and around Innsbruck, resolved to occupy the military barracks in Innsbruck as soon as the United States Seventh Army launched its attack from Bavaria.[11] On May 2, the resistance carried out its major coup. Between 9:25 a.m. and 11:30 a.m., its troops captured all four barracks with two thousand men.[12] The next day the insurgents took possession of the seat of the provincial government.[13] In the early evening, in a festive mood, thousands

---

[9]The military staff was headed by Major Werner Heine, a highly decorated (*Ritterkreuzträger*) commander of the Mountain Troops Reserve Battalion 136. Heine was assisted by his adjutant, Lieutenant Ludwig Steiner, *Obergefreiter* Oskar Görz, *Major* Josef Schneeberger, *Oberleutnant* Anton Huber, Dr. Emil Eckl and their associates. The civil staff included Dr. Friedrich Würthle, Jörg Sackenheim, Helmut Heuberger, Karl Hirnschrott, Laugges, Görz and their associates. Dokumentationsarchiv des österreichischen Widerstandes (DÖW). Vienna No. 7093; *Bericht H. Heuberger,* OM.

[10]*Bericht H. Heuberger,* OM.

[11]Ibid., DÖW 7093; R. Mackowitz, *Kampf um Tirol. Entscheidende Taten zur Befreiung Innsbrucks im Frühjahr 1945* (Innsbruck: Wagnersche Universitätsbuchdruckerei, 1945), p. 38.

[12]*Major* Heine, *Oberleutnant* Huber, *Hauptmann* Guido Todeschini, Eckl, *Rittmeister* Winkler, and, above all, Sackenheim bore the brunt of the fighting. Otto Molden, *Der Ruf des Gewissens. Der österreichische Freiheitskampf 1938-1945* (Vienna: Herold, 1958), pp. 319-323; Gruber, *Leben,* pp. 37-43; Bericht Jörg Sackenheim, OM; *Bericht Ludwig Steiner,* OM, *Bericht H. Heuberger,* OM.

[13]Luža, *The Resistance,* pp. 251-252; Gruber, *Leben,* pp. 43-44; Mackowitz, *Kampf,* pp. 51-54; Molden, *Der Ruf,* pp. 322-327, *Bericht Görz,* OM, *Bericht Dr. Praxmarer,* OM. The representatives of the three main overlapping movements around *Ing.* Anton Hradetzky, Prof. Dr. Hans Gamper and Prof. Eduard Reut-Nicolussi formed a unified political organ in the first days of May 1945. This temporary underground coalition was named the Executive Committee of the Austrian Resistance in Tirol. Mackowitz, *Kampf,* pp. 48-49; Molden, *Der Ruf,* pp.

Tirol and the Austrian Resistance 215

of Austrians welcomed with flowers the advancing columns of the United States 103rd Infantry Division.[14] The reports of the victory of Innsbruck's armed resistance reverberated through the entire land. Spontaneous open rebellion spread across the Tirol.[15] Successively, the chiefs of the local resistance took over the administration of the self-liberated communities.[16] Like the people in Paris and soon in Prague, the Tiroleans themselves silenced the German guns.[17]

Contrary to its European counterparts, the Austrian resistance did not precipitate the national split, whose reverberations would continue for years to play a role in the political life of the country. The passage of time and circumstances had little effect on the

---

323-325; *Namensliste,* OM; Luža, *The Resistance,* pp. 250-251.

[14][United States Army] *Report of Operations. The Seventh United States Army in France and Germany 1944-1945,* III, 845-846. Major Schneeberger and Lieutenant Steiner assisted the American troops in the Seefeld-Zirl area. For the enthusiastic reception of the United States troops in Innsbruck, see Ralph Mueller and Jerry Truk, *Report After Action. The Story of the 103rd Infantry Division* (Innsbruck, 1945), p. 143: "It was like the liberation of Paris. The ovation was tremendous. Men, women and children screamed greetings and threw flowers before the advancing troops. Bottles of cognac and wine were offered the doughs, puzzled as to whether or not they should accept . . . Pretty girls climbed aboard tanks and jeeps to kiss [the soldiers]. Austrian flags fluttered in the town. There were no white flags. The people seemed to consider it a liberation . . . The *Wehrmacht* troops still in uniform stood at the curbside. They still carried weapons, but wore 'Free Austria' armbands, and shouted 'Heil Americans!' The scene was totally different from anything the doughs had ever seen in any German town."

[15]DÖW, ed., *Widerstand und Verfolgung in Tirol 1934-1945. Eine Dokumentation* (Vienna: Dokumentationsarchiv des österreichischen Widerstandes, 1984), II, pp. 584-608; Holzner, *Untersuchungen,* pp. 120-131; DÖW, 7802-7804, 8385.

[16]The nuclei of some local cells had been built since 1943, but most of them emerged into the open in late April 1945. The underground co-operated with the conscripted foreign workers and prisoners of war.

[17]The resistance forces released all the prisoners from the Innsbruck Gestapo Camp in Reichenau.

distinctive features of Tirolean regionalism. In adversity or prosperity, peace or war, under democratic or authoritarian regime, the mixture of cultural and social semi-isolation, and the fearsome loyalties of community proved extraordinarily potent. The resistance brought home some vital aspects of the Tirolean outlook. For generations the Tiroleans had resented outsiders in any other than an unquestionably supportive role. The resistance managed to transcend both regionalism and personal exclusiveness. The old-fashioned personalized character of the Tirolean movement for liberation did its best to conceal party differences. Unlike in the other *Länder,* the political parties of the Tirol failed for some time to recapture their legitimacy. In fact, the prestige of the resistance has glittered further and longer in the Tirol than anywhere else in the country.

Austria's geographical position determined to a large extent the type of clandestine activities that would be conducted there. Landlocked and isolated within the Reich, with long lines of communication to the outside, the country could not easily reach out. Switzerland and Yugoslavia were the natural outlets. Fortunately, the Alpine forests provided a favorable terrain for insurgency. Outside Vienna, the capital of the resistance, the Tirol, with its extremely strong local patriotism, became the center of clandestine activities. With 5.26 percent of the population and 10.4 percent of the resistance, the Tirol became a bastion of the liberation-movement.[18] Resisters with strong native ties were generally active in the *Land* where they were born. In contrast to Vienna, the Tirolean underground was largely composed of the single non-party, patriotic All-Austrian formation headed by Dr. Gruber.[19] The Communists were dispropor-

---

[18] Luža, *The Resistance,* p. 335.

[19] Radomír Luža, *The Resistance in Tyrol 1938 to 1945. Incidence of Variables, April 10-11.* 22 (1985). The percentages may be considered as orders of magnitude. They reflected the trends and patterns. The original computer-assisted investigation focused on 3,058 resisters in Austria. See Luža, *The Resistance,* pp.

tionately weak, and the other political parties wielded less influence than elsewhere in the country. Firmly entrenched in a cluster of rural communities in the mountain valleys of the Alps, the underground remained largely fragmented, self-contained, and insulated. The segregated local cells failed to expand beyond local boundaries and were unable to transform the local engagements of their groups into a central organization with a regional character. The loosely structured resistance featured some specific characteristics of its own. It became very difficult to unify this diversity of clandestine cells. The isolated groupings were more easily activated by outsiders who could maximize their Tirolean connections and upgrade local activities.[20] The almost unanimous endorsement of the central command in April 1945 for the person of Dr. Gruber lessened the impact of geographical barriers and the influence of local interests. Tirol's distinct historical consciousness became the instrument through which Austria's identity reasserted itself.

Initially, the movement was largely a heterogeneous, assortment of diverse and inexperienced elements, with a constantly changing cast. Arrests continued to erode its ranks. The resisters were more concerned with ideas about Austrian independence and the system's violence and inhumanity than with specific political objectives. Looking more to the past than to the future, the activists lacked a bold vision of change. The resistance was for them primarily a national struggle and a moral commitment. In a computer-assisted analysis of the membership in the resistance, one detects nine affiliates in the resistance on the basis of political and ideological commitment. Several major tendencies could be identified in the Tirol, all of them identical with formations in

---

291-322. In April 1985, 310 resisters from the Tirol were selected from this sample. The author is indebted to a Tulane student in sociology, Miss Cynthia Gentry, who helped to handle the computer-work.

[20]For example, Karl Gruber, Fritz and Otto Molden, Waldemar von Knoeringen, and Robert Uhrig.

the other *Länder*.[21] The Communists (KPÖ) and the Revolutionary Socialists (RS) were numerically weak, and outside of urban areas in the Lower Inn Valley, of little importance. The Legitimists (L) established a reputation for political courage by linking their activities with the efforts of Otto Habsburg in the West. The defeat of France in 1940 and the destruction of legitimist cadres by the Gestapo put the movement adrift and caused it to fold by winter of 1942. The Traditionalists (T) made up the fourth political current with about 16 percent of the sample. The largely Catholic conservatives and former Christian Socials, who formed the Austrian People's Party (ÖVP) in 1945, enjoyed strong support among the peasants. They turned away from their former anti-Socialist stance. The fifth affiliate, a medley of patriotic activists of apolitical backgrounds, became predominant after the arrests of 1943 hit the Innsbruck underground. Central to these various independently minded groups (here called the All-Austrian tendency, AA, with about 64 percent of the sample) were the widely dispersed patriotic groups from the umbrella organization O 5, the Gruber network and the cluster of various local cells. Ultimately, its organization united with the military and energetically pushed forward the preparations for a popular uprising in and around Innsbruck. A handful of determined military men (4.6 percent of the sample) set up the sixth tendency (M). A few of them were of German origin, some of them had served in the old Habsburg army, but the majority were disaffected young *Wehrmacht* officers and non-commissioned officers. They detested Hitler's mismanagement of the war and of their Austrian homeland. After 1943 individual officers and non-commissioned officers formed nuclei around which clandestine military cells organized. Curiously, the *Wehrmacht* constituted the power base that enabled them to plot against the regime. They tried to clear out pro-Nazi elements from selected military

---

[21]Luža, *The Resistance in Tyrol. Variables.* For Austria, see Luža, *The Resistance, passim.*

units, to replace them with Austrian soldiers and to ensure thereby the reliability of the units stationed in or near Innsbruck. When the United States troops advanced in 1945, toward the Tirol, the military established contacts with the civilian networks whom they had supplied with arms. In Innsbruck they joined forces with the civilians in their preparations. The military's position of power and the men's trust in one another made them the most effective force for resistance in 1945.

In April 1985 this writer conducted an analysis of the data concerning membership in the underground.[22] The proportion of women in the Tirolean sample was much lower, 7.4 percent of the sample, than in the Austrian resistance sample with 11.6 percent. Their contribution to the resistance was much below the female proportion of the population, 51.9 percent. The great majority of the militants, 81.3 percent, was composed of youthful cohorts born in 1900-1909. Persons born between 1910 and 1929 formed 9.1 percent of the sample. The largest Tirolean affiliate of the resistance, the AA, commanded the support of more than 95 percent of the 1900-1909 cohort; 76.4 percent of the resisters of this generation belonged to this tendency. Almost one-half of the T affiliate consisted of the 1920-1929 cohort. One-half of the sample resided in the rural areas. The area of Innsbruck was the capital of the Tirolean resistance. Yet 93.3 percent of the AA members and 34.8 percent of the T formation, and 72.2 of all the resisters, were born in the countryside.[23]

The militants engaged in various types of clandestine work. Eight various categories of activities are defined on the basis of the available data.[24] Both in Austria and in the Tirol, the organizational activity, consisting mainly of the formation and adminis-

---

[22]Ibid.

[23]The percentages may not be precise because of a number of missing observations (187) and can be considered as orders of magnitude, i.e., as a general, rather than a specific, indication.

[24]One person could have been engaged in several types of parallel activities.

tration of the clandestine groups, appeared to have been the most essential part of the underground work, 90.4 and 77.4 percent (Tirol). In contrast to the Austrian resistance (20.7 percent), the underground press and political propaganda in the Tirol did not play any significant role (8.7 percent of the sample). Passive and active sabotage involved 21.6 percent of the sample in the Tirol and 10.6 percent in Austria. Some 27 percent of the sample in the Tirol and 13.8 percent in the country took part in direct actions. About 10 percent of the sample in the Tirol, and 7.2 percent in Austria, established communication with Allied officials and agents. The AA formation was responsible for 64.5 percent of the contacts abroad, for 91.6 percent of direct actions, 84.9 percent of the guerilla actions, 80.4 percent of acts of sabotage, and 54 percent of the organizational-administrative work. Its political propaganda was insignificant. The sample shows as an exception the high incidence of propaganda written by Jehovah's Witnesses. The percentage for the Jehovah's Witnesses in written propaganda was disproportionately high. They accounted for 44.4 percent of all activities in propaganda.[25]

The resistance evolved in three stages during the course of the Second World War. In its *first* phase, after March 11, 1938, the leading members of the Tirolean *Heimwehr,* former Christian Socials, and the followers of Kurt Schuschnigg were taken into protective custody by the Gestapo.[26] The silent opposition hoped for signs of protest, but the majority of the population apparently endorsed the National Socialist rule.[27] In 1938-1939, politically diverse groups spread throughout the *Land* and established an embryonic community of resistance. The Legitimists reached their peak during this stage but declined rapidly in 1941-1942, while the Communists and Socialists recorded their highest level of

---

[25]Luža, *The Resistance in Tyrol. Variables.*

[26]See DÖW, ed., *Widerstand in Tirol,* II, pp. 391ff.; DÖW 1575, 4236.

[27]For the persecution of the Jews, see Gad Hugo Sella, *Die Juden Tirols. Ihr Leben und Schicksal* (Tel Aviv, 1979).

clandestine work in 1941-1942, before they were decimated by the Gestapo. The Traditionalists continued to grow. In the *second* stage from 1943 to the last week of winter 1944, the scattered underground started to advance. During the final stage the resistance reached its peak. During the first stage, the Tirolean resistance grew more slowly than in the rest of the country: 1938 = 12.3 percent in the Tirol and 20.8 percent in Austria; 1939 = 8.5 and 18.1 percent; 1940 = 4.8 and 15.3 percent; 1941 = 6.1 and 9.2 percent; 1942 = 8.9 and 8.3 percent. By contrast, during the second and the final phases the growth of the Tirol's resistance was faster than in the rest of the country: 1943 = 21.1 and 11.5 percent; 1944 – 27.6 and 10.9 percent; 1945 = 9.2 and 5.7 percent of the sample.[28]

The resistance's attitude hardened after the German reverses in the Soviet Union and Italy in 1943. With the establishment of reliable lines of communication with American authorities in the wake of the invasion of France in 1944, cooperation among the main underground formations resulted in unity of action between the military and civilian segments. This sign of unity was welcomed by the United States authorities and changed the character of clandestine actions which had become more effective and more practical. The military and All-Austrian formations shot up to become the most effective elements of the resistance. At the final stage, the unified underground directed successfully, in close cooperation with the United States military and intelligence organs, the uprising in Innsbruck and helped to wrest the *Land* from Nazi hands. In the closing weeks of the war it was estimated that the active core of the Tirolean resistance amounted to well over one thousand activists. The liberation-movement claimed to have saved 89 bridges from destruction, to have kept over five thousand German soldiers from the battlefield and to have saved

---

[28]Luža, *The Resistance in Tyrol. Variables.*

thirty-four localities and numerous public installations from damage. The final death toll of the Tirol's uprising was twenty one.[29]

---

[29] See the low estimate given by the Bund der Tiroler Freiheitskämpfer in 1948, in Holzner, *Untersuchungen,* pp. 134-135. Wolfgang Pfaundler offered his estimate of the number of the Tirolean fighters before the liberation, no more than 1,500 persons. *Zum Problem des Freiheitskampfes 1938-1945 an Hand von Beispielen, insbesondere des Widerstandes eines Tiroler Tales* (Ph.D. Dissertation, University of Innsbruck, 1950), p. 86. Fritz Molden gave the most up-to-date figures, *Die Feuer in der Nacht. Opfer und Sinn des österreichischen Widerstandes 1938-1945* (Vienna: Amalthea, 1988), pp. 194-195.

The Perception of the Anschluss after 1945

Anton Pelinka

The topic of this paper is not the Anschluss as a political event, but as a political issue between 1945 and 1955. How was the Anschluss of 1938 treated after 1945—not by historians, but by political actors? The analytical idea is that the political treatment of the Anschluss permits an insight into political motives and political interests—the Anschluss as an indicator of the quality of the political system after 1945.

On April 27, 1945, representatives of the three antifascist political parties—the conservative Austrian People's Party (ÖVP). the social democratic SPÖ, and the communist KPÖ—declared Austria's annexation, executed by a military occupation by German troops in March 1938, to be null and void. Austria declared herself the first victim of Hitler's aggressive foreign policy.

In a proclamation, which prefaced the declaration of independence itself, the Austrian political parties elaborated on the main direction of the interpretation of the historical events: The Anschluss as a consequence of military blackmailing, of military occupation, of military force.

Typical of that direction of the Austrian position was that the proclamation quoted the Moscow Declaration of November 1, 1943—with the exception of the last sentence of that declaration. The representatives of the independent republic of Austria, the representatives of the antifascist political parties, did not want to use the following paragraph in the proclamation: "Austria is to be reminded that she is responsible for participation in the war on the side of Hitler Germany, a responsibility she cannot escape, and that on the occasion of the final accounting the consideration of how much she added to her liberation will be unavoidable."[1] That omission is significant for the construction of a truth the second republic always relied on whenever it seemed to be opportune, especially in international affairs. The other truth— the participation and responsibility of a significant number of Austrians in the military occupation of Austria by Germany— was to be hidden, repressed, forgotten too easily.

The second part of the Moscow Declaration was mentioned at the end of the declaration of independence, but with a significant terminology; it was called a "postscript" (*Nachsatz*) of the Moscow Declaration, a characteristic not to be found in the Allies' document itself. The Austrian government at its very beginning was anxious to emphasize Austria's role as a victim.

This official position, which was aimed at the Allied Powers especially and which was designed to influence public opinion in foreign countries, accompanied the negotiations for the reestablishment of full Austrian sovereignty, the negotiations which led to the State Treaty of May 15, 1955. Official Austria between 1945 and 1955 was consequently in pursuit of extinguishing the historical interpretation of the Anschluss as it was formulated in the final paragraph of the Moscow Declaration. Austria should be depicted as a victim, she should not be shown as an accomplice of the Nazi criminals. On the eve of the signing of the Austrian State Treaty, at the foreign minister's conference in Vienna on May 14, 1955, the Austrian government finally succeeded in eliminating the offending paragraph from the preamble

---

[1] For the declaration of independence see "Staatsgesetzblatt für die Republik Österreich," 1. Mai 1945, 1. St. Published in *Rot-Weiss-Rot-Buch. Gerechtigkeit für Österreich! Darstellungen, Dokumente und Nachweise zur Vorgeschichte und Geschichte der Okkupation Österreichs* (nach amtlichen Quellen). Erster Teil. Verlag der österreichischen Staatsdruckerei, p. 200f. The Moscow Declaration is quoted after Gerald Stourzh, *Kleine Geschichte des österreichischen Staatsvertrages*. (Graz: Styria, 1975), p. 152.

of the treaty. It had been the very precise wording which gave Austria "a certain responsibility," the very same interpretation of the Anschluss as was included in the formulation of the Moscow Declaration.[2]

For ten years official Austria fought for the fixing of Austria's role as a victim; it required the full ten years before Austria was able to free herself from responsibility for the crimes of Nazism.

But this assertion was contradicted many times, especially for domestic reasons. Beginning in 1948 those Austrians who, in 1938 during the Anschluss, had been on the other side, who had jubilantly welcomed the occupation of Austria by German troops, started to be again of some interest as voters. The shades of the 1949 general elections could be seen in advance. More than 500,000 "Ehemalige" (former Nazis) got back their voting rights.[3] And now, suddenly, the other side of the truth became part of the official, collective memory: Austria was a country which had not defended itself militarily; many Austrians—not only the true believers in Nazism, but also the Catholic bishops and the social democratic State Chancellor Karl Renner as well—had welcomed the Anschluss; Austria had a Nazi Party which in 1938 was already an extremely successful party whose membership was about the same as the membership of the Social Democrats.

In the rather official *Rot-Weiss-Rot* book, the Austrian government did not mention the behavior of the bishops and did not mention Renner's pro-Anschluss declaration of 1938 either. Despite a reference to a certain opportunism, which some Austrians demonstrated in 1938, the official consequence in that government document was:

---

[2] Stourzh, *Kleine Geschichte*, p. 121.
[3] Max E. Riedelsperger, *The Lingering Shadow of Nazism: The Austrian Independent Party Movement since 1945* (New York: Columbia University Press, 1978).

> But the Austrian people didn't go over to Nazism, even at that period. Everybody who knows the Austrians at least a little understands and accepts that Prussianism, militarism and Nazism are basically as alien to the Austrian as to any other people in Europe. Prussia's military cult, the idea of totalitarianism and the perfect control of the individual by the government, have been and still are in permanent contradiction to the Austrian's nature.[4]

The Anschluss was an occupation. The nature of the Austrian was irreconcilable with Nazism because that very nature was a contradiction to Prussia and militarism. The specific Austrian roots of Nazism simply could be forgotten. Nazism was against the Austrians' nature. But as soon as the "Ehemaligen" re-entered the political process, history became less simple, became more complex again.

The most prominent representatives of the two main political, ideological pillars which dominated the first decades of the Second Republic reflected in different ways after 1945 the events of the spring of 1938 in Austria. Perhaps the most important description is from Adolf Schärf. Schärf had been arrested on the morning of March 12 and he had spent altogether fifteen days in prison. At first, he thought he had made a political mistake:

> I thought my imprisonment had been a misunderstanding because I expected that the Nazis would take their revenge on the representatives of the Patriotic Front— an erroneous estimation. Soon I had to realize that the new regime con-

---

[4]"Und dennoch ging das österreichische Volk auch in diesen Tagen nicht zum Nationalsozialismus über. Jeder, der die Österreicher auch nur ein wenig kennt, weiss und versteht, dass ihnen Preussentum, Militarismus und Nationalsozialismus im Grund nicht weniger fremd und verhasst sind als irgendeinem anderen Volke Europas. Der militärische Kult des Preussentums, der Gedanke der Totalität und der völligen Erfassung des Einzelnen durch den Staat, waren und blieben der Natur des Österreichers entgegengesetzt." *Rot-Weiss-Rot-Buch,* p. 71f.

sidered as well Social Democrats as its enemies.⁵

After five years of Nazi terror in Germany, Schärf had observed, he was surprised by the attitude the Nazis had concerning Social Democrats. Karl Kraus had watched, analyzed, published—but Adolf Schärf was still not prepared to recognize the reality.

Renner's propaganda statement from April 1938, promoting the Anschluss slogan the Nazis had put forward, was not mentioned by Schärf. But his evaluation of the Anschluss was expressed in the description of his meeting with Wilhelm Leuschner in early summer 1943, when Leuschner had tried to win Schärf over for a (pan-German) resistance against Hitler. Schärf's response became famous—for good reasons: "The Anschluss is dead: the love for the German Empire has been extinguished in Austria."⁶

Schärf's attitude toward the Anschluss was of specific domestic importance because of its meaning for the interpretation of the concordat. Schärf was interested in denying any legal validity of the treaty between the Dollfuss regime and the Holy See based on the argument that the Anschluss was not an occupation by definition in international law, but was an annexation in the legal sense. Owing to such an annexation, the public law, as it had existed before the annexation, ceased to exist along with the concordat as part of public law.⁷

---

⁵"Ich glaubte. dass meine Verhaftung auf einem Missverständnis beruhe, dies in der irrigen Meinung, dass der Nationalsozialismus seine Rache an den Angehörigen der Vaterländischen Front nehmen werde. Aber bald entdeckte ich, dass für das neue Regime die Sozialdemokraten ebenso als Feinde galten wie die 'Vaterländischen'." Adolf Schärf, *Erinnerungen aus meinem Leben*. (Vienna: Verlag der Wiener Volksbuchhandlung, 1963), p. 158

⁶"Der Anschluss ist tot, die Liebe zum Deutschen Reich ist den österreichern ausgetrieben worden." *Ibid.*, p. 167.

⁷Karl R. Stadler, *Adolf Schärf. Mensch - Politiker - Stattsmann* (Vienna: Europaverlag, 1982), p. 358f.

Schärf's interpretation of the Anschluss did not become the official position of the Austrian government of the grand coalition between ÖVP and SPÖ. Schärf's attitude demonstrated, nevertheless, how much he was prepared to change the interpretation of the Anschluss as an occupation for the much less favorable interpretation of the Anschluss as an annexation (at least less favorable for the international Austrian interests) on the basis of certain domestic political interests. The change within the leadership of the Austrian socialists in 1957, when Schärf lost his chairmanship for the more or less ceremonial position of federal president, was extremely helpful for the breakthrough in the direction of a compromise concerning the issue of a concordat. Schärf had tried to use the interpretation of the 1938 events as a partisan instrument against the Church.

Ernst Koref mentions in his memoirs Renner's Anschluss declaration only in a marginal note. Koref explains a certain feeling—which can be seen as one of the roots of Renner's declaration—a feeling representative of republican pan-German attitude many Social Democrats had: "The feeling of the loss of our country's independence was paralyzed by pan-German national emotions and hopes . . . The acceptance of a German identity tempted many Austrians to welcome the Anschluss out of the strong effect, after all, of Hitler's successes at his beginning."[8]

After this remark, Koref mentioned Renner briefly, without quoting the latter's declaration itself.[9]

Johann Böhm, too, described specific Social-Democratic as-

---

[8]"Das Gefühl des Verlusts der Eigenstaatlichkeit unserer Heimat wurde durch deutschnationale Gefühle und Hoffnungen paralysiert. . . Das Bewusstsein der Zugehörigkeit zum deutschen Volke verleitete manchen—nicht zuletzt auch unter der starken Wirkung der Hitlerschen Anfangserfolge—zum Anschlussbekenntnis." Ernst Koref, *Die Gezeiten meines Lebens* (Vienna: Jugend und Volk, 1980), p. 224.

[9]Ibid., p. 225.

pects of 1938: "'The masses of our people were alienated by the years of the green (Austro)-fascism. They were passive and tired out from the economic crisis.'[10] Böhm emphasized the manipulative character of the plebiscite of April 1938: 'The almost 100 percent Yes was the consequence of the strongest pressure.'"[11]

The tendency of Social Democrats not to stress or even mention Renner's behavior in 1938 is paralleled by the tendency of Christian Socials to overlook the bishops' behavior. Lois Weinberger wrote about the evening of March 11, 1938: "Some were speaking of resistance, but soon it became clear that resistance would be madness and self-sacrifice without reason. German troops were already invading Austria."[12]

The German soldiers, of course, did not come before dawn of March 12. Weinberger did not mention at all the domestic, the Austrian roots of the Nazis' seizure of power. Weinberger's reflection upon the events of March 1938 was colored by a kind of pan-German-flavored Austrian patriotism. He wrote that it already had been obvious before 1938 that "Of the so-called pan-German nationalist students, about 80% had non-German, mostly Slavic, names, while on the Catholic, non-nationalist side, there were a lot of true German names, indicating that here were good

---

[10]"Die grosse Masse unseres Volkes aber war verbittert durch die vorhergegangenen Jahre des grünen Faschismus. Sie war durch die grosse wirtschaftliche Not stumpf und müde geworden . . ." Johann Böhm, *Erinnerungen aus meinem Leben* (Vienna: Europaverlag, 1964), p. 173.

[11]"Das fast hundertprozentig 'Ja' ist unter stärkstem Druck zustande gekommen." Ibid., p. 174.

[12]"Einige sprachen von Widerstand, doch war klar, dass er Wahnsinn und sinnlose Selbstaufgabe gewesen wäre. Schon marschierten ja die deutschen Soldaten in unser Land ein." Lois Weinberger, *Tatsachen, Begegnungen und Gespräche. Ein Buch um Österreich.* (Vienna: Österreichischer Verlag, 1948), p. 68f.

Austrians, children of workers, farmers, artisans."[13]
Like Schärf, Weinberger also had illegal contacts with the German resistance. He had several meetings with Jakob Kaiser before July 20, 1944, and, like Schärf, Weinberger gave a description of his opposition to any resistance with a pan-German intention:

> Jakob Kaiser, Goerdeler and Leuschner are pressing to cooperate with the new, human empire of the Germans, to keep us connected with them. But, in spite of our respect for their goals and in spite of our acceptance of many arguments they used, we did not hesitate one second to emphasize that our goal has to be a free, independent Austria, completely independent from Germany.[14]

Like Weinberger, Josef Klaus also did not mention at all Innitzer's behavior in spring 1938. Klaus admitted his friendship with and his promotion by Wilhelm Wolf.[15] But Klaus omitted in his memoirs the fact that Wolf, representing the strongly pan-German wing among Austrtian Catholics, had been appointed

---

[13]"Von den sogennanten deutschvölkischen Studenten ungefähr 80% undeutsche, meist slawische Namen hatten, während auf der katholischen, als 'nicht nationalen' Seite lauter brave. . . kerndeutsche Namen schon äusserlich nachwiesen, dass hier gute österreichische Arbeiter-, Bauern- und Bandwerkerkinder wohnten." Ibid., p. 75.

[14]"Jakob Kaiser, Goerdeler und Leuschner dringen, ihrem Deutschland, dem neuen, dem menschlichen Reiche der Deutschen treu zu bleiben oder doch in engster Verbindung mit ihm zu marschieren. Wir aber liessen, bei aller Achtung und Anerkennung ihres Wollens und bei aller Einsicht in die Richtigkeit sehr vieler ihrer Argumente, nicht eine Sekunde lang einen Zweifel darüber, dass wir das nicht könnten und dass wir Österreich wollten, nichts anderes als ein freies, unabhängiges, auch ein von Deutschland unabhängiges, wirklich selbständiges Österreich." Ibid., p. 124.

[15]Josef Klaus, *Macht und Ohnmacht in Österreich*. (Vienna: Fritz Molden Verlag, 1971), especially pp. 23, 28f., 71. Concerning Wilhelm Wolf's position see Gerhard Seewann, *Österreichische Jugendbewegung 1901-1938*, 2 vols (Frankfurt am Main: dipa-Verlag Kurt Werner, 1971), pp. II, 771, 847.

foreign minister of Seyss-Inquart's Anschluss cabinet on the evening of March 11, 1938. Considering his friendly relationship with main actors of the Anschluss, Klaus' picture of the real events was surprisingly brief: "But March 1938 came. The new, brown-shirted rulers expelled me from my working place in the chamber of labor as they had many others on the first day of their power."[16]

A much more intense description of the March events was given by Alfred Maleta. Maleta mentioned his surprise at seeing former friends going over to the Nazis and in witnessing Innitzer's behavior: "In spite of all attempts to understand politically, I remembered how difficult it was for us, fighters for the Church and for Austria, really to accept it. In our anger we agreed that we never again would be willing to commit ourselves to that extent for the Church."[17]

In its first, general program, the "Aktionsprogramm" of 1947, the SPÖ did not say much about the Anschluss and what it did say was not at all directly stated. Indirectly, the Anschluss was mentioned by the following sentences:

> After the liberation from fascist rule, Austria has to regain her full political sovereignty. She must be free from the occupation.
>
> The socialists are opposed to the idea of any collective responsibility of whole nations for the crimes of their political elites. They are opposed for that reason to the indiscriminate ostracism of the whole German people, whose

---

[16]"Doch der März 1938 nahte. Die neuen braunbehemdeten Herren der Arbeiterkammer entfernten mich mit...vielen anderen gleich am ersten Tag ihrer Machtübernahme." Ibid., p. 30.

[17]"Bei allem Bemühen um politisches Verständnis erinnerte ich mich daran, wie schwer es uns, den Kämpfern für die Kirche und für Österreich, fiel, dies innerlich zu verkraften. In diesem Zorn schworen wir einander damals, dass wir uns nie mehr sonderlich für die Kirche exponieren würden." Alfred Maleta, *Bewältigte Vergangenheit. Österreich 1932-1945.* (Graz: Styria, 1981) p. 196f.

democratic parts had been victims of the Nazi terror even before the Austrian people.

Expiation for the fascist and Nazi crimes, integration of the former "Mitläufer" (fellow travelers) of both fascist parties into the community of all citizens.[18]

The term "both fascist parties' indicated a combined classification of the Nazi Party and of the "Vaterländische Front" as two parts of the same concept of fascism.

The ÖVP published its first general party platform in 1945. There, too, the Anschluss was mentioned only indirectly: "The Austrian People's Party is taking over the heritage of those groups which had always stressed Austrian tradition and always defended Austria's independence."[19]

In its platform "Alles für Österreich," published in 1952, the ÖVP said: "The denial of voting rights of individual citizens or specific groups of citizens has to be opposed forever as an undemocratic instrument."[20] This formula from the ÖVP program of 1952 had the very same intentions as the SPÖ program of 1947. The SPÖ stipulated in 1947 the "integration of the former fellow-travelers" of Nazism, a phrase with about the same mean-

---

[18]"Nach der Befreiung von der faschistischen Herrschaft muss Österreich endlich seine volle politische Souveränität wiedererlangen. Es muss frei werden von der Besetzung."

"Die Sozialisten . . . lehnen ebenso ab den Gedanken an eine kollektive Verantwortlichkeit ganzer Völker für die Verbrechen herrschender Schichten. Sie wenden sich darum auch gegen die unterschiedslose Ächtung des ganzen deutschen Volkes, dessen demokratische Teile noch vor dem österreichischen Volk ein Opfer der nationalsozialistischen Gewaltherrschaft wurden.

"Sühne der faschistischen und nationalsozialistischen Verbrechen. Eingliederung der früheren Mitläufer der beiden faschistischen Parteien in die Gemeinschaft der Staatsbürger." Klaus Berchtold, ed., *Österreichische Parteiprogramme 1868-1966*. (Vienna: Verlag für Geschichte und Politik, 1967), p, 268-277.

[19]Ibid., p. 376.

[20]"Eine aberkennung des Wahlrechtes einzelner Staatsbürger oder bestimmter Gruppen von Staatsbürgern wird für alle Zukunft als undemokratische Zwangsmassnahme abgelehnt." Ibid., p. 380.

ing as the ÖVP's opposition to the denial of the franchise to any "group of citizens." Both declarations aimed at the former Nazis; both parties were interested to get the "Ehemaligen" votes.

Between 1945 and 1949 the Anschluss was reinterpreted for domestic reasons. During the electoral campaign in the fall of 1945, both major parties tried to outbid each other in rejecting the Anschluss. As a campaign slogan, the ÖVP, for instance, formulated: "The Anschluss, the hobby of Austrian Social Democracy and its sore point. From Dr. Bauer in 1919 to Dr. Renner in 1938." And the SPÖ suggested the exchange of Austrian Nazis for Austrian prisoners of war in Siberia.

In 1949 everything seemed to have changed. Neither party tried to outbid the other any longer in anti-Nazism; they did not criticize each other any more for having a traditional inclination toward the Anschluss. Instead of anti-fascist rhetoric, the major parties competed for the votes of the former Nazis. The new interpretation was symbolically emphasized by the suddenly different attitude the SPÖ had toward its "Siberia-slogan" from the 1945 camapaign. The ÖVP in 1949 strongly criticized the socialists precisely for that slogan of 1945, and the SPÖ tried to keep its distance from its own slogan of four years past.[21]

What had mattered in 1945 that did not matter any more in 1949? In 1945 both major antifascist parties separated themselves from the Anschluss, and they tried to compete in this separation. In 1949 both major parties demonstrated a completely different attitude; the ÖVP and the SPÖ now were interested to win over as many voters as possible from among the half-million reenfranchised former Nazis.[22] These voters functioned, as newcomers to the political market, as an irresistible spoil. And the parties

---

[21] Norbert Hözl, *Propagandaschlachten. Die österreichischen Wahlkämpfe 1945-1971.* (Vienna: Verlag für Geschichte und Politik, 1974), p. 122.

[22] Ibid., p. 145.

responded to such a temptation by changing their view of the Anschluss.[23]

Significant for the parties' changing attitudes was, on the one side, the substantial assistance socialist politicians gave for the foundation of the "League of Independents" (VdU); and, on the other side, the concessions the ÖVP made to attract former Nazis, especially to win their outspoken support for propaganda reasons.

Viktor Reimann reports about a former leading Nazi who criticized the ÖVP for cooperating with the "reds" before "March 13, 1938." "March 13, 1938" was used as a synonym for the Anschluss. The position of this specific former Nazi leader was significant for the complete change of the historical evaluation. The consequence of the newly established attitudes of the parties was perhaps perfectly expressed by the already mentioned former Nazi leader, who in his talks with the ÖVP, openly refused to sit at the same table with a member of the Austrian resistance.[24]

The interpretation of the Anschluss formulated in 1945 to impress the Allied Powers had to yield to a completely different interpretation, a completely different view. The very same politicians who, in 1945, had declared Austria to be the first victim of aggressive German imperialism, did not hesitate to declare now almost the opposite views. They almost apologized for their "antifascist" attitudes of 1945.

By reevaluating the Anschluss, the politicians just took into account the fact that the events of March 1938 had been the result of a deep cleavage within Austria, within Austrian society. The reentrance of the former opponents, of the former Nazis, into the political process had to have the consequence of a reinterpretation of history. Even if Austria as a sovereign state had

---

[23] See the different articles in Anton Pelinka, Erika Weinzierl, eds., *Das österreichische Tabu* (Vienna: Verlag der österreichischen Staatsdruckerei, 1982).

[24] Viktor Reimann, *Die Dritte Kraft in Österreich*. (Vienna: Fritz Molden Verlag, 1980), p. 161.

been the victim of an occupation—called Anschluss—by Nazi Germany, hundreds of thousands of Austrians had seen the occupation by Germany as a liberation, as a liberation from a not truly desired independence and from a not fully accepted regime. The occupation had been, in the eyes of a large portion of the Austrian population, the realization of a long-standing dream. And those jubilant Austrians had not allowed their joy to be dimmed by the real occurrence of events—the open persecution of political opponents, the open deprivation of rights of all Jewish citizens, the open transformation of an authoritarian into a totalitarian dictatorship.

Those Austrians who had welcomed Hitler jubilantly and those who, referring to Renner's or Innitzer's behavior, had been satisfied positively by the accomplishments of the Anschluss were never reeducated or resocialized by the founding fathers (and mothers) of the Second Republic. On the contrary, those Austrians, hundreds of thousands of believers in Nazism as well as hundreds of thousands of Nazi fellow-travelers, irresistibly attracted the founders of the Second Republic. The masses did not adapt to the politicians; the politicians did adapt to the masses.

And the politicians demonstrated the contradiction of the two sides of historical truth. The protocols of cabinet meetings after 1945 are full of proof that the coalition government clearly distinguished between the international and the domestic side of truth. Internationally, Austria had to be the victim, as well as accessible to the individual victims, especially to the Jews; domestically, Austria was not interested at all in helping those victims, in reintegrating Jewish victims. The contradiction of two different sides of truth was characteristic of the Second Republic from its very beginning.[25]

---

[25] Robert Knight, ed., "Ich bin dafür, die Sache in die Länge zu ziehen." *Die Wortprotokolle der österreichischen Bundesregierung von 1945 bis 1952 über die Entschädigung der Juden.* (Vienna: Athenäum, 1988).

The Anschluss as a (negative) thesis was dead. The foundation of the Second Republic was the necessary, positive antithesis. But thesis and antithesis became amalgamated into an untidy synthesis, a synthesis for domestic reasons already established in 1949, and beginning with 1955 all the more useful because of international interests. It is an amalgam between the role of victim and the role of accomplice, between military occupation and voluntary annexation, between liberation in 1945 from the Germans and liberation in 1955 from the liberators. This amalgam blocked, and still blocks, the open view, the frank analysis of the historical reality of March 1938.

In the fifth decade of the Second Republic, at last, we are becoming more and more painfully aware of the contradictions hidden in the untidy synthesis. This delay is a result of a fundamental political carelessness. The handshake between an Austrian defense minister and a hardly pardoned mass murderer? But so many politicians, from both major parties, had been active for decades in their efforts to help the "last Austrian prisoner of war." The election of Kurt Waldheim as Federal President? But Waldheim had been "not even" a Nazi. And the appointment of five former Nazis to Kreisky's cabinet? That is, that has been Austrian reality.

The double reality, the double truth of the Anschluss is still dominating the Second Republic. And this republic is all the more paralyzed, the less it openly faces both sides of reality, of truth. The reason for that is indicated by the almost arbitrary interpretation of the Anschluss, an interpretation which follows the daily needs of market-oriented political parties and politicians.

The Political Effects of the Anschluss on the Austrian Second Republic

Melanie A. Sully

Fifty years after, the Anschluss still brings back memories of pain and guilt. Was Austria a victim of a military invasion and Nazi occupation or a willing partner in a welcomed union? Around 200,000 turned up on the Heldenplatz in near-hysteria to cheer the *Führer,* yet thousands of Austrians were soon to be on their way to concentration camps and many others perished in the following seven years of Nazi tyranny. There were those who undoubtedly were exhilarated by the prospect of Anschluss with the German Reich whilst for others it meant sorrow, tragedy, exile or getting on as best they could with the new regime. A confusing and contradictory picture emerges of a country which has been in search of a mission and a national identity since the end of the Great War.

The peace settlements had endorsed the principle of self-determination, yet banned a union of Germany and Austria. This was an attractive ideal for those in all political camps of the First Republic, including the Social Democrats. The ties were emotional, cultural and practical. The Habsburg Empire's collapse had left a void in the minds and hearts of German-Austrians who had never aspired to establish such a small and economically inviable state. Unlike Switzerland, there was no tradition here of a small state nor a republic. The Austrian First Republic, democracy and the economy subsequently foundered in the turbulent days of the inter-war period.

After the horrors of a bloody civil war in 1934, Austria had a corporate state dominated by the Fatherland Front, a patriotic but unpopular unitarian movement.[1] Both the illegal Socialists and the Nazis carried on their own private wars against first Dollfuss and then Schuschnigg. Even today interpretations of this past are divisive. The two main parties currently in coalition clash bitterly in their views of the period 1934-1938 and on whether these were years of resistance or oppression. How strong was the idea of "Austria" and independence, or was this subservient to a *grossdeutsch* element in a regime vying at best with Nazism, but hopelessly outmaneuvered by it on all counts? The two *Lager* agree to differ. A portrait of Dollfuss still hangs in the parliamentary *Klub* of the Austrian People's Party (Österreichische Volkspartei, ÖVP), where he is regarded as an Austrian patriot and a victim of National Socialism. The Socialist Party of Austria (Sozialistische Partei Österreichs, SPÖ) will never forget him as the chancellor who gunned down the workers in the civil war of 1934 and paved the way for Hitlerism.

From 1934 to 1938 Austrians lived under a dictatorship which failed to tackle the problem of chronic unemployment. Morale and the economy had been weakened by Hitler's Thousand Mark Tax on Germans visiting Austria. The country felt lonely and isolated, squeezed between German Nazism and Italian Fascism, and little sympathy or assistance seemed likely to come from the Great Powers. The Third Reich with a modern, dynamic pseudo-egalitarian image had admirers even in Britain. The Anschluss seemed a panacea for all ills, both economic and emotional.

The experience of occupation bred disillusion as the country was exploited, wiped off the map, and Vienna reduced to the status of an insignificant provincial town. In the darkest depths of Dachau where former opponents shared a common vision of a better tomorrow, the formative phase for the new Austria was

---

[1] See Bruce F. Pauley, *Der Weg in den Nationalsozialismus* (Vienna: Österreichischer Bundesverlag, 1988).

born. Consensus and tolerance seemed to be the only solution and formed a central element in the emergent Austrian identity.

In 1945 the Second Republic was established on the basis of a spirit of tolerance and its very being and institutions were officially deemed to be a direct response to the years of National Socialist occupation. The need to pull together was fostered by Four-Power occupation which lasted until 1955. It was easy to shelve an examination of Austria's role in the Holocaust, and reconstruction was a more urgent task. The nascent national identity was too fragile to withstand such introspection. The immediate past was in a psychotic way repressed, and nostalgia for faded imperial grandeur filled its place. The latter was sufficiently distant, less distasteful and, above all, did not seriously threaten the basic consensus of political life in the infant Second Republic. It was possible with the Moscow Declaration of November 1943 to be shielded under the idea of Austria as a victim and conveniently to neglect responsibilities and complicity. Austria was simply a victim of Nazi aggression, a notion encouraged by the Allies, who found it increasingly attractive when confronted with the need to build a stable, prosperous country along the Iron Curtain.

However, in 1945 there could be no *Stunde Null* as old constitutional forms and political groups and elites reemerged. Many old racial and religious prejudices and authoritarian attitudes on law and order also remained, as a study undertaken at the Institute of Contemporary History, Linz University, in 1978 revealed.[2] The ghosts of Austria's Nazi past were never sufficiently exorcised, and an open discussion about what had gone on during and after the war was until the 1980s tabu.[3]

---

[2] "Der 'Hitler in uns' lebt noch," *Arbeiter-Zeitung*, 7 March 1978 and "Adolf im Hirn," *Extrablatt*, n. 6, June 1978.

[3] See Anton Pelinka and Erika Weinzierl, eds., *Das grosse Tabu—Österreichs Umgang mit seiner Vergangenheit* (Vienna: Österreichische Staatsdruckerei, 1987).

Austria's treatment of other victims showed a crass indifference to their plight. Compensation to Jews was parsimonious in comparison to that by Germany and subject to long bureaucratic delays. The two main parties showed tolerance and understanding, although this often seemed to be applied more eagerly to winning the votes of the *Ehemaligen.*

In the mid-1960s the tragic case of Ernst Kirchweger, a sixty-seven-year-old pensioner and committed anti-fascist, occurred as a brutal reminder of an unsavory past.[4] Kirchweger met his death in scuffles with right-wing students and sympathizers who were shouting "Hoch Auschwitz" during demonstrations against the anti-Semitic sentiments of a university professor, Taras Borodajkewycz, an ex-Nazi who had cultivated good relations with members of the People's Party. No doubt such assimilation was necessary, but it is questionable whether equally imperative lessons from the past were sufficiently internalized. The Second Republic's first victim of neo-Nazism cast a cloud over its twenty-year birthday celebrations, but Austrian schizophrenia on the war and moral responsibility was allowed to drift on until the fiftieth anniversary of the Anschluss.

The Kreisky-Peter affair, the support for Burger in 1980, the Reder-Frischenschlager handshake in 1985 all exposed the vulnerability of groups in Austria on the question of overcoming the past. Austrians preferred to regard these cases as private, family squabbles which had little to do with "uninformed" outsiders, and, for the most part, foreigners obliged, even going so far as to manufacture a Hollywood version of the glorious myth.

No one can deny that the events surrounding 1938 and its consequences are involved and complex. The interlude 1934-1938 saw to this. This is especially relevant in the context of the attitude of Social Democracy to this period. Workers were alienated from the corporate state after the civil war, a fact quickly

---

[4] See K. Horak and F. Klar, *Hitler ist nicht tot* (Vienna: Verlag Jungbrunnen, 1968).

realized by the Nazis and exploited by them to buy support, and, in this effort, anti-Semitism was a powerful instrument of propaganda. The tragedies of 1934 lived on to divide the country four years later as Social Democrats sought revenge. In many ways the Nazis could claim to offer the workers more than their predecessors. Jobs and food were non-ideological slogans, but, it was very appealing if one had neither. Apartments, too, seemed more plentiful with "aryanization" and were available to those who had been deprived of accommodations after the civil war. It also partly explains the reluctance to have Jewish émigrés return to Vienna after the war. The Nazis portrayed themselves as the true Socialists, showing sympathy for the workers, who had after all only been misguided in the past by evil Jewish intellectuals of Viennese bourgeois background.[5]

In Austrian political life Nazi propaganda played on important themes such as anti-clericalism and opposition to the Habsburgs, stressing the importance of the *Volk:* "Das Volk regiert" was the banner displayed on the Ringstrasse's Parliament. Nazism was populist and understood very well the raw points of the workers' history. After the war this affected the attitude of the Socialist Party toward the Nazi period and blunted the Socialists' capacity for criticism. This was particularly apparent before the presidential election of 1986 when the SPÖ seemed unable or unwilling to take the lead in directing the discussion on the war-time past of Kurt Waldheim.

The Anschluss had important consequences for Austrian Socialism. Many in the Revolutionary Socialists (RS), the radicals who had broken with the Social Democratic Party after 1934 went into exile, where they abandoned active politics. It was the end of this particular interregnum in the party's history, and it meant in 1945 that the party of the Second Republic was to be

---

[5]For further details see H. Safrian and H. Witek, *Und keiner war dabei* (Vienna: Picus Verlag, 1988), and E. Tálos, E. Hanisch, and W. Neugebauer, *NS-Herrschaft in Österreich* (Vienna: Verlag für Gesellschaftskritik, 1988).

shaped by pragmatists and those on the right. After 1934 there had been a new beginning and an experimentation with more radical socialism. This came to an end in 1936. Those who left Austria joined others who had got out in 1934. The first wave of exiles had become influenced by the principles of Swedish Social Democracy and British laborism.[6] They had the advantage of having worked abroad for four years and had adapted to the new situation. The new émigrés found that they too were now identified with the failures and mistakes of the past and their moral authority to lead a new party was weakened. Many also seemed weary of politics, unable to muster enough strength to meet the demands of reconstruction. The years 1934-1938 had taken their toll, and exile and re-adjustment were harder for Revolutionary Socialists to accept. The year of the Anschluss was to mean the end of Austro-Marxism, as symbolized by the death of Otto Bauer in July of that year. The appeal of the all-German revolution gradually evaporated, and from then on the party would not tolerate the luxury of dualism and ambivalence on questions such as the nature of democracy, the state, and participation in government. The post-war left was to remain isolated and insignificant. The way was clear for the "Renner" men. The party was also dependent on experts from the Nazi period. The socialist "New Man" that had been the product of the dream of the 1920s had perished or stayed in exile. There had not been sufficient time to mature and to provide recruits for the postwar era. Help was sought from *Ehemaligen,* and they eagerly accepted the favors of party patronage in return for respectability and acceptance in active politics.[7]

After 1945 the SPÖ was in many ways successful, although some observers complained that the party had lost passion and

---

[6]See K. H. Ritschel and P. Lendvai, *Kreisky* (Vienna: Zsolnay, 1972) and Melanie Sully, *Continuity and Change in Austrian Socialism* (New York: Columbia University Press, 1982).

[7]See J. Haslinger, *Politik der Gefühle* (Darmstadt: Luchterhand, 1987).

spirit. The emphasis was on reformism and gradual consolidation. This course lacked ideological intensity and helped spawn a moral vacuum. This contributed to the party going astray in the 1970s and 1980s and to the Androsch syndrome. It promoted a certain lack of imagination and contributed an intellectual deficit. Even with repeated absolute majorities the SPÖ could not overcome income differentials or radically alter the economic infrastructure.

The legacy of 1938 for the SPÖ led to a lack of vision and socialist idealism. The fashionable fetish of economic growth ultimately lost the party credibility with ethnic minorities, the handicapped, women, environmentalist groups and the peace movement.

The experience of Nazism was also to affect political life in the Second Republic in the form of a downgrading in the importance of the class struggle. The notion of the entire *Volk* coexisting together in the same boat in a kind of national community, or *Volksgemeinschaft*, was carried on in the form of economic and social partnership, along with the Great Coalition, one of the hallmarks of the post-war era. The Socialist Party was on the way to becoming a *Staatspartei* and a *Volkspartei* and participated quiescently in this process. This trend was reinforced by an older tradition, no doubt strengthened after 1938, viz. anti-communism.

Obviously not everything since the war has derived from the experience of 1938. Much of Austrian political culture, associated with a high degree of deference and a penchant for compromise, had longer roots going back even to the monarchy. The experience of 1934 is also arguably more traumatic for the politics of the Second Republic. This influenced the SPÖ and the trade unions to seek a place at the green table and made the idea acceptable to industry. It was, however, re-inforced by the neutralization of the class enemy which had occurred under the Nazis. The Anschluss also meant for Austria the loss of an entire culture, the lost rich input from Jewish intellectuals which affected arts and politics alike. A void seemed to replace this cultural ferment, and politics became more businesslike and scientific.

These changed conditions were important in the phase of reconstruction of the republic and in what has been referred to as the growth of the Second Republic's myth. It was necessary for the visibility of the republic for both sides to indulge in selective amnesia with respect to the foibles of the other camp. Coalition politics necessitated coalition history and this meant dodging the tricky issues of the past. School teachers let history end in 1918 and recommenced history again in 1955, just in time to capture the gloss and glamour of the new age.

Each camp protected the other from embarrassment. Everything was split in accordance with the principles of *Proporz*. Even bi-partisan involvement in the resistance was acknowledged along these lines.

Failure to agree on interpretation of the events leading to the civil war has posed a latent threat to the cozy stability and bonhomie of Austrian politics and has sporadically surfaced to disturb the charm of a post-war success-story. The myth of 1938 has its forerunners in the myths of February 1934 and July 1934. What was different about 1938 was that it provided something to cling to and to unite around. Even socialists could afford to be more relaxed about the Anschluss than they ever could be about 1934. The other myths were divisive and could not have generated the consensus and success of the Second Republic. Recent attacks on the myth of the foundation have undermined confidence and led to problems of integration.

After 1945 the country developed a reputation for tolerance and stability, but this was based on a young democracy and excessive conflict-avoidance which regarded criticism and debate as essentially negative. The failure to confront the past adequately and the weakness of this formal democracy meant that Austria was ill-equipped to face the trauma and complexities of the Waldheim affair.

The republic's democracy was also vulnerable because the

main arena of political conflict had always been dominated by the *Lager,* the Church and the federal provinces. This is where the greatest activity and mobilization occurred and where loyalties were strong. A striking continuity in *Lager* voting support, carrying over from the First Republic, is apparent in the first election in 1945, despite considerable demographic and socioeconomic changes since 1938. After 1945 the nation-state was slow to generate the same kind of engagement and commitment in political life.[8] The May Day parades and religious festivals continued to attract popular support. Austria's democracy, therefore, was imbalanced and only partially developed. Old, fragmented sub-systems co-existed with newer forms of elite accommodation introducing an element of disguised tension.[9] Conflict could be tolerated so long as it was regulated by the main elites and not broadcast beyond mutually accepted boundaries. In this way stability could be maintained and the pitfalls of the First Republic avoided.

The dangers of this setup lay dormant but surfaced during the Waldheim controversy. Waldheim was a representative figure of the Anschluss period; neither a convinced Nazi nor a great hero, he was driven on by the need to survive. His Catholic family suffered in 1938 and his experiences seemed to personify the agony in Austrian history. Like many others he did his "duty," believed in the myth, and was guilty at the very least of gross self-deception. Austria was hurt and outraged by this outside condemnation of Waldheim. It was felt as a slight on an entire nation which had shown itself to be a good partner in the western world and a reliable opponent of communism. Once

---

[8] See Gerhard Botz, "Anschluss an die Vergangenheit," in *Jahrbuch des Dokumentationsarchivs des österreichischen Widerstandes* (Vienna: Österreichischer Bundesverlag, 1987), pp. 23-44.

[9] For the typology of political systems in the First and Second Republics see Rudolf Neck and Anton Pelinka, *Bürgerkrieg–Sozialpartnerschaft* (Vienna: Verlag Jugend und Volk, 1983).

again, Austria was lonely and shunned, resentful of foreign intrusion in its affairs and desiring to show its independence and pride. Waldheim was elected in 1986 by 54 percent of the electorate who believed he stood for the restoration of decency in public life and traditional Christian values. Many were tired of socialist mismanagement, corruption, and party patronage. Frustration with the established parties was widespread amongst the youth, while the workers felt their party had let them down by introducing lay-offs in the nationalized industries. A large reservoir of protest had accumulated long before the escalation of the Waldheim controversy. Electoral volatility was on the increase and new issues relating to peace, sexual discrimination, and the environment were becoming more prominent.

The Second Republic's reliance on conflict-avoidance and on an overprotective attitude to democracy, which had tended to regard criticism as negative, deprived the country of a ready mechanism to respond to the crisis unleashed by the Waldheim controversy.

It is appealing but facile to believe that Waldheim's resignation could have brought about a return to "normalcy." The crisis was symptomatic of a deeper malaise and more profound cleavages. Reforms in archaic decision-making structures were long overdue. Some believe, in a desperate attempt to be optimistic, that the Waldheim case could ultimately be positive in so far as the past will be openly re-examined and the new generation will honestly debate past shame and guilt. This may be, but it still could hinder progress that otherwise may have taken place without too much scrutiny—a process which involved the modernization of Austria and liberalization. More flexible opening times for shops and a loosening of Chamber–Party links are signs of these new trends; greater discussion within the Church and industry also seemed possible. Austria could have become more relaxed about conflict and active participation, but now this may seem to be too much like a dangerous experiment and the temptation will surely be to withdraw, play safe, go on the defensive and overreact to the views of the outside world. The Anschluss experience is again cited in this context in so far as it is believed that Austria should not yield to outside pressure and bullying, but the danger that this attitude brings is increasing insularity.

The Anschluss anniversary and Waldheim's unconquered past unfortunately coincided with a backlog of pent-up frustration with the stagnation in political life and threatens, paradoxically, to hold up progress which might otherwise have occurred more smoothly.

There is still a chance, however, that Austria can go forward by accepting and recognizing the mistakes of the past. The Waldheim controversy provided this opportunity, although the president himself repeatedly failed to respond in a helpful and sensitive way.

The Anschluss anniversary gave Austria another chance. Because of the delicacy surrounding the president's role in the war, it was decided that Waldheim should not give an official speech on the day of commemoration, March 11, 1988. It was felt that such an act would be inappropriate and that Waldheim anyway would not find the right words for the occasion. Instead, the president was to be content with addressing the nation the evening before on television.

Waldheim's broadcast was, surprisingly, a respectable performance, even if it was too late and lacked conviction in its presentation. The speech recognized the Holocaust as one of the greatest tragedies in world history in which Austrians had participated and acknowledged that there were those who had welcomed Hitler, "There were hundreds of thousands of Austrians who greeted the Anschluss, cheered Hitler and the occupation, and cherished many false hopes." He denounced fanaticism and intolerance, recalled the victims, including civilians and resisters, and referred to the dual role of Austria and its people, "There were Austrians who were victims and others who were accomplices."[10]

It had to be accepted that Austria was the first victim of Nazi aggression, but "let us not create the impression that we had nothing to do with this. Obviously there can be no collective guilt, but as Head of State of the Republic of Austria, I want to apologize for the crimes of National Socialism committed by Austrians.[11] President Waldheim expressed respect for the victims, adding that Austria was a victim too, but that lessons had been learned and Austria had contributed to peace and freedom. Commenting on contemporary events, he spoke of the need for a moral regeneration to root out financial scandals and corruption in public life. He promised a political clean-up and a new start, although no one seemed quite sure what he had in mind by moral reform. Waldheim's own credibility had long since been destroyed and the general verdict on his speech was that it had come too late.

Even as he spoke, thousands of demonstrators were calling for his resignation on Vienna's Ringstrasse. The ceremonies and public speeches continued and Bruno Kreisky, Erhard Busek for the Conservatives, and the Mayor, Helmut Zilk, were amongst those who addressed the crowd. They warned against the dangers of intolerance and fanaticism in this solemn, often emotional recollection of the horrors of the past.[12]

Chancellor Vanitzky stressed, in a special meeting of the cabinet, the *dual* role of Austria as victim *and* partners in the tragedy. The former was accepted, but the latter was not; a balance was needed. Anti-Semitism had found willing and ready accomplices on hand after the Anschluss and, although soldiers were not volunteers, many had gone along with the Third Reich and some even today did not feel that they had served in an alien

---

[10] *Wiener Zeitung*, 11 March 1988.
[11] Ibid.
[12] *Wiener Zeitung*, 12 March 1988.

uniform. Vranitzky dismissed the idea of collective guilt but insisted that there was personal guilt, responsibility and shame. Some had kept the Nazi machine going with inhuman enthusiasm, and this had to be accepted, and, Vranitzky continued, "many Austrians at that time—and often even today—did not see service for a foreign and unjust cause as a matter of shameful compulsion but as a simple test in which they had to protect themselves, and in which, for the most varied motives, they carried out the duties allocated to them."[13] It was a sober conclusion to a depressing occasion, and the relevance to the *causa prima* was inescapable.

It had taken fifty years and Waldheim for this acceptance of dualism in Austrian history with respect to the Anschluss to be acknowledged by a leading political figure. It has to be admitted that anti-Semitism fell on fertile ground in Austria, and did not suddenly appear with the Germans. An honest re-examination of Austria's role in the Holocaust can no longer be avoided, but it must come from within and include all sections of society, including schools, factories, and others. External pressure has often in the past proved to be counterproductive, but its absence induces slumber and the inclination to hide behind the old myths. The fact that Herman Göring is still an honorary citizen of Mauterndorf in Salzburg shows the extent of the problem. Apparently it has been possible to dissociate the Nazi character and actions of Göring from his role in providing jobs, as if this was a separate item from the Nazi war machine. The ÖVP provincial governor, Wilfried Haslauer, believed this decision had to be respected, although this was contested by the Green Party in Parliament. The Greens were concerned about the educational effect on the young and were also protesting against the fact that Adolf Hitler was still recorded as an honorary citizen in the Styrian town of Leibnitz.[14] Such incidents may only be of importance in a

---

[13] *Austria Today*, 1/88, p. 5.

[14] As reported in the *Salzburger Nachrichten*, 7 May 1988.

symbolic sense, but they indicate a reluctance to make even a simple gesture in the process of *Vergangenheitsbewältigung*.[15]

It is no longer plausible to indulge in a simplified view of history which states that Hitler came, saw, and conquered as if the masses on the Heldenplatz were passive recipients of an alien message. This leads to the even more simplistic view that the problem disappeared with the collapse of the Third Reich in 1945. A concentration on Hitlerism has fostered this particular myth. This resulted in a tendency to shy away from the Nazi problem, for logically it was not necessary to confront the problem if it was believed to have been imported by means of force. Much needs to be done in honestly reassessing the past. The year 1938 presents historians with the classic Viennese problem of distinguishing between myth and reality and establishing "historical truth." Politics and history coincide at this point where interpretations of the past have proved to be so controversial.

Where does all this leave Austria today? If Waldheim had resigned and the country had confessed its guilt and shame and acknowledged its part in the Holocaust—would that have been the end of the matter? The country must be left some pride and a set of recognizable rules by which to govern. The old myth of the consensus had this virtue and helped Austrians overcome a crisis of identity. New ways forward must recognize this. Often it is asked if Austria has learned from the past, but it too has a right to expect that the world has learned from its mistakes and will not again neglect the predicament of a small state in the heart of Europe, struggling to consolidate its own identity and control its own destiny.

In addition, this process of coming to terms with the past has

---

[15]It was eventually decided that Göring's honorary citizenship had lapsed and was invalid, although this was a technical and legal decision rather than action born of a genuine desire to come to terms with the past. See the *Salzburger Nachrichten*, 14 June 1988.

to be a kind of permanent revolution and does not end with Austria. It is not enough to (as the Austrians are readily criticized for doing) point the finger and be self-righteous. The defensive reaction of Austria has been to quote the darker side of other countries' history. This is not convincing on the grounds that it cannot exonerate Austria. But often there is a grain of truth in some of the missives. To an extent British, and no doubt American, imperialism too requires a process of *Vergangenheitsbewältigung,* but the Germans and Austrians have not been on the side of the angels and have had the misfortune of being on the losing side. Every country has its myths and past to overcome. These are the lessons for Austria and the world on the anniversary of the Anschluss.

A Jewish View of the Anschluss and the Second Republic

Paul Grosz

This essay appears only after the author overcame considerable reluctance to present his ideas here. An illustrious company of learned academics and accomplished political professionals is daunting for one who is himself neither the one nor the other. Further, the Foreign Ministry of Austria was one of the sponsors of the symposium to which these papers were first presented, and, if there were an *apologia* for Austria, participation would have seemed to be an endorsement of the official position. But to have the president of the Jewish Community of Vienna write on the Jews of Vienna in a foreign publication, especially an American one, under the auspices of the Austrian Foreign Ministry seemed less than palatable.

Now, it is quite legitimate for Austria to try to present herself to the world as favorably as possible. My country has exerted much effort in the field of education. Austria has conducted an exemplary humanitarian policy toward refugees, including Jewish refugees from the East, keeping her borders open despite the obvious difficulties and costs that go with such a policy. One must acknowledge the real, if belated, efforts of elements of the Austrian government, of some of the media, some of the dignitaries of the Catholic Church, some of the teaching establishment in the schools and universities, and quite a few of the young people to take a new, more realistic look at their past and to accept and further an open discussion about it. "To do good and speak about it" is legitimate.

An earlier president of the Vienna Jewish Community, Dr. Desider Friedmann, was appointed to membership in the *Staats-*

rat in the government of Dr. Kurt Schuschnigg. This fact was recently cited and offered as evidence of the comparative liberality of Schuschnigg's policy toward the Jews when contrasted with that of the National Socialists. Dr. Friedmann died a dreadful death in a German concentration camp; one must speculate whether he would much appreciate being offered in evidence, fifty years later, attesting to the liberality of treatment of Jews.

Presidents of the Austrian Jewish Community seem prone to lend their considerable reputations to validate one or another policy or particular act concerning the Jews of Austria. The presidents are frequently called upon to perform symbolic functions of approval, even if only by being present at a given ceremony or the like. But that does not alter realities. It would be redundant to mention what is so clearly shown in many other of the essays in this book: Anti-Semitism was a fact of Austrian life, politically, socially, and morally. It was based on Christian, especially Roman Catholic, religious teachings and understandings, but was also fed by economic greed and other rationales that were used to mask simple hatred for Jews.

Should yet another president of the Jewish Community participate in yet another, possibly exculpatory, exercise? Misgivings would have to be overcome, and the answer would have to be "yes." Although many others could do as well or better, *someone* has to write for the Jews, for, otherwise, after all the ink had been spilt and many viewpoints on the theme "1938 to 1988" had been offered, there might still have been no Jewish point of view presented. So, without claiming to speak for all Jews and not expecting to please everyone, this president will make some observations and offer some opinions. Since the office of president of the Jewish Community does not confer infallibility (any more than that of president of other entities), there may be errors in fact or judgment or wrong conclusions may be drawn. If that should be the case, then challenge is quite in order; Jews seem to thrive on challenge.

The assigned purpose of this essay was to treat the role of

the Jews of Austria during the period of examination—a forbiddingly daunting task even if one were permitted a volume, rather than just a brief chapter of writing. The Jews of Austria and all their troubles in ten pages! Nevertheless, there may be value in presenting a very brief (one hopes not abortive) review of the history of the Jews in Austria in order to gain some sort of perspective on recent times and events. Then observations on the present Viennese and Austrian Jewish community and its prospects will be more understandable.

If one consults a chronology of the Jews and their presence in Vienna from the tenth century until 1938, one finds that it begins with the earliest mention of Jews in an Austrian historical document, the so-called "Raffelstettener Zollordnung" of 903 (the exact date is in dispute). This document, concerned with taxes and customs fees, refers to Jews for the first time as rightful merchants. No individual was cited by name.

The first Jew in Vienna to be known by name was Shlomo, the mintmaster. He won this first mention in 1190, when his assigned duties were to mint the silver extorted from King Richard I of England, the Lionhearted, who had been abducted by Leopold V and thrown into the dungeons at Dürnstein. There Richard languished until his loyal minstrel Blondel found him and negotiated his ransom. This is a tale that every schoolchild in Austria knows; it is perhaps not surprising that, although Duke Leopold played the knave and extortioner, all the sympathies are with him, the Austrian, and there is very little compassion for the victim, a foreigner.

Shlomo the mintmaster would receive notice in the documents yet another, and final, time six years later. In the course of events, a horde of crusaders were passing through Vienna on their way to the Holy Land. Their religious fervor to fight the infidel was so great that they could not contain themselves until they reached Jerusalem; in their ardor they slew fifteen Jews whom they encountered in Vienna. Shlomo was one of those slain.

In 1215 the Catholic Church, in the Lateran Council of that year, saw fit to announce the requirement that the Jews wear the pointed *Judenhut* in order that they could be distinguished from good Christians. This was a clear indication that the fact of their being infidels and damned was not, by itself, enough to identify them as apart from the rest of society. This outward sign of exclusion, the compulsory hat, was applied to the Jews of Vienna as well as to the other European Jews.

Some time later, the good gentry, clergy and burghers of Vienna began to experience a diminishing liking for those to whom they owed money and they figured that it might be to their advantage to drive the Jews out. So, on 23 May 1420, following the order of Duke Albrecht V, all Jews were seized, and, two days later, many of the poorer ones were packed onto small boats and rafts and sent down the Danube to Hungary, where King Sigismund took them in; those who drowned on the way were spared the harassment which the survivors suffered later.

Of the Jews who remained in Vienna, many were tortured to get at their valuables, including evidence of debts owed them. They were completely dispossessed and finally driven out— except for the many who committed suicide.

Less than a year later, on 12 March 1421, Jewish men and women were carted from their habitats to a place called Erdberg, at that time a small hamlet outside Vienna, now a part of the third district of Vienna. There they were invited to forswear their religion and to become good Catholics. When they declined this invitation, as most of them did, they were burned at the stake. This hideous procedure took place much to the gaudium of these unfortunate Jews' Viennese neighbors, who attended the spectacle, picnicking there with their families and quite enjoying it all. More than 110 Jews died in what was then called the "Great Gesera."

Thirty years later, Pope Nicholas V issued a bull to confirm that Jews might settle on Austrian lands.

It would become tedious to continue the dreary narrative. It is a chronology of continuing, monotonous repetitions after a pattern. That pattern was one of hatred for Jews, of abuse and extortion, of religious persecution, of dispossession and expulsion, even of outright murder. This went on and on over the centuries; it was not until the eighteenth century that Jews could ever stay in Vienna for longer than three generations before being driven out, being burned or drowned or otherwise being removed from the society of Vienna.

The chronology comes to an end in 1938 at which point one finds the following notation: On 1 April 1938, a transport of 151 "Schutzhäftlinge" (prisoners in protective custody) was dispatched to Dachau and the concentration camp. Sixty of the prisoners were Jews. In the next month, on 24 May, another fifty Jews followed their unhappy fellows. Approximately 120,000 Jews were expelled or were allowed to flee to save their lives, but they had to lose their homes, their friends, their livelihoods and their homeland. Unfortunately, 65,000 others could not or did not flee and, therefore, also lost their lives as well. They became the victims of what is variously called the *Endlösung* (final solution), the Holocaust or *Shoah;* one can choose the denominating word depending on one's point of view.

So much for the past; what of our own times?

A *very* few Jews, this writer among them, were not caught up in the Holocaust and survived the war in Vienna. Such a survivor could believe that he had lived through a great, terrible accident of history. Here a personal account seems appropriate:

I lived in a house where the other inhabitants knew me to be a Jew. They did not go to the police and denounce me—and it was dangerous for them not to have done so. But, despite that demonstration of solidarity, we were divided in our outlooks and by circumstances. When the first invading Russian soldier came into the house, I was, and I felt myself to be, liberated; my good neighbors felt themselves to be occupied. This is not a moral indictment; what one feels, he feels. It was simply a fact.

The years 1938 to 1945 had been a nightmare, then to be forgotten as some terrible accident in the otherwise straight way into the future. It had been just seven years, but all had been lost or destroyed. Nevertheless, in 1945 it was time to get on with things (the influences of the Cold War played a role here), anti-Nazism was *de rigueur* and anti-Semitism was taboo. Nobody was a Nazi anymore; nobody was anti-Semitic. And nobody talked about it.

Well, there were some outbreaks that troubled the waters. There was the Professor Taras Borodajkewycz affair,[1] for instance, and there was the matter of Dr. Friedrich Peter in the *Nationalrat* and the accompanying sharp exchange between Dr. Simon Wiesenthal and Chancellor Bruno Kreisky,[2] Then Dr. Josef Klaus, when he was a candidate for the chancellorship, described himself as "ein echter Österreicher" as if an Austrian

---

[1] In the early 1960s, Professor Taras Borodajkewycz, in his lectures at the University for International Commerce (now the University for Economics) defended Nazism and the Third Reich, boasted of his support of the Nazis, and made blatantly anti-Semitic statements in and out of the lecture hall. His statements were not only provocative, they were also in violation of Austrian law. There were demonstrations against Borodajkewycz, and, on one occasion, in a confrontation between protesters and supporters, a demonstrator was struck and later died from his injury. Finally, when Borodajkewycz expressed his inflammatory views in an interview on television, there arose such a furor that the University Senate took notice, and he was required to take early retirement—Ed.

[2] Dr. Friedrich Peter was leader of the *Freiheitliche Partei Österreichs* (FPÖ, the Liberal Party of Austria) and a member of parliament. As head of the party's faction in parliament, he was to become one of the vice-presidents of the body. It was pointed out that he had been a decorated member of a notoriously vicious SS unit. Among the many who cried out against such a man being an officer of parliament, Dr. Simon Wiensenthal called for Peter's removal. Bruno Kreisky argued that Peter had conducted himself above reproach in republican politics and that he had been duly elected and ought to be allowed to hold his position. The dispute between Wiesenthal, head of the Nazi-hunting Documentation Center in Vienna, and Kreisky, leader of the Socialist Party (and also Jewish) became acrimonious—Ed.

citizen of Jewish heritage was *not* a genuine Austrian.[3]

There were incidents, it is true, but, generally speaking, Austrians did not apply themselves to "Vergangenheitsbewältigung"" (coming to grips with the past). And the Jews, who should have known better, did not either. There were no barricades, there was nothing worth fighting for; no, one did not let the past interfere with the present. Democratic Austrians, and Austrian Jews among them, were all pursuing the same goals; they were all taken with making a good living—or at least a better living. And the fault may lie with those who should have known better.

An excerpt from a recent report of the Federal Press Service is revealing of the attitudes and spirit of the time just after the war:

> The great majority of the Austrian Jews who were driven out of their businesses or dwellings were not invited to return to their homeland after the war.
>
> The government in Vienna has occupied itself several times with the question of bringing back (the Jews).
>
> The recently made known minutes of the Ministerial Council from the time of 1950 cast a shadow over politicians who until now have stood in nearly unassailable reputation.
>
> Federal Chancellor Figl warned against bringing back Jewish citizens and, with regard to compensation and reparation, offered the opinion that: "The Jews should just quickly become rich people." His Vice-Chancellor, Schärf, in 1952 made light of the number of Jews who had lost their lives as being relatively small. In 1945 State Chancellor Renner excused the attitude of the petty officials, bourgeoisie, and small businesspeople at the time of the Anschluss by observing that they had in no way thought that a world war could

---

[3] In the parliamentary election of 1970, Dr. Josef Klaus, leader of the conservative *Österreichische Volkspartei* (ÖVP, Austrian Peoples Party) was described as "ein echter Österreicher,." It availed him nothing; Klaus and the ÖVP lost the election to the Socialists and Kreisky—Ed.

break out, but rather, at the most, something might happen to a few Jews.

Expressions of politicians of the second rank were still worse.

But on to the present and a few vital facts about the Jewish community of Austria. Currently, there are about six thousand Jews who are members of the *Kultusgemeinde* in Vienna, and there are another two hundred in the provinces. There is about an equal number—possibly a few more—of Jews who are not directly affiliated with the community, but, eventually, they all come to the community for one reason or another. They are mostly immigrants from the Soviet Union, or some are Viennese Jews who have lived in the city for years but do not want to be registered as Jews. However, in time, they come to the community because they want their children to go to the Jewish school, or the aged come to the home for the elderly, or, finally, because they want to be interred in the community's cemetery.

The Viennese Jewish community was once among the wealthiest of its kind, the proud center of Jewish development in Europe. Practically nothing of that has been left. One reason is that, in 1945, there were only about two thousand surviving Jews in Vienna. Mostly they were *Mischehen* (people who had intermarried with Gentiles) and *Unterseeboote* ("submarines," or people who lived under cover), and some were *Funktionsjuden* (people who had been used by the Gestapo). In succeeding years only those Jews applied to come back home who had emigrated to lands where they were received in an unfriendly manner (and here there are tales that could be told), or where they could not earn their livelihood, or where life was simply not inviting enough to stay on.

The *Kultusgemeinde* was, naturally, a reflection of the population of that time. The people decided to do what they thought was the right thing under the circumstances. They decided to use up whatever property and wealth they had left, because they thought there would be no future. They reasoned that within ten years the only people still living would not be able to bring forth another generation. In twenty years time, there would be nobody left at all. So, by what is now called the "Second Arisierung" in the community, all was practically given away. The recipients were mostly the Gemeinde Wien or affiliates of the Socialist Party. Over the years, the *Kultusgemeinde* was being run, to a large degree, by a Socialist.

Finally, in the mid-1970s a change occurred for reasons that stemmed from the past. In 1956 a wave of Hungarian immigrants came to Vienna as a consequence of the revolution. They came in thousands upon thousands, including Jews. About a thousand Hungarian Jews stayed in Austria. And then, in following years, many more Jews came from Poland, from Czechoslovakia, from Romania, from all the Eastern countries. They flocked to Vienna not intending to stay there, but they were captured by the charm of Vienna, one must assume. Beginning in the mid-1970s, these people commenced to "invest in the walls," that is, they then began to buy homes. Until that time, they had, so to speak, sat on their valises and trunks, expecting to leave momentarily. But they had founded businesses, and their children had started to school; they decided in the 1970s to remain in Vienna.

One can imagine—or perhaps one cannot imagine—what a shock it was to the young people who had been brought up in Vienna, to the offspring, then twenty years old and more, when all of a sudden, in 1986, they were confronted with a completely open anti-Semitic attitude, coming not just from the streets, but from the very highest echelons of society and public life. For them, it was the first time they had experienced such a thing, and it was shattering. The Jews of Vienna do not decry what happened, or what was supposed to have happened, during wartime, or the situation or actions of President Waldheim, so much as they decry what has been happening from March 1986 until today.

One must grant the fact that Austria has certainly done a lot of work in the field of education, in the field of disseminating information, and in the media (especially television and radio) to combat anti-Semitism. It is not so certain, however, that this will have the desired results because there is still one serious deficiency. It is a number with a decimal point. It is not so important what the first, second, third, or fourth digit beyond the decimal point is; what is important is that digit that is up front, before the decimal point. It is the responsibility of the one at the front to set the tone and the pace and establish the worth of the figure.

In arguing Austria's worth, much has been made of Austria as a bulwark against communism, but this must be without consequence now; simply being anti-communist does not carry any weight nowadays. I think that one goes in the wrong direction if one attempts, by reiterating that Austria is anti-communist, to establish Austria in the eyes of the world as a trustworthy ally and desirable colleague.

Practically on the same day that the newspaper notices alleged that Dr. Waldheim had been a member of the *Sturm Abteilung* (SA), friend and foe alike decided that Waldheim embodied Austria or that Austria equaled Waldheim. It was surely not true then or ever, but later the negative characteristics that—rightly or wrongly, fairly or unfairly—were attributed to Dr. Waldheim were more and more transferred to all of Austria. To allow that to happen was a piece of political *Fahrlässigkeit* (negligence).

Unfortunately, Dr. Waldheim became the "ugly Austrian," or rather the symbol of the "ugly Austrian." Judging from the results, it seems that all the great efforts to make Dr. Waldheim acceptable without reservations did not change the picture to his advantage; rather, in the process, the picture of Austria worsened.

But to return to the matter of how the Jews live today in Austria, one must say that they fare very well again. It might be that the whole rekindling of anti-Semitism will slumber off eventually. But there is still a disturbing question: What will happen the next time that the flames of anti-Semitism are fanned? What may ensue if there is a marked passion-arousing difference between what is presumed to be the good Austrian's, the patriotic Austrian's point of view and the viewpoint of a Jew? There is quicksand here for a Jew. For example, in the last presidential election, 53.9 percent of the electorate cast their votes for President Waldheim. Since 100 percent is the whole, that means that 46.1 percent of the Austrians who went to the polls did *not* vote for him. One did not question the Austrianness or the patriotism of the 46.1 percent who opposed Waldheim, but if a Jew gets up and says that he is not for Waldheim, the question is raised whether he is acting as a Jew and not as an Austrian. That is a profoundly wrong attitude from which to regard and judge Austrian Jews. One cannot continue with such a seriously and fundamentally flawed attitude.

To illustrate further the kind of dilemma an Austrian Jew may have to face, it is useful once again to recount a personal experience:

I will stand up in defense of Austria, or in defense of the Jews, or in defense of a principle whenever I see them wronged. But even the most principled enterprise can be hazardous.

When Dr. Waldheim became a candidate for the Austrian presidency, the World Jewish Congress joined in alleging Nazi associations and complicity in war crimes in Waldheim's past. Some urged that the Congress' vigorous campaign against Waldheim might have had a great positive effect in that it prompted a thorough search into the question. I did not see it quite that way. I can defend my judgment all the more easily by reason of the fact that we Austrian Jews became, somehow, the victims of the affair. I think that the World Jewish Congress, any other organization, or, for that matter, any humanitarian organization ought not to be reproached if it should initiate or participate in such a controversy, if it does so in good faith. But there should be a sense of measure, a sense of propriety. After Dr. Waldheim had been elected to the presidency of Austria, the president of the World Jewish Congress, Mr. Edgar Bronfman, said in a meeting in Brussels that (with Waldheim as its president) Austria was unfit to be a member of the European Community. I took exception to that statement, for I believed it to be beyond the proper boundaries of criticism. I emphasized that I thought that Mr. Bronfman had the right to be critical; but he had on that occasion gone beyond the proper bounds.

That which ensued made me feel somewhat uneasy—no, it made me *very* uneasy. After I had said my piece concerning the events in Brussels, my reception back in Vienna was something that I did not relish. I was roundly congratulated and hailed as if I were a knight in shining armor, defending Austria against a world conspiracy. I was not and am not a knight in shining armor, and congratulations were completely out of place. Being an Austrian, however, I accepted those congratulations gracefully—we Austrians are such nice, congenial people that we cannot bring ourselves to reject gestures of a friendly or generous nature. And besides, even if I had declined the accolades, my declination would not have been reported in the press or in the news broadcasts, no matter what!

To stand silent when one's country is wrongly condemned is no service to one's country; to be a wholly uncritical patriot does not serve one's country well either. To be a Jewish citizen of Austria puts one in danger of being impaled on one horn of a dilemma or the other.

Interpreting the Anschluss

Lonnie R. Johnson

For Austrian historians as well as the general public, the Anschluss era is one of the most sensitive topics of Austrian contemporary history. Punctuating the end of the First Republic and prefacing the beginning of the Second Republic, it casts a long shadow over antecedent and subsequent events. The discussion of controversial issues, such as the consequences of the demise of Austrian democracy in 1933-1934 or the adequacy of denazification in Austria after 1945, inevitably ends or begins with a discussion of the Anschluss. Changes in Austria's domestic political situation as well as Austria's position in international constellations also have provided different frameworks for interpreting the Anschluss. Perspectives on the Anschluss were obviously different before 1938 and thereafter, just as they were before and after 1945, 1955, or, to take a recent example, the advent of the so-called "Waldheim affair" in 1986. The purpose of the following series of observations is to outline selected problems of interpretation which have arisen in the course of the last five decades and to illustrate to what extent they have been influenced by changing circumstances of interpretation.

Each of Austria's three political "camps" (*Lager*) supported the Anschluss idea at some time during the interwar period, and it was in this respect that the idea was one of the few political common denominators of the First Republic. Gerhard Botz has identified six distinct "Anschluss movements" between 1918 and 1938, four of them non-National Socialist.[1] The political and

---

[1]Gerhard Botz, *Der 13. März 38 und die Anschlußbewegung. Selbstaufgabe,*

ideological motivations for each camp's aspiration for an Anschluss diverged, but they generally agreed that it was the solution to the then questionable political and economic viability (*Lebensfähigkeit*) of Austria, a problem aggravated by the virtual absence of an Austrian national identity.

An attitude of resignation characterized the initial interpretation of the Anschluss. Austria's lack of domestic cohesion, international isolation, and the western democracies' "policy of appeasement" put her at the mercy of Nazi Germany. Retrospectively Schuschnigg justified his decision not to resist the Anschluss militarily in the following manner: "Resistance by Austrian forces alone had not the smallest prospect of success. There can therefore be little doubt about the answer to the question whether resistance in these circumstances, even symbolic resistance, made any sense and whether its inevitable consequences were morally defensible."[2]

Given the Western responses to the Nazi dismemberment and occupation of Czechoslovakia and the invasion of Poland, one can understand Schuschnigg's reasoning. Erwin Schmidl's recent study documents how bleak the military prospects of resistance were,[3] and one can only theorize about what the domestic or

---

Okkupation und Selbstfindung Österreichs 1918-1945 (*Zeitdokument* 14 of the Dr. Karl Renner Institut; Vienna: Verlag der SPÖ, 1981), p. 9.

Translations of German texts have been made by the author unless noted otherwise. Parts of this article are based on the author's "Die österreichische Nation, die Moskauer Deklaration and die völkerrechtliche Argumentation: Bemerkungen zur Problematik der Interpretation der NS-Zeit in Österreich" which appeared in the Austrian Resistance Archive's *Jahrbuch 1988*, pp. 40-51.

[2]Kurt von Schuschnigg, *The Brutal Takeover: The Austrian Ex-chancellor's Account of the Anschluss of Austria by Hitler*, trans. Richard Berry (London: Weidenfeld and Nicholson, 1971), p. 281.

[3]See Erwin Schmidl, *Der deutsche Einmarsch in Österreich* (Vienna: Österreichischer Bundesverlag, 1987), pp. 43-69. The conjecture in the conclusion of Schmidl's book that armed resistance would have resulted in a civil war in Austria (p. 253) has been a source of controversy. See Félix Kreissler, "War der 'Anschluß' im März unvermeidlich?: Soll die Geschichtsschreibung normalisiert

military costs of defending Austria might have been. Nevertheless, it is conventional wisdom that armed resistance would have clearly established Austria's political and moral status of a victim of Nazi Germany in 1938, an issue which was in many respects unclear in 1945.

Nazi propaganda successfully portrayed the Anschluss as an affirmation of Nazi ideology by creating the impression that the entire matter was merely a question of Germans dealing with Germans and managed to camouflage the economic, military, and strategic interests Nazi Germany had in Austria.[4] Anti-capitalism, anti-liberalism, anti-clericalism, anti-Marxism, and anti-Semitism had their various clients in Austria, although for different ideological reasons, and the Nazis successfully rearticulated Austria's own traditions of Anschluss in their propaganda, a fact that is best briefly illustrated by two of Hitler's speeches in Vienna.

On March 15, 1938, three days after the first Nazi units had entered Austria, Hitler gave his famous speech on Vienna's Heldenplatz, witnessed by an estimated audience of 200,000. He accused the Schuschnigg regime of attempting to "obstruct the creation of a truly Greater German Reich, and, in doing so, blocking the path of the German people into the future." Reinterpreting the bastion or bulwark metaphor, which had been part of Austrian self-definition from the Turkish sieges right up to the Christian Corporate State's struggle with Bolshevism and National Socialism, Hitler also outlined Austria's new national and historical role: "From this point on, I proclaim a new mission for this land. The oldest Eastern province of the German people should, from this point onward, be the newest bastion of the German nation and herewith the German Reich. . . . With history

---

werden?" in the Austrian Resistance Archive's *Jahrbuch 1988*, pp. 15-30.

[4]For a detailed analysis of the Nazi military, economic, and strategic objectives that were obscured by propaganda see Norbert Schausberger, *Der Griff nach Österreich. Der Anschluß* (Vienna: Jugend und Volk, 1978).

as a witness, I now proclaim the entrance of my homeland into the German Realm."[5]

The pathos of historical destiny and national mission was reinforced by the issues of Austrian viability and national identity. In a speech on April 9, 1938, one day before the plebiscite the Nazis organized to justify the Anschluss after the fact, Hitler said:

> This country is a German country, and its people are German [the racial or national argument] . . . This country cannot live for long without the Reich [the viability argument] . . . After the collapse in 1918, German-Austria wanted to return immediately to the Reich [the Versailles-St. Germain or dictated peace argument] . . . Finally, if all of these reasons are not sufficient, this is my homeland. [the voluntaristic or *Führer* argument].[6]

The Nazis summed up this broad spectrum of issues in one slogan, *Ein Volk, ein Reich, ein Führer;* however, the unification with Germany, the Hitler cult, and Nazi ideology were three separate issues for many Austrians in 1938. Only in the course of the war did they learn to see how they were fatally interrelated. It is important to differentiate among the various motives which inspired Austrians to vote "Ja" for the Anschluss in 1938 and not to assume that they had the insights of 1945 in 1938.

The experience of the Anschluss with Nazi Germany was largely responsible for creating the basis for an unprecedented Austrian national consciousness and the postwar political consensus in Austria, both of which are generally recognized as the foundation for the success of the Second Republic.[7] In this re-

---

[5]Max Domarus, ed., *Hitler: Reden und Proklamationen,* 2 vols. (Munich: Süddeutscher Verlag, 1965), II, 832-834.

[6]Max Domarus, ed., *Hitler,* II, 848-849; for a detailed analysis of the Nazi propaganda for the plebiscite see Gerhard Botz, *Wien vom Anschluß zum Krieg: Nationalsozialistische Machtübernahme und politisch-soziale Umgestaltung am Beispiel der Stadt Wien 1938/39* (Vienna: Jugend und Volk, 1978), pp. 113-175.

[7]See, e.g., William T. Bluhm, *Building an Austrian Nation: The Political Interpretation of a Western State* (New Haven: Yale University Press), pp. 46-50;

spect, the Austrians' disillusionment with the Anschluss was a productive national learning experience just as their disillusionment with National Socialism was a productive political learning experience. However, the Austrians' change of spirit created national and political illusions about the *historical* role many Austrians played during the era of the Anschluss. The Anschluss turned Austria's interwar German-Austrians into Germans, but after having become Germans, they became Austrians; however after having become Austrians, many people frequently could not understand having been German. A similar phenomenon existed for some Austrians in the sphere of political attitudes. In 1945, many of Austria's recent converts to democratic pluralism had trouble understanding their previously having been anti-democratic, and the immediate postwar era was not a good time to admit having been German or anti-democratic. In other words, Austrian disillusionment with National Socialism created some Austrian illusions about National Socialism in Austria.

National stereotypes played a considerable role in how the Allies perceived Austria and how Austrians began to perceive themselves after the Anschluss. For seven years, Nazi and Allied propaganda identified National Socialism as something quintessentially German which led to an equivocal ideological usage of the concepts "Nazi" and "German" on both sides and made it terminologically difficult to identify Austria with Nazism. Despite the considerable size of Austria's indigenous pre-1938 Nazi movement, which Bruce Pauley has documented so well,[8] and

---

Lonnie Johnson, *Introducing Austria* (Vienna: Österreichischer Bundesverlag, 1987), pp. 120-127; Wolfgang Neugebauer, "Zur Entwicklung des österreichischen Nationalbewußtseins" in the Austrian Resistance Archive's *Jahrbuch 1987*, pp. 42-62; Karl Stadler, *Austria* (London: Benn, Ltd., 1977), pp. 181-204; Kurt Steiner, *Politics in Austria*, (Boston: Little, Brown, and Co., 1972), pp. 11-21.

[8] Bruce Pauley, *Hitler and the Forgotten Nazis: A History of Austrian National Socialism* (London: Macmillan, 1981); revised German edition: *Der Weg in den Nationalsozialismus. Ursprünge und Entwicklung in Österreich* (Vienna: Österreichischer Bundesverlag, 1988).

the fact that there were, according to Gerhard Botz, by 1942 almost 700,000 members of the NSDAP in what had been Austria.⁹ By 1945, Austrians, as budding patriots and democrats, perceived German National Socialism as something foreign, and Allied policy reinforced this mode of perception by distinguishing between the way Austria and Germany as states as well as Austrians and Germans as individuals were treated.

It is also hard to estimate the importance of what may be called the *Gemütlichkeit*-effect. Generalizations about national character are as notoriously dangerous as they are notoriously effective. Despite the fact that Austrians considered themselves to be Germans in a broad sense of the word, they had a long tradition of distinguishing themselves from Germans, the Prussian being the epitome of Germanness from the Austrian point of view. However, the Austrian sense of Austrianness (*Österreichertum*) seldom corresponded to the idea of a small, independent Austrian state before 1938, and the development of the Austrian sense of nationhood can be described as a gradual process of collectively aligning an Austrian sense of historical particularity with the idea of political independence from Germany.

Hugo von Hofmannsthal classically formulated the differences between Prussians and Austrians in *Preusse und Österreicher* in 1915, and the type of distinctions he made were psychologically operative from 1938 to 1945 (and still are today), the *Piefke*, a perjorative expression in Austrian dialect for Northern Germans, being the epitome of the German.¹⁰ One brief example suffices

---

⁹Gerhard Botz, "Die österreichischen NSDAP Mitglieder" in Reinhard Mann, ed., *Die Nationalsozialisten. Analysen faschistischer Bewegungen* (Frankfurt: Klett-Cotta, 1980), pp. 109-118.

¹⁰Hugo von Hofmansthal, "Preusse und Österreicher" in Bernd Schoeller, ed., *Reden und Aufsätze II: 1914-1924* (Frankfurt: Fischer, 1979), vol. IX in *Gesammelte Werke*, pp. 459-461. For examples of the antipathies between Austrians and Germans during the era of Anschluss see Bruce Pauley, *Hitler and the Forgotten Nazis*, pp. 216-223; Karl Stadler, *Österreich 1938-1945 im Spiegel der NS-Akten* (Vienna: Herold, 1966), pp. 123-130; Maurice Williams, "The After-

to show how national stereotypes influenced the Allies. The epic brooding operas of a German composer like Richard Wagner can easily be identified with National Socialism. It is difficult to do the same with Johann Strauss' waltzes, and it would be equally difficult to deny the existence of a certain Austrian quality and the "subtle and disarming influence" it exercised on the Allies.[11] Gordon A. Craig once expressed the conjecture that Roosevelt and Churchill "were privately agreed that the Austrians were a jolly people who deserved much better treatment than the awful Germans,"[12] an assumption which has not been proved, but, it corresponds well to prevailing stereotypes nonetheless.

It has been argued that the Austrian state was a victim of National Socialism, but that the Austrian people were victims and accomplices of National Socialism. It is important to dis-tinguish between two levels of argumentation here: the first deals with Austria as a subject of international law, a state that was occupied by a foreign power and illegally deprived of its organs of government, not a democratic state in 1938 but a state nonetheless; the second deals with the history of the Austrian people—not in black-and-white categories that apparently mutually exclusive concepts like victim and accomplice tend to evoke, but rather sees that history in the many shades of gray that exist in between those extremes. One of the major problems in the immediate postwar years was that the legal framework of Austria's occupation by Nazi Germany was used by representatives of the Second Republic as the historical framework for interpreting the status of the Austrian people during the Anschluss, which, in

---

math of the Anschluß: Disillusioned Germans or Budding Austrian Patriots?" *Austrian History Yearbook,* XI (1978), 129f.

[11]Michael Balfour and John Mair, *Four Power Control in Germany and Austria 1945-1946* (London: Oxford University Press, 1956), p. 319.

[12]Gordon A. Craig, "The Waldheim File" in *The New York Review of Books,* October 9, 1986, p. 3.

turn, produced a number of terminological and historical distortions.

It was a fortunate coincidence that Allied tactical planning for postwar Europe corresponded to the national aspirations of the Austrian people because "weakening Germany, and not the support of an Austrian national idea, was the actual motivation for those [Allied] plans for the reestablishment of Austria."[13] The foundations for the Second Republic were laid in Moscow in October 1943 at a conference of the Allied foreign ministers, and the first jointly formulated Allied policy statement on Austria, the Moscow Declaration, *dictated* the conditions for the reestablishment of Austria and simultaneously established a framework through which Austria had to interpret the Anschluss. Despite its brevity, the Moscow Declaration was a complicated document that combined psychological warfare with a statement of Allied policy using terminology that had far-reaching legal implications in the postwar era.[14] It consisted of five individual clauses—an introductory cluster of three separated by an ominous "however" from a subsequent conditional cluster of two:

> The Government of the United Kingdom, the Soviet Union, and the United States of America are agreed that Austria, the first free country to fall victim to Hitlerite aggression, shall be liberated from German domination [victim clause]. They regard the annexation imposed on Austria by Germany on March 15, 1938, as null and void [annulment clause]. They consider themselves in no way bound by any changes effected in Austria since that date. They declare that they wish to see reestablished a free and

---

[13] Fritz Fellner, "Die außenpolitische und völkerrechtliche Stellung Österreichs 1938. Österreichs Wiederherstellung als Kriegsziel der Alliierten" in Erika Weinzierl and Kurt Skalnik, eds., *Österreich. Die zweite Republik*, 2 vols. (Vienna: Styria, 1972), I, 64.

[14] For a pregnant analysis of the political genealogy of the Moscow Declaration and its consequences see Gerald Stourzh, *Geschichte des Staatsvertrages 1945-1955. Österreichs Weg zur Neutralität* (Graz: Styria, 1975; 2nd rev. ed., 1980), pp. 1-5.

independent Austria [reestablishment clause], and thereby open the way for the Austrian people themselves, as well as those of neighboring states which will be faced with similar problems, to find that political and economic security which is the only basis for lasting peace. Austria is reminded, however, that she has a responsibility which she cannot evade for participation in the war on the side of Hitlerite Germany [responsibility-accomplice clause], and that in the final settlement account will inevitably be taken of her own contribution to her liberation [incentive-contribution clause].[15]

The most important clause in the first part of the declaration was the annulment clause because it provided the legal basis for Austria's status as a victim and retroactively established the continuity of Austria as a subject of international law, that is as an occupied state that was to be reestablished. (Up until the Moscow Declaration, the Western Allies, tacitly at least, had recognized the Anschluss.) However, the second part of the declaration was inconsistent with the first part because it made Austria as an occupied state responsible for participating in the war on the side of Nazi Germany. The exact wording of the Moscow Declaration is exceptionally important because it addresses *Austria,* not *the Austrians,* and it left the status of Austria unclear. Was Austria an enemy state and quasi-ally of Nazi Germany that had to be defeated or an occupied state that had to be liberated? It could not be both.

The "Proclamation of Independence (*Selbstständigkeit*)" issued by the representatives of the Socialist Party of Austria (SPÖ), Austrian People's Party (ÖVP), and Communist Party of Austria (KPÖ) on April 27, 1945, provided the domestic basis for the reestablishment of the Second Republic and referred to the individual clauses of the Moscow Declaration. The proclamation closed by quoting the clauses of the Moscow Declaration

---

[15]*Foreign Relations of the United States,*1943, I, 761 (hereafter cited as *FRUS*).

that were concerned with Austria's responsibility and contribution, which were interpreted in the spirit of the exact wording of the Moscow Declaration in the following manner:

> ... the impending state government will without delay initiate measures in order to make every possible contribution to its [Austria's] liberation; however, it sees itself compelled to ascertain that this contribution, in light of the exhaustion of our people and the exploitation (*Entgüterung*) of our country, regretably can be only modest.[16]

In other words, the state of Austria could assume a responsibility for contributing to her own liberation only after the proclamation of April 27, 1945, established an Austrian government that could act as an agent of the state.

Representatives of the Second Republic did not formally have an opportunity to discuss the issue of responsibility with the Allies until a meeting of Allied "deputies" responsible for the negotiation of a treaty with Austria in London in January 1947, but in the immediate postwar period a dual argument was formulated to deal with the question of responsibility as a legal issue which went as follows: Despite the Anschluss, Austria as a subject of international law had never ceased to exist [the argument of legal continuity]. However, the Anschluss had robbed Austria of its legal organs of government and representation [the argument of factual discontinuity]. Austria was in fact reestablished on April 27, 1945, with the proclamation of independence and establishment of the provisional government under Karl Renner's leadership in the spirit of the Constitution of 1920-1929. However, according to the argument of legal continuity, Austria was neither a territorial nor a legal successor to the Third Reich, nor parts thereof, nor a new state, but was juridically identical with the First Republic. Consequently, April 27, 1945, marked

---

[16]*Staatsgesetzblatt für die Republik Österreich*,1945, St. 1, Nr. 1, May 1, 1945, p. 2.

the reestablishment of a *status quo ante* in terms of international law and with regard to the Austrian constitution.[17]

The purpose of the argument for legal continuity was to affirm Austria's status as a state despite the Anschluss and Allied occupation: it was to justify Austria's status as a victim of Nazi Germany, on the one hand, and to make the conditions of Austria's reentry into the community of nations after a seven-year absence appear less negotiable than they actually were, on the other. Given the fact that there was no Austrian government between March 1938 and April 1945, representatives of the Second Republic viewed the legal responsibility for the war either as a question of Germany's state responsibility as an aggressor that had occupied Austria or as a question of individual Austrians' responsibility in service of Nazi Germany. In this manner, the issue of responsibility was split into issues of domestic and foreign policy, each of which, however, was subject to inter-Allied and Austrian-Allied negotiations: the State Treaty and denazification.

As an issue of foreign policy, Austria did not demand reparations from Germany, although there technically was a legal basis for this claim, nor did Austria as an occupied country feel legally bound to pay reparations to other states, although the moral obligation to have done so is a different issue. Within the context of the negotiation of the State Treaty, Austria insisted on being treated as a victim of Nazi Germany as stated in the Moscow Declaration, and the fact that there was a clause concerning Austrian responsibility in the preamble of the draft of the treaty

---

[17] See Stephan Verosta, *Die internationale Stellung Österreichs. Eine Sammlung von Erklärungen und Dokumenten aus den Jahren 1938 bis 1947* (Vienna: Manzsche Verlagsbuchhandlung, 1947), pp. 1-9; Wilhelm Brauneder and Frederich Lachmayer, *Österreichische Verfassungsgeschichte*, 3rd ed. (Vienna: Manz, 1978), pp. 248-255; Ludwig Jedlicka, "Verfassungs- und Verwaltungs-Probleme 1938-1945" in *Vom Alten zum neuen Österreich* (St. Pölten: Niederösterreichisches Pressehaus, 1977), pp. 399-426.

was a source of concern.[18] As a domestic issue related to the Allied occupation and administration of Austria, the Austrian government insisted that denazification and the prosecution of former Nazi Party members as well as Nazi war criminals of Austrian origin fell into the Austrian, not the Allied, realm of legislative and executive jurisdiction, a point which the Allies conceded in the fall of 1946.[19]

In the immediate postwar period, one of the dilemmas Austrian politicians confronted was that of wishing to deny Austrian state responsibility for the war as a principle of foreign policy but, simultaneously, also wanting to assume responsibility for the domestic prosecution of a considerable number of former Nazis—536,000 were registered after the war—and to do so without jeopardizing, in the eyes of the Allies, Austria's status as victim.

When the negotiation of the State Treaty began, the Yugoslavian delegation forced the issue of responsibility by demanding the cession of 2600 square kilometers of territory inhabited by Slovene minorities in Carinthia and Styria and based part of its claims on the assumption that Austria had a responsibility for participating in the war on the side of Hitlerite Germany.[20] In a memorandum circulated to the Allied deputies responsible for

---

[18] *FRUS*, 1947, 11, 518.

[19] See Dieter Stiefel, *Entnazifizierung in Österreich* (Vienna: Europaverlag, 1981), pp. 94-100.

[20] The Yugoslavian memorandum circulated to the Allied deputies asserted: "Two principles had been laid down in the Moscow Declaration: the reestablishing of independent Austria and the responsibility of Austria for taking part in the war on the side of Hitlerite Germany." An abbreviated version of this memorandum has been reprinted in *Documents on the Carinthian Question*, (Beograd: Ministry of Foreign Affairs, 1948). Based on the exact wording of the Moscow Declaration, the Soviet Union supported the Yugoslavian argument, partly because its logic reinforced Soviet claims to the "German assets" in Eastern Austria. See *FRUS*, 1947, II, 114-124 and Gerald Stourzh, *Geschichte des Staatsvertrages*, pp. 27-32.

the negotiation of the State Treaty, the Austrian delegation outlined its position:

> Austria desires that the preamble of the treaty clearly state that Austria is a liberated country and that her independence be formally reestablished.... Austria rejects the conception that she can be made responsible for actions which were committed by German occupational force because no Austrian state and no Austrian government existed after March 1938. The Austrian position is that Austrians were forced into the service of German war organizations just as the citizens of other occupied territories were. Therefore, she hopes that the principle will be laid down in the treaty that Austria should not be burdened with reparations.[21]

On January 30, 1947, Federal Chancellor Leopold Figl addressed the Allied Deputies, and his argumentation provides a good example of Austria's official postwar legal and historical interpretation of the Anschluss:

> The forced annexation of Austria took place in a period in which the Fascist regimes had reached their apex [the argument of geopolitics of fascism]. The fact that there was no military reaction on the part of the Great Powers and that the diplomatic reactions were very weak was bound to discourage the Austrians even further [the argument of split responsibility or policy of appeasement]. It would therefore be unfair to hold those Austrians who were forced into the service of Hitler's war machine fully responsible for their now tragic fate [the argument of the force of totalitarian circumstances]. Austria herself could not be forced into Hitler's war, as she had been totally occupied by the invaders and deprived of her Government [the argument of factual discontinuity], but Austrians were finally forced indi-

---

[21] "Memorandum der österreichischen Bundesregierung, der Konferenz der Sonderbeauftragten für den österreichischen Staatsvertrag in London vorgelegt am 19. Jänner, 1947" cited in Eva-Marie Csáky, ed., *Der Weg zur Freiheit und Neutralität: Dokumente zur österreichischen Außenpolitik 1945-1955* (Vienna: Österreichische Gesellschaft für Außenpolitik, 1980), p. 121.

vidually to serve Hitler's war machine [the argument of individual responsibility]. Austria was not the only country with Quislings[22] [the argument citing collaboration elsewhere]; on the contrary, this species existed in numerous European countries. Therefore, it would be completely unjustified to judge Austria upon the basis of that small minority which voluntarily served the German policies of aggression [the argument of the minority or minimalization].[23]

The plausibility of this form of argumentation has to be seen in light of the backgrounds of the Austrian delegation. Figl, for example, was on the first transport of Austrian prisoners the Nazis sent from Vienna to Dachau on April 2, 1938, and he spent the duration of the war in concentration camps. Vice Chancellor Adolf Schärf came out of the underground, and Foreign Minister Karl Gruber had been active in resistance from 1938 on and was responsible for the liberation of Innsbruck before American soldiers arrived in the city. Given their experiences, they could, with clear consciences, speak of Austria as a victim.

Figl argued with the insights of 1945 and attempted to portray the majority of Austrians as victims of National Socialism, which involved minimalizing the degree of the Austrians' collaboration—be it forced or voluntary—and drawing parallels between Austria and other occupied countries. This form of argumentation extended the logic of the theory of Austria as an occupied country or victim of the Anschluss from the state level to the one of individuals. If, in international law, the state of Austria had a status similar to that of other states occupied by Nazi Germany—and after the Moscow Declaration in 1943 it did— then the population of Austria had a status similar to that of other occupied states, like the Belgians or the Czechs.

---

[22]Vidkun Quisling (1887-1945), a Norwegian fascist who collaborated with the Nazis during the occupation of Norway.

[23]Excerpt cited in *FRUS*, 1947, II, 120; full text in Eva-Marie Csáky, *Der Weg zur Freiheit*, p. 123.

However, the factual differences between the Austrians and the populations of other occupied territories were enormous. Although the Austrians increasingly began to perceive the Anschluss as a foreign occupation in the course of the war, the German occupiers were not as foreign as they were elsewhere, nor were the conditions of occupation in Austria comparable in many respects to those prevailing in other occupied states. Within the framework of the Third Reich, Austrians had, for example, a juridical and, in many cases, psychological position as Germans, which was an essential feature of their self-perception. Consequently, both the quantity and the quality of Austrians' involvement in National Socialism and the Nazi war effort was different from what others did. Almost 700,000 Austrians were members of the National Socialist Party, and approximately 1.2 million Austrians served in German units during the war, ranging from the *Schutz Staffel* (SS) to the regular armed forces. These facts make a liberal application of the theory of occupation historically incredible; at this point, the historical inadequacy of the legal terminology of the theory of occupation is most evident. Nevertheless, the interpretation of Austria as an occupied victim of the Anschluss corresponded well to the way many Austrians felt after the war and reflected Austria's nascent national consciousness to a certain extent.

Three phenomena converged at this point: the legal terminology of the occupation-victim theory of the Anschluss, an Austrian postwar psychology that had been colored by the hardships and sufferings of the war and the immediate postwar period, and an Austrian national consciousness that was non-German or, in some cases, even anti-German. The Germans were the Nazis and the Austrians were the victims. This attitude, a national delusion that was psychologically understandable but historically untenable, hindered, to a great extent, an accurate appraisal of Austrian's involvement in National Socialism. It also leveled crucial moral, political, and historical distinctions among (1) the Austrian victims of National Socialism who were systematically murdered for racial and political reasons, as were 65,000 Austrian Jews or some 30,000 Austrians involved in resistance who were executed or died in Nazi concentration camps and prisons; (2) the Austrian victims of the war as one of the circumstances of National Socialism, such as the 250,000 Austrians who died in German uniform and the 30,000 Austrian civilians killed in Allied bombing and military action; and (3) the Austrian victims of the immediate postwar period which, in many respects, was harder on the civilian population than the war itself. (Immediately after the war, Austrians had to survive on 500-800 calories per day. In a speech on Christmas Day, 1945, Federal Chancellor Figl told the Austrians: "I can give you nothing; not a piece of bread, no coal to heat, no glass to repair your broken windows.")[24]

The greatest inadequacy of the victim-theory of the Anschluss was that it did not adequately distinguish between the logic of the concentration camps, the logic of the battlefield, and the consequences of the war, and it consequently allowed Austrians who may have been accomplices of National Socialism before 1945 to consider themselves bona fide victims thereof thereafter. Not only the experience of the Anschluss and the war psychologically colored Austrians' attitudes towards the years between 1938 and 1945. Their postwar experiences did so as well. A recent opinion-poll in Austria revealed that the percentage of Austrians who consider Austria a victim of National Socialism is highest in Lower Austria and Burgenland, two provinces where the conditions of occupation were especially severe because they were occupied by the Soviet Union.[25]

---

[24]Figl cited in Roman Sandgruber, "Vom Hunger zum Massenkonsum" in Gerhard Jagschitz and Klaus-Dieter Mulley, eds., *Die 'wilden' fünfziger Jahre*, (St. Pölten: Niederösterreichisches Pressehaus, 1985), p. 112. According to Sandgruber, the average number of calories per normal consumer was 3,200 before the war, 2,000 in 1944, 500-800 in the summer of 1945, 1,183 in the summer of 1946, and 1,800 in the summer of 1947.

[25]Gerhard Jelinek, "Sinneswandel," in *Die Wochenpresse*, Nr. 14, April 8,

A series of international and diplomatic factors contributed to inhibiting a full-fledged discussion of the Anschluss era in postwar Austria. As long as the conditions of the Austrian State Treaty were negotiable—until 1955—it was a matter of national interest and common sense for Austria to use the victim-status granted in the Moscow Declaration as the basis for self-representation. Austria and Austrians' roles in the Third Reich, and the consequences thereof, were issues related to the negotiation of the State Treaty, and those issues became entangled in the dynamics of the Cold War.

The Cold War brought the negotiation of the State Treaty to an impasse, and it also shifted the priorities of United States policy in Austria. The United States was the occupational power which had come to Austria with the most ambitious program of denazification. Despite the fact that the Soviet Union had pursued a relatively lax program of denazification in its own zones of occupation, it began to use denazification as an obstructive issue in the joint administration of Austria and the negotiation of the State Treaty. Aside from wanting to deprive the Soviets of this tactical ploy, by 1947 anti-communism had become a much higher priority of the United States than was anti-Nazism. The Cold War, Austria's western orientation, and Austria's own indigenous anti-communism made the Anschluss era and denazification secondary issues for the United States, which subordinated its policy of denazification in Austria to the tactical demands of the "containment" of communism on national and international levels. The Cold War made reliable anti-communists more important than reeducated former Nazis.[26]

1988, p. 32. According to the results of the poll, Lower Austria and Burgenland had the highest provincial averages of respondents calling Austria a victim of National Socialism (66%) and the lowest provincial averages for calling Austria an accomplice of National Socialism.

[26]See Oliver Rathkolb, "U.S.-Entnazifizierung in Österreich. Zwischen kontrollierter Revolution und Eliten Restauration, 1945-1949" *Zeitgeschichte*, 11. Jahr, Heft 9/10 (June/July 1984), 302-323; Robert Knight, "Kalter Krieg, Entnazi-

The final draft of the Austrian State Treaty contained a reiteration of the responsibility-clause of the Moscow Declaration which read:

> Whereas, following this annexation, Austria, as an integral part of Nazi Germany, participated in the war against the Allied and Associated Powers and other United Nations, and whereas Germany made use for this purpose of Austrian territory, troops, and material resources, and Austria cannot avoid a responsibility arising from this participation in the war; . . . .[27]

Austria found this passage politically and legally unacceptable because it stated that the Republic of Austria had participated in the war on the side of Nazi Germany. On the eve of the signing of the State Treaty, May 14, 1955, Austrian Foreign Minister Leopold Figl requested that the assembled Allied foreign ministers strike this clause from the preamble, arguing in the following manner:

> [If Austria] should appear from this point on as a principally neutral state with the special political and moral tasks and responsibilities of such a state and find and realize in this role her future political *raison d'être* (*Staatsidee*) in a certain respect, . . . [then it would be] . . . inappropriate and contradictory to brand this new Austrian neutrality and peace factor with a mark of guilt, and, in doing so, to burden Austria's internal and external development with a moral mortgage.[28]

The Allied foreign ministers honored Figl's request.

Technically speaking, Figl's request was legitimate because it was based on the legal argumentation of the occupation-theory of

---

fizierung und Österreich" in Sebastian Meissl, Klaus-Dieter Mulley, and Oliver Rathkolb, eds., *Verdrängte Schuld, Verfehlte Sühne. Entnazifizierung in Österreich 1945-1955* (Vienna: Verlag für Geschichte und Politik, 1986), pp. 37-51.

[27] *FRUS*, 1947, II, 518.

[28] Cited in Gerald Stourzh, *Staatsvertrag*, p. 167.

the Anschluss and the factual discontinuity of an Austrian government from 1938 until 1945. However, the deletion of this passage appears to have the status of an official historical revision, which was sanctioned by the signatory powers, because Figl argued against branding Austria with a "mark of guilt" or burdening it with a "moral mortgage." Figl acted as a politician representing Austria's national interest, not as a historian, arguing for Austria's future against part of the Austrians' past. Nevertheless, he seems to have been well aware of the political and historical implications of this passage and apparently was willing legally and historically to dispense with the issue of responsibility—which meant that it was something that the Federal Republic of Germany would have to carry alone.

The political rationale for portraying Austria *and* Austrians as victims of National Socialism outlived its pragmatic justification—the signing of the State Treaty which led to the reestablishment of full Austrian sovereignty in 1955—to become a component of Austria's history and national identity. In 1945, the victim-clause of the Moscow Declaration functioned as a positive point of orientation for the development of the Austrian national identity which was reinforced in 1955 by Austrian neutrality.

The persistency of the official Austrian interpretation of Austrians' history is perhaps best illustrated by the fact that on May 8, 1985, the fortieth anniversary of the defeat of Nazi Germany, no official commemorations were held in Austria because, I assume, Austria had not participated in the war. Nevertheless, many Austrians did, and there were almost 100,000 victims of National Socialism and almost 300,000 victims of the war to commemorate, victims and "victims." However, the president of the Federal Republic of Germany, Richard von Weizsäcker, son of a leading Nazi diplomat and a former officer in the German Wehrmacht himself, gave an unprecedented speech in which he asked his countrymen "to look the truth straight in the eye—without embellishment and without distortion" and in which he called May 8, 1945 ". . . a day of liberation. It liberated all of us from the inhumanity of the National Socialist regime."[29] In light of the fact that Germany was defeated, occupied, and divided, von Weizsäcker's speech established new historical standards. High-ranking representatives of the Second Republic have not yet found such an unprecedentedly clear terminology. Austria was "liberated" in 1945, occupied, and—to use Anton Pelinka's phrase— "liberated from the liberators in 1955."[30]

A number of domestic and institutional factors contributed to postponing the discussion of the Anschluss era. First and foremost was the pragmatic consensus, after the war, between the political elites of the SPÖ and the ÖVP, which provided the basis for coalition governments up until 1966. Having fought a civil war against each other in 1934, the Socialists and the Conservatives had to bury many of their ideological and historical differences in 1945 in order to co-operate, and in 1948, when an amnesty for the so-called "less-incriminated" Nazis reinstated them with their right to vote and spilled a half million new voters into the political arena, the Socialists and Conservatives pragmatically buried the years 1938 to 1945 as well. Austria's initial programs of denazification between 1945 and 1948 were rigorous; whether they were followed by a creeping renazification after 1949 is a controversial issue. One point of view is that the SPÖ and ÖVP indiscriminately courted former Nazis; the other is that they helped reintegrate them into a democratic society.[31]

Another factor is that the low-friction-atmosphere of coop-

---

[29] *Bulletin: Presse und Informationsdienst der BRD*, Nr. 52, Bonn, May 9, 1985, pp. 441-442.

[30] See Anton Pelinka's contribution to this volume, pp. 173.

[31] Compare, for example, the pointed criticism of Anton Pelinka, *Windstille. Klagen über Österreich* (Vienna: Medussa, 1985), pp. 88-102, or Josef Haslinger, *Politik der Gefühle. Ein Essay über Österreich* (Darmstadt: Luchterhand, 1987), pp. 65-81, with Dieter Stiefel's pragmatic approach in his *Entnazifizierung in Österreich*, pp. 325-333 or his "Nazifizierung plus Entnazifizierung = Null? Bemerkungen zur besonderen Problematik der Entnazifizierung in Österreich" in Sebastian Meissl, et al., eds., *Verdrängte Schuld, Verfehlte Sühne*, pp. 28-36.

eration and consensus, which has been one of the keys to the economic and political success of the Second Republic, has not been conducive to conflicts, especially the kind that a discussion of National Socialism involves because it is not the type of issue that is either raised or resolved in the spirit of neocorporative bargaining. The term "coalition historiography" has been frequently used to describe the convenient interpretation of the Anschluss era that prevailed in Austria up until the Waldheim affair, its main shortcoming being that it implies some sort of active conspiracy to conceal the past and downplays how stormy the coalitions were. Nonetheless, a recent study of Austrian secondary-school history books, which can be regarded as official history in so far as they have to be approbated before publication by the Ministry of Education and serve as the basis of instruction in schools, showed to what extent a distorted picture of the Anschluss era still officially prevails.[32]

The fact that the study of contemporary history was institutionalized much later in Austria than in the Federal Republic of Germany certainly also played a role in Austria's belated confrontation with the Anschluss era, and a direct comparison of Allied policy in each country is one explanation for this phenomenon. The Allies granted the Austrian government the responsibility for denazification in Austria in 1946-1947, but they executed the programs of denazification and reeducation themselves in Germany. In other words, the Germans were forced to look at their immediate past in a manner which the Austrians were spared. As a matter of national identity and political legitimacy, the Germans had to explain National Socialism as a historical aberration, not a logical consequence of German history,[33] and

---

[32] See Peter Malina and Gustav Spann, "Der Nationalsozialismus im österreichischen Geschichtslehrbuch" in Emmerich Tálos, Ernst Hanisch, and Wolfgang Neugebauer, eds., *NS-Herrschaft in Österreich 1938-1945* (Vienna: Verlag für Gesellschaftskritik, 1988), pp. 577-600.

[33] For an analysis of the changes in the German historiography of National

German interpretations of National Socialism could not avoid the question of responsibility. Austria, in comparison, could avoid the question because, according to the occupation-victim theory of the Anschluss, the years between 1938 and 1945 were, technically speaking, a matter of German responsibilitiy.

The fact that Austrian institutions dealing with the research of National Socialism and contemporary history were founded sixteen years later than their counterparts in Germany may reflect the lack of political immediacy that historical justification and explanation had in postwar Austria. In Germany, for example, the Institute for the Research of National Socialist Politics (*Institut zur Erforschung der National-Sozialistischen Politik*) was chartered in Baden-Würtemberg in 1947 and the Institute of Contemporary History at the University of Munich was founded in 1950. The initiative of Herbert Steiner led to the foundation of the Austrian Resistance Archive (*Dokumentationsarchiv des österreichischen Widerstandes* in 1963, and in 1966, Ludwig Jedlicka founded the Institute for Contemporary History at the University of Vienna. The practitioners of contemporary history in Austria today are in many respects Jedlicka's academic children and grandchildren.

Jedlicka, his succsssor as chairman at the Institute of Contemporary History, Erika Weinzierl, and Karl Stadler were the first Austrian historians to do case-studies on National Socialism in Austria in the early and mid-sixties,[34] and monographs by Gerhard Botz and Radomír Luža, *Die Eingliederung Österreichs*

Socialism, see Hans Mommsen, "Aufarbeitung und Verdrängung. Das Dritte Reich im westdeutschen Geschichtsbewußtsein" in Dan Diner, ed., *Ist der Nationalsozialismus Geschichte? Zu Historisierung und Historikerstreit* (Frankfurt: Fischer, 1987), pp. 74-88. In the same volume, Gerhard Botz discusses the Austrian relationship to the Nazi era in "Österreich und die NS-Vergangenheit. Verdrängung, Pflichterfüllung, Geschichtsklitterung," pp. 141-152.

[34] For a brief overview of the problems related to the Austrian interpretation of the Anschluss, see the introduction to Emmerich Tálos, et al., *NS-Herrschaft in Österreich*, pp. ix-xiii.

in das Dritte Reich (1972) and *Austro-German Relations in the Anschluss Era* (1975), broke new historical ground in the early seventies. The 1978 commemoration produced a wave of publications;[35] 1988 has resulted in a virtual flood: a tentative bibliography of Anschluss-related literature listed 132 (predominately book-length) publications by May 1988.[36]

However, one obstacle historians face in their research work in Austria is the fact that many relevant documents do not become part of the public domain for fifty years. Archivists also may use—and have used—the stipulations of Austria's laws on privacy of information to restrict access to documents, whether they fall under the stipulation of the laws or not, and there is no uniform legislation regulating the use of archives because some of them fall into the federal realm of competence, others into the legislative and administrative discretion of the provinces or local authorities. In other words, in 1988, fifty years after the Anschluss, historians in some cases do not have access to the documents they need to study 1939. A revision of Austrian legislation dealing with archives is urgently needed, a fact recognized by politicians, scholars, and archivists alike. Scholars hope that new legislation will anchor their right to use archival material, shorten the limitation of time before they have access to materials, and provide for an instance that will be able to mediate disputes between scholars and archivists related to the interpretation of laws on privacy of information.

The interpretation of the interwar circumstances that led to the demise of Austrian democracy in 1933-1934 overshadows how Austrians interpreted 1938. The issue at stake here is who was domestically responsible, or more responsible, for creating

---

[35]The most notable 1978 monographs were Gerhard Botz's *Wien vom Anschluß zum Krieg* (note 6) and Norbert Schausberger's *Der Griff nach Österreich* (note 4).

[36]See *Dokumentationsarchciv des österreichischen Widerstandes Mitteilungen*, Folge 86, May 1988, pp. 8-14.

a state of affairs that facilitated the Anschluss in 1938—the Austrian Social Democrats with their Austromarxism or the Conservatives with their authoritarian ideology of political Catholicism? Divergent interpretations of two events suffice as brief illustrations.

In February 1934, a three-day civil war that ended with the defeat of Austrian Social Democracy prefaced the establishment of a one-party regime, the Christian Corporate State, under Engelbert Dollfuss' leadership—a regime which its Conservative proponents called authoritarian and its Socialist opponents called Austrofascist. In July 1934, there was an attempted *Putsch* by Austrian Nazis which the Christian Corporate State put down but which also cost Dollfuss his life.

The Socialist interpretation of February 1934 and the Conservative interpretation of July 1934 each reflect how they view their own merits and their opponents' shortcomings. In February 1934, the Socialists defended Austrian democracy, and in July 1934 Dollfuss' authoritarian regime defended Austrian independence; the Socialists fought the Austrofascists and lost, and the Dollfuss regime fought the Nazis and won, for the time being at least; for Socialists, Dollfuss was a fascist who presided over the bloodbath of February 1934, but for Conservatives he was a martyr for Austrian independence in July 1934. For the Socialists, fascist rule began in Austria in 1934, but for Conservatives it began in 1938. To date, Socialists and Conservatives have not agreed on what kind of regime the Christian Corporate State was. Socialists subsume it with Hitler's Germany and Mussolini's Italy under the term "fascist," a designation the Conservatives reject. The Socialists were the victims of the Austrofascists in 1934, and the Austrians were the victims of Nazi Germany in 1938.

From the Conservative point of view, one of the Socialists' greatest shortcomings was that they inhibited the development of an Austrian national consciousness because, up until Hitler came to power in 1933, the Socialists had been the proponents of an

Anschluss with Germany. In addition to this, Dr. Karl Renner, the senior Social Democrat statesman in Austria in 1938, gave an interview shortly before the Nazi plebiscite on April 10, 1938, in which he objected to the method in which the Anschluss was executed but nevertheless called it "a satisfaction for the humiliations of 1918 and 1919" and said that he would vote *Ja*.[37] After the Anschluss, the Socialists reassumed the Anschluss as a traditional goal, which Otto Bauer reformulated. Shortly before his death in Parisian exile in 1938, Bauer called the reestablishment of Austria a "reactionary slogan" and called for a "unified German revolution" (*gesamtdeutsche Revolution*)—a maintenance of the Anschluss after the German-speaking proletariat's envisioned victory over Nazism.[38]

Apologists for Austria's authoritarian regime stress the fact that it strived to maintain Austrian independence and contributed to the development of an Austrian national consciousness.[39] However, the domestic unpopularity of the Christian Corporate State was one of the prime sources of its weak foreign policy with Nazi Germany. The Christian-corporate ideology of Austrian independence also should not be confused with Austrian nationalism as we see it today. In Schuschnigg's speech of resignation on March 11, 1938, the day before the Anschluss, he justified his decision not to defend Austria militarily by saying " . . . we are not willing, even in this dire hour, to spill German blood, . . ."[40]—German blood being Austrian and German.

---

[37]*Wiener Tagblatt*, April 3, 1938, p. 1, cited in Gerhard Botz, *Wien vom Anschluß zum Krieg*, p. 143.

[38]Otto Bauer, *Werkausgabe*, vol. IX (Vienna: Europaverlag, 1980), p. 855.

[39]See Gottfried Karl Kindermann, *Hitler's Defeat in Austria: Europe's First Containment of Nazi Expansion*, trans. S. Brough and D. Taylor (London: C. Hurst, 1988).

[40]"Abschiedsrede des Bundeskanzlers Dr. Schuschnigg am 11. März 1938 um 20 Uhr" in *Rot-Weiß-Rot Buch: Gerechtigkeit für Österreich*, Erster Teil, (Vienna: Österreichische Staatsdruckerei, 1946), p. 63.

Shortly before the Nazi plebiscite in April 1938, the Austrian bishops, former pillars of the Christian Corporate State's Catholic-authoritarian ideology, issued a pastoral letter which stated that it was a "self-evident national duty" for "believing Christians" to profess their allegiance as "Germans to the German Reich."[41]

It is a moot question whether more democracy in Austria or more Austrian patriotism would have changed the course of events in 1938, but the fiftieth anniversary of 1934 in 1984 showed how sensitive and unresolved these issues still are. One of the key terms in the 1984 debate about 1934 was "divided guilt" (*geteilter Schuld*)[42] which reflected a certain inability to discuss the fate of the First Republic either in the spirit of mutual responsibility or in less politically and morally loaded terms like "historical causality."

Austrian academicians abandoned the victim-theory of the Anschluss long before the Waldheim affair erupted in 1986. Despite its numerous controversial domestic and international manifestations, the Waldheim affair provided historians with an unprecedented amount of access to public opinion which, conbined with the fiftieth anniversary of 1938, became the basis for an unprecedented national debate about the Anschluss era. The manner in which Kurt Waldheim dealt with his past polarized Austria between apologetic and critical schools of thought, and, for the latter, Waldheim's inability to deal critically with his own past came to symbolize an indefensibly apologetic interpretation

---

[41] This pastoral letter appeared in various newspapers on March 18, 1938, such as the *Reichpost* and the *Völkischer Beobachter*. Cited in Erika Weinzierl, "Kirche und Nationalsozialismus in Wien im März 1938" in Felix Czeike, ed., *Wien 1938* (Vienna: Verein für die Geschichte der Stadt Wien, 1978), pp. 169-170.

[42] See Norbert Leser, "Eine Kronzeuge der historischen Wahrheit: Wilhelm Ellenbogen und die These der 'Mitschuld' der Sozialdemokratie," *Zukunft*, Heft 2 (February 1984), 13-23.

of the Anschluss era. How he dealt with his personal history began to represent how Austria had officially dealt with hers.

The bitter controversy not only about what Waldheim had done in the past but, more important, about what he knew about the past and how he interpreted it contributed to the dissemination of the results of research and to the propagation of a critical interpretation of the Anschluss era. His candidacy and election helped publicly to dismantle the victim-theory of the Anschluss, and his presidency marked a turning point in the official Austrian interpretation of the Anschluss as well as the Austrian public's general awareness of what happened in Austria and Europe between 1938 and 1945.

A comparison of the nationally televised address dealing with the fiftieth anniversary of the Anschluss that Waldheim gave on March 10, 1988, with Figl's statement before the Allied deputies responsible for the negotiation of the State Treaty in 1947 is revealing because Figl's statement, despite its age, is symptomatic of the official interpretation of the Anschluss that prevailed in Austria up into the eighties. Like Figl, Waldheim stressed the fact that "... although Austria resisted the political and economic pressure of Hitler for years as no other country did, it went under [the argument on the geopolitics of fascism]." He mentioned that "... the international community of nations gave us no help against the aggression [the argument on the policy of appeasement]," and stressed the fact that "... As a state, Austria was the first victim of Hitler ... [the argument of legal continuity-factual discontinuity." However, unlike Figl, Waldheim did not attempt to minimize Austrians' participation in or responsibility for the Anschluss and National Socialism, and he made the following important observations and qualifications:

"... But there were hundreds of thousands of Austrians who greeted the Anschluss, cheered Hitler and the occupation, and nurtured false hopes ... There were Austrians who were victims [of National Socialism] and others who were accomplices ... We may not forget that many of the worst myrmidons [*Scher-*

gen; base servants] of National Socialism were Austrians."
Waldheim's speech also contained an unprecedented apology: "Let us not create an impression that we did not have anything to do with this. It is evident that there is no collective guilt; nevertheless, as the Republic of Austria's Head of State, I want to apologize for the crimes of National Socialism commited by Austrians."[43] The personal aversion many people feel for the man Waldheim undoubtedly obscured the importance of what he said, and although Waldheim's lack of personal credibility lessened the impact of his speech, he spoke as Austria's head of state nonetheless.

An opinion-poll conducted in Austria by Gallup and the Austrian weekly, *Die Wochenpresse,* at the end of March 1988 showed the effects of the events surrounding the fiftieth anniversary of the Anschluss. Compared with the results of an identical poll held in September 1987, the March 1988 survey revealed that fewer Austrians were prepared to call Austria "the first victim of Nazi Germany" (1987: 48%, 1988: 45%) and more Austrians were willing to recognize Austria as "an accomplice (*Mittäter*) coresponsible for events up until 1945" (1987: 24%, 1988: 35%). This shift reflects a drop in the number of people who previously had had no opinion (1987: 28%, 1988: 20%) and the critical impact of the 1988 commemoration.

The poll revealed also to what extent the interpretation of the Anschluss is a generational and an educational issue. Among the Austrians questioned who were under thirty years of age, 37% opted for the victim-interpretation of the Anschluss, 37% for the accomplice-interpretation, and 26% were undecided, whereas among Austrians over fifty years old, the majority chose the victim-interpretation (51% victim, 31% accomplice, and 18% undecided). Levels of education also played a considerable role in responses. Among the Austrians surveyed who had a second-

---

[43]The full text of Waldheim's speech is reprinted in *Wiener Zeitung,* March 11, 1938, p. 4.

ary (*Matura*) or university degree, the majority (46%) chose the accomplice-theory (41% victim, 13% undecided).[44]

Whether the results of this poll are symptomatic of a long-term trend is something only time will tell, but many observers find this change in public opinion encouraging. Certainly there are a fair number of Austrians who would like to quit "tearing open old wounds," and for pessimists the changes achieved thanks to the Waldheim affair and the fifty-year-commemoration of the Anschluss are too little and too late. Optimists, however, have recognized them as being better late than never.

---

[44]See Gerhard Jelinek, "Sinneswandel," *Die Wochenpresse*, Nr. 14, April 8, 1988, pp. 30-32.

Austria Then and Now

Wolfgang Waldner

The commission of this article is to describe the present-day situation and the mood in Austria in comparison with Austria of fifty years ago. Since the author is neither a historian nor a witness of the Anschluss-period, this comparison will necessarily be an amateur's undertaking.

The point of view here is that of a young Austrian citizen who is deeply interested in his country's past, present and future, one who is also a diplomat, committed for the past seven years to serving his country.

A diplomat has the opportunity, on the one hand, to keep track of what is going on in Austria while witnessing, on the other hand, the process of change in international public opinion towards Austria. It has been extremely painful and upsetting to realize how easily an entire country and people can be exposed to misperception, misjudgment and even have their reputation seriously tarnished.

Contemporary Austria is entirely different from the Austria of fifty years ago, a difference which has been developing gradually ever since the end of World War II. This difference becomes rather obvious if one compares the commonly known circumstances which facilitated the Anschluss in 1938 with the present-day situation in Austria. In contrast with the 1920s and 1930s, Austrians of today have no problem of identity as a people or a nation. One could even go so far as to say that Austrians are sometimes too self-assured and too self-centered, which can create negative effects. The recent international criticism of their country caught many Austrians off guard. For some fifteen years they had lived under the illusion that Austria was an "island of the blessed" detached from the untoward things that happened in the rest of the world.

The Waldheim controversy, which many Austrians initially perceived as being forced upon them, constituted an unpleasant awakening for quite a number of people (or a slap in the face, as Professor Sully has put it). Not only were they forced to engage in discussions which they were not used to, or which they had avoided for years, Austrians all of a sudden were confronted with a more realistic view of their country and its possibilities in the international context. Austria, even to its less educated or naive citizens, is not the center of the world anymore, or the "heart of Europe," a notion which at least jokingly permitted the conclusion that Europe could not exist without that heart.

An Austrian may acquire a more realistic view of Austria when he notes that he may read *Le Monde* daily and be sobered by the knowledge that only after three months might one discover an article dealing with Austria. Such was the experience of this writer as a student in Paris. Although it was not a scientifically reliable indicator, it was the kind of experience that influences one's view about Austria's place and position in the international community.

Many Austrians, as a consequence of the international debate *in re* Waldheim, have adopted a more realistic view of their country, its power, its vulnerability, its exposure to international media and international politics. This is probably one of the lessons Austrians have learned, at least to some degree, from the events that have occurred since 1986.

Austria today has such a strong sense of national identity that the simple thought of a new Anschluss, even if it occurs only as a theoretical aspect with regard to Austria's ambition to join the European Community, can be called absurd. There can be no doubt that, despite many shortcomings, Austria of today holds a firm place among the most stable countries in the world in terms of social peace, a working pluralistic society and parliamentary democracy as well as a functioning market-oriented economy.

Professor Sully has remarked that the Austrian system is a "partially developed" and "deceptive democracy" where important decisions were taken in "substructures such as the so-called social partnership." It might be correct that this social partnership is not a perfect example of a highly democratic decision-making body, and it was not meant to be. On the other hand, it is largely owing to this social partnership that Austria became an economic success story after World War II. Although this forum for creating a behind-the-doors consensus among the major actors in the economic field, the "social partnership," might be outdated, it certainly helped Austria, over a number of decades, to become a prospering and socially stable country, and it was admired and studied by delegations from numerous foreign countries. François Mitterand in the late 1970s advocated a similar system for France during the campaign which led to his first election as president. All political parties represented in the Austrian parliament adhere to the principles of a pluralistic society and a western style parliamentary democracy. There is also, by and large, a consensus among the major parties concerning the most important issues of national interest particularly in matters of foreign policy and defense. This characteristic certainly distinguishes present-day Austria from 1938.

Austria's international activities in the fields of science and research, within the framework of the United Nations, and with regard to human rights, constitute another major difference compared with Austria of the 1930s. These international activities enable our country to play a considerable role in the community of nations, be it on a bilateral or a multilateral level, and thus add to the stability of our political, economic, and social system.

Contrary to a number of reports in foreign mass media, anti-Semitism is definitely not rampant in Austria, which is another difference from the 1930s. The definition of anti-Semitism is as controversial among scholars, politicians and opinion-poll-takers as are the methods of correctly measuring it. However, there is probably what has been called a generational aspect of anti-Semitism in Austria which means that Austrians of the world war generation are more likely to be anti-Semitic than young Austrians, born during or after World War II, who constitute today two-thirds of the total population. It is fairly safe to say that the overall degree of anti-Semitism in Austria today is not higher than in other western countries, including the United States. This is, of course, of little help to the victims of anti-Semitism, be they in Austria or elsewhere in the world. One must not underestimate or overlook certain undertones in the language of newspapers and politicians or the regrettable anti-Semitic incidents which became known and received special attention and coverage in the media over the past months and years. Austrians do have a special moral obligation to point their fingers at and to condemn every single incident of this kind.

Austrians, to a considerable degree, have come to terms with their past as far as the 1930s, the Anschluss, and their attitudes towards the Jewish population are concerned. This process is certainly not completed yet and it probably will never be, but which people can boast of truly having accomplished a similar task? And dealing with the past should not be primarily a collective activity. It should rather be the voluntary and continuing personal exercise of every thinking individual, a constant reevaluation and reexamination of one's thoughts, needs, and values with the purpose of finding proper guides for future conduct.

The process of overcoming the past, or *Vergangenheitsbewältigung*, has to some degree been going on in Austria for more than fifty years. It is a well-known fact that numerous Austrians started to regret and to reverse their attitudes towards the Nazi ideology already shortly after the Anschluss. The number of Austrians disappointed or disillusioned with Hitler grew as the end of the Nazi era approached. This number was added to those thousands who were willing to fight the Nazi regime from the very beginning, as did Mr. Fritz Molden and Minister Karl Gruber.

On the other hand, it is also an undeniable fact that hundreds of thousands, maybe millions, of Austrians have gladly accepted the Allied thesis in the Moscow Declaration of 1943 that Austria had been the first victim of Nazism. A large majority of Austrians has considered this thesis a most welcome excuse for not dealing with their own involvement or personal attitude during that period. And those hundreds of thousands who underwent the procedures of denazification probably also thought that they had in that way paid the price for their previous involvement. The predominant feeling and consensus of most Austrians at that time, for one or the other reason, was that it was better not to talk too much about the unpleasant past but rather to consider how to manage the present and future problems.

The new generations born after World War II were, for almost fifteen to twenty years, to a large extent excluded from information as well as debate about this dark chapter of Austrian history. Many Austrian parents and teachers were simply reluctant to talk about that time and their personal involvement. This writer's own experience in this context is a rather common one. The history taught in the schools until the end of the 1960s did not go beyond the year 1918. On the contrary, now students all learn and are taught from books that also cover the Nazi period.

The national and international discussion about the wartime-years of President Waldheim has certainly triggered and considerably sharpened the phenomenon which has now been taking place in Austria for more than two years: That is a very intensive debate of Austrians of all ages and social strata about Austria's role in the 1930s and during the Nazi period. Painful processes of soul-searching and heated discussions with colleagues, friends, and family members affected and still do affect, in one or the other way, most Austrians. In many instances parents suddenly were, and still are, confronted with embarrassing questions by their children and even grandchildren.

It is important to stress that, contrary to some simplifying reports in the mass media, the two discussions (Waldheim and

Austria's role in general) are essentially separate ones although they coincide and influence each other to a large extent. In particular, the events observing the fiftieth anniversary of the Anschluss were very often decoupled from the emotionally conducted debate concerning our president.

To the great relief of many Austrians, most of these events in remembrance took place in a calm and disciplined atmosphere and with a great deal of dignity. But there were also some unhappy incidents, one for example during a Sunday morning event in the Theater in der Josefstadt. Simon Wiesenthal, who participated as a guest of honor, was interrupted or insulted by someone in the audience. He remained calm and said: "There is one positive aspect already to be seen in these recent developments—the number of indifferent people has decreased." The whole audience rose and gave him a long applause while the people who had staged the incident left the theater or were led away by police.

The number, kind, and quality of events in this context is very impressive. They range from a so-called "Mahnwache" or commemorative guard near St. Stephen's Cathedral that went on for months in 1987, to hundreds of books, articles, radio and television reports, interviews, documentaries, and the like, dealing with that topic. Nobody can tell for sure how many discussions, lectures, symposia, and films were and still are being dedicated to that period of our history.

The culminating point was reached in March 1988, when one had the impression that officials were virtually racing from one event to the next. A number of prominent speakers, ranging from top representatives of government, political parties, religious communities, and cultural life to worldwide-known victims of the Nazis like Viktor Frankl and Simon Wiesenthal recalled that period on various occasions. The union of Austrian university students organized a several-days-long series of speeches, discussions, concerts, readings and exhibitions in numerous locations. A number of galleries and theaters had exhibitions and readings.

The Vienna State Opera had a nationwide broadcast featuring several speeches, one by Cardinal Koenig, and music by the famous composer Ernst Křenek, who had to leave Austria in 1938 and now lives in California. For many Austrians, one of the most moving experiences was the personal account of Alfred Maleta, a politician who later became president of the parliament. He described in a long interview on a prime-time radio transmission his tragic and horrible years in Mauthausen concentration camp.

Most of the speeches in one way or another referred to the dual role of Austrians in 1938. We were victims of Nazi aggression, as acknowledged by the Allies in 1943 and after the war. But we were also culprits. President Waldheim certainly found the right words in his speech on March 10, 1988, when he said:

> The mirror of our history does not reflect a single image. A people's image is multi-faceted. We must not forget that many of the worst Nazi torturers were Austrians. Austrians were victims and perpetrators. Let us not pretend that we have nothing to do with it. Of course, there is no such thing as collective guilt. Nevertheless, as the head of state of the Republic of Austria, I should like to apologize for Nazi crimes committed by Austrians....

In spite of various shortcomings and setbacks, such as anti-Semitic incidents or lack of understanding on part of the population, Austria is undergoing a purgative and healthy process. Through consciously facing up to its past, Austria is laying a solid foundation for its future.

There are several signs that Austria is currently at the threshold of a new era and a comprehensive renewal: The two major parties (Social Democrats and Christian Democrats) which hold a solid three-fourths majority in parliament formed a grand coalition in 1987 and started to implement an ambitious program. The long-expected tax reform recently adopted by parliament is one of the most modern in Europe. It entered into force on January 1, 1989, and resulted in a streamlining of the progressive system, a general lowering of income tax, and scrapping of many exemptions. Budget consolidation plays a central role in the government's economic strategy. The aim is to reduce the net federal deficit as a percentage of nominal Gross Domestic Product by 0.5 percent per year to 2.5 percent in 1992. In 1987 the net deficit had decreased according to this plan (to 5.0 percent, 1986: 5.1 percent). An ambitious privatization program was started in 1987 which is designed to develop Austria's capital markets. Österreichische Industrieverwaltung, A.G.—the state holding company—sold part of its interest in Austria's largest oil company. Starting in 1988, the government began to sell up to 49 percent of its shares in the profitable Austrian Airlines and the national electricity company. The Austrian National Bank continues to conduct its traditional hard-currency policy, which is held in high esteem by international organizations like the International Monetary Fund. For years the Vienna Stock Exchange has been becoming more attractive to international traders. Its governing body performed a major reform in 1987 which became effective in 1988.

Science and research policies have become a national priority of our government.

The cultural scene is blossoming; new laws favoring tax deductions for art-sponsoring were adopted. The federal budget for culture is one of the very few that have been increased in spite of budgetary cuts in most other ministries.

Probably the most ambitious and comprehensive goal of the government grows out of Austria's new attitude towards the European Community. The government has adopted a program designed to prepare Austria's participation in the huge internal market of 320 million people envisaged to be established by the European Community. New laws adopted by the Austrian parliament were designed to conform with laws of the European Community, and the Austrian government has made application for full membership in the Community, which would have been almost unthinkable a few years ago.

In spite of—or maybe because of—the purgative process of *Vergangenheitsbewältigung,* many Austrians, in particular the younger ones, recognize these signs of renewal in the areas mentioned as well as in the judicial and moral fields and with regard to democratic reform. Austrians are increasingly willing and ready to look into the future, to take new roads, to break with taboos and to build a new and modern Austria capable of dealing with the problems of the 1990s and the twenty-first century. Many of them were born after World War II, but they have, at least over the past few years, consciously and extensively dealt with their country's history and are still doing so. They are the Austrians who for many years to come will have the opportunity and the challenge to live according to the high principle formulated by Israeli President Chaim Herzog on the occasion of his conciliatory visit to Germany: "Not to forget the past - not to ignore the future."

Index

Abel, Emil, 131
Abel, Othenio, 154
Academy Award, 115n
Academy of Sciences (Akademie der Wissenschaften), Vienna, 164
Ackerl, Isabella, 6
"Adabeis," 11
Adel und Untergang, 108
Adenauer, Konrad, 44
Adler, Max, 149
Administrative Supreme Court (Verwaltungsgerichtshof), 124, 125, 130, 132
Akademie Theater, 96
Albrecht V, Duke of Austria, 256
Albrich, Thomas, 31n
Allied Powers, personnel, 3, 9, 22, 59, 113, 114, 167, 170, 172, 173, 182, 183, 185-187, 191, 192, 196, 211, 212, 221, 224, 234, 239, 269-277, 280, 282, 285, 291, 299, 301
Alpenland, 186
"Alte Kämpfer," 149, 173
"Altreich" (Old Reich), 8, 178, 180, 187, 195
Amann, Klaus, 91, 92, 95n, 102, 113n
Americans, 5, 8, 55, 62, 110-113, 122, 185, 188, 204, 205, 211, 221, 251, 253, 278
Amstetten (Niederösterreich), 192
An uns glaubt Gott nicht mehr (film), 105
Andics, Helmut, 65n
Andrian, Leopold von, 104, 109
Androsch, Hannes, 243
Anglo-Saxons, 59, 107
Angola, 204
Anti-Semitism, 24, 41, 42n, 68, 88, 92, 96, 105, 123, 125, 128, 135, 139, 140, 151, 159, 160, 204, 240, 241, 248, 249, 254, 258, 261, 262, 267, 297, 298, 301
Arbeiter Zeitung, 25, 26n, 131
Arbeiter Verein, 68
Arbeitsgemeinschaft national sozialistischer Studentinnen, 140
Arendt, Hannah, 42n
Argentina, 42n
Arneth, Alfred Ritter von, 19
Aryanization (Arisierung), 12, 131, 194, 241, 261
Aspern (Niederösterreich), 50, 55
Asylverein, 139
Auch das war Wien, 114
Auernheimer, Raoul, 92, 93, 94n, 98, 99, 104, 107, 111-113
Augustinian Chorherren, 42
Austrian Freedom Front (Österreichische Freiheitsfront), 186
Austrian Institute, New York, ii, 6
Austrian National Bank (Österreichische Nationalbank), 302
Austrian-American Tribune, 114
Austro-fascism, 86, 229, 242, 288
Austro-German Relations in the Anschluss Era, 287
Austro-Hungarian Monarchy (Habsburg Empire, Danubian Monarchy, Dual Monarchy), 1, 16, 19, 20, 33, 37, 40, 45, 57, 58, 67, 115, 122, 125, 126, 138, 184, 194, 209, 237, 243
Austro-Marxism, 242, 288
Austro-Prussian War (1866), 58
Autorenversammlung, 97
Avars, 121
Baden, 186, 187

Baden-Württemberg, 286
Bajuvarians, 125
Balfour, Michael, 271n
Balkans, 57
Barbie, Klaus, 204
Barea, Ilke, 109
Bärnthaler, Irmgard, 78n, 153n
Bartsch, Rudolf Hans, 96, 108
Basil, Otto, 101, 102, 106, 107
Bauer, Otto, 19n, 25, 26n, 72, 233, 242, 289
Bauer, Wilhelm, 38n
Baum, Vickie, 109
Bavaria, 36, 176, 183, 186, 214
Becker, Carl Heinrich, 126
Becker, Hans, 213n
Beer-Hofmann, Richard, 91, 97
Beide Sizilien, 107
Beitzke, Hermann, 130
Bekenntnisbuch, 116, 117
Belgians, 278
Beneš, Eduard, 87n
Berchtesgaden, 28, 30, 48, 50, 154
Berchtold, Klaus, 79n, 232n
Berger, Albert, 113n
Berlin, 20, 29, 47, 94, 104, 119, 140, 143, 147, 172, 184, 202, 213
Bern, 212
Berner, Hans, 149
Beust, Ferdinand Graf, 20
Bielka, Erik, 23n
Billinger, Richard, 96, 106, 108
Billroth, Theodor, 123
Bischoff, Norbert, 16, 17
Bismarck, Otto von, 123
Blei, Franz, 104
Bluhm, William, 168n, 268n
Blut und Boden, 96, 101, 108
Boberach, Heinz, 169n, 179n, 185n, 188n

Böheim (Niederösterreich), 180
Bohemia, 126
Böhm, Johann, 228, 229
Bolshevism, Bolsheviks, 93, 179, 192, 194, 196, 267
Bonitz, Hermann, 119
Borkenau, Franz, 18, 19n, 33, 109
Bormann, Martin, 193
Borodajkewycz, Taras, 240, 258
Bosnia, 57
Bossi-Fedrigatti, Anton, 95
Botz, Gerhard, 23, 30n, 32, 40, 42n, 168n, 171n, 245n, 265, 269, 270, 286, 287n, 289n
Brasslof, Stephan, 162
Bratislava, 101
Braun, Felix, 103, 104, 111
Brauneder, Wilhelm, 275n
Brazil, 109
Brehm, Bruno, 93, 95, 96
Brenner Pass, 59, 61
Breuning, Klaus, 38n, 144n
Brief an eine Unbekannte, 110
British, 50, 112, 121, 242, 251
Brno (Brünn), 15
Broch, Hermann, 104, 105, 109, 112, 115
Brod, Max, 104
Bronfman, Edgar, 263, 264
Broucek, Peter, 144n, 166n
Bruck an der Leitha (Niederösterreich), 51
Bruck an der Mur (Steiermark), 178
Bruckmüller, George Ernst, 168n
Bruckner, Ferdinand, 104
Brussels, 263, 264
Budapest, 21, 55, 56
Bukey, Evan, 8, 66, 67n, 141n, 169n, 170
Bund der deutschen Schriftsteller

Österreichs, 95, 96, 116
Bund Oberland, 156
Bundeskulturrat, 100
Bundesverlag, Österreichischer, 100
Bürckel, Josef, 163
Burgenland, 51, 58, 280
Burgtheater, 96, 99
Burkert, Günther, 74n
Burschenschaften (Student corporations, fraternities), 123, 124, 129, 140, 144, 153, 155, 158
Busek, Erhard, 248
California, 111, 301
Carnegie Endowment for International Peace, 122
Carolingian March, 38
Carsten, Francis, 30, 31n, 60n
Cartellverband (CV), 140, 155
Catholic Nationals, 144-148, 162, 163
Central America, 204
Central Europe, 6, 33, 55, 59, 60, 62, 145, 148, 165
Chaimowitz, Thomas, 41n
Chamber of Commerce, 2, 246
Chamber of Labor, 82
Chamberlain, Neville, 33
Chargaff, Erwin, 166n
Cherbourg, 189
Chorherr, Thomas, 41n
Christian Science Monitor, 111
Christian Socials, 2, 6n, 27, 28, 64, 66, 68, 73-75, 79, 194, 218, 220, 229, 288
Christian, Viktor, 164
Christmann, Hans Helmut, 162n
Church, Roman Catholic, 6, 10, 29, 54, 75, 177, 186, 196, 228, 231, 245, 246, 253, 254, 256
Churchill, Sir Winston, 183, 271

Cisleithania, 18, 20, 24
Civil War (1934), 50, 66, 69, 80, 237, 238, 240, 241, 243, 244, 284, 288, 290
Clergy, 9, 176, 203, 207, 225, 256, 290
Coalition government, 1, 2, 3, 73, 75, 78, 228, 235, 238, 243, 244, 285, 301
Cold War, 3, 258, 281
College of Agriculture (Hochschule für Bodenkultur), Vienna, 136, 156, 162
College of Mining (Montanistische Hochschule), Leoben, 136, 141, 159
College of Veterinary Medicine (Tierärztliche Hochschule), Vienna, 159
Colorado College, 111
Columbia University, 121, 122
Committee of Seven (Siebener Ausschuss), 148
Commonweal, 47
Commonwealth of Great Britain, 60
Communists, Communist Party of Austria (KPÖ), 62, 78, 115, 141, 156, 167, 178, 183, 186, 193, 196, 216, 218, 221, 223, 245, 262, 273, 281
Compromise of 1867 (Ausgleich), 18, 19
Concordat, 10, 227, 228
Constitution, 1, 21, 22, 71, 72, 76, 82-86, 88, 152, 167, 239, 274, 275
Constitutional reform, 72, 82
Constitutional Supreme Court (Verfassungsgerichtshof), 24-25, 77
Cornell University, 122

Corporative State, 6, 66, 67, 79, 82, 83, 86, 88, 152, 196, 237, 240, 267, 288-290
Corti, Axel, 105
Corti, Egon Caesar, 92
Coudenhove-Kalergi, Richard, 26
Craig, Gordon, 271
Crinis, Max de, 126
Croats, 88
Csáky, Eva-Marie, 277n, 278n
Csokor, Franz Theodor, 21, 92-95, 99, 103, 104
Czechoslovakia, Czechs, 21, 24, 28, 33, 53, 59, 61, 67, 87, 88, 122, 160, 211, 261, 266, 278
Czeike, Felix, 290n
Czermak, Emmerich, 144
D-Day (6 June 1944), 188, 189, 191-192
Dachau, 52, 104, 111, 113, 155, 162, 238, 257, 278
Daladier, Edouard, 33
Danubian Monarchy, 33, 40 (*see also* Austro-Hungarian Monarchy)
Darwin, Charles, 120
Das deutsche Leid, 96
Das Neue Reich und seine Begründung, 37
Das Neue Österreich, 29
Das Neue Reich, 37
Das Wirtshaus zur verlorenen Zeit, 111
Daviau, Donald, ii, 7
Deggenfeld-Schonburg, Ferdinand, 138
Denmark, 47
Der Anschluss österreichischer Schriftsteller an das Dritte Reich, 91
Der Augarten, 107

Der Christliche Ständestaat, 29
Der Engel mit der Posaune, 110
Der von der Vogelweide, 96
Der Wahre Staat, 144
Deutsch-sozialer Volksbund, 148
Deutsche Lehr- und Forschungsstätten, 125
Deutsche Studentenschaft, 136, 140, 143, 157, 158
Deutsche Wissenschaft, 120, 127
Deutsches Historisches Museum, Berlin, 38
Diamant, Alfred, 66n
Die Eingliederung Österreichs in das Dritte Reich, 286-287
Die Furche, 42n
Die Rückkehr (Return to Vienna), 110
Die Tür geht auf, 110
Die Warte, 147, 148
Die Wochenpresse, 292
Die Zeugin (A Woman is Witness), 110
Diner, Dan, 286n
Doderer, Heimito von, 106, 115
Dokumentationsarchiv des österreichischen Widerstandes, 33n, 40n, 105, 286
Dollfuss, Engelbert, 25-27, 29, 63, 65-67, 71, 73-85, 87, 131, 135, 136, 227, 238, 288
Dollfuss-Schuschnigg regime, 25, 26, 69, 71, 174
Domarus, Max, 268n
Drach, Albert, 104
Drimmel, Heinrich, 142, 155n
Dritter November 1918, 99
Dual Monarchy, 57 (*see also* Austro-Hungarian Monarchy)
Dualism, 20
Dubrovnik (Ragusa), 92, 98
Dürnstein an der Donau (Nieder-

Österreich), 255
Eötvös, Josef Freiherr von, 40
Eckl, Emil, 214n
Ehemaligen, 225, 226, 233, 240, 242
Ehrenstein, Alfred, 104
Eibl, Hans, 144, 148
Eichmann, Adolf, 42n, 200, 207
Eisenstadt (Burgenland), 188, 192
Eisterer, Klaus, 31n
Elias, Herbert, 149, 150
Endlösung (final solution), 257
Engel-Janosi, Friedrich, 164
England, 33, 41, 105, 109, 111, 114
Eppel, Peter, 145n
Eppinger, Hans, 153
Erdmann, Karl Dietrich, 43, 44
Ermächtigungsgesetz, Kriegswirtschaftliches (War Economy Powers Act), 72, 73, 76
Erste Österreichische Spar-Casse, 32
Ertl, Emil, 93
Ethiopia, 61, 100
European Community, 263, 296, 302
Exner, Franz, 119
Fachidioten, 166
Falta, Otto von, 161
Fatherland Front (Vaterländische Front), 28, 66, 78, 79, 81, 84, 100, 101, 137, 139, 141, 153, 155-157, 165, 226, 232, 237
Feldkirchen (Oberösterreich), 179
Feldmann, Angela, 74n
Fellner, Fritz, 21n, 272n
Fellner, Günter, 38n
Fichte, Johann Gottlieb, 131
Figl, Leopold, 17, 259, 277, 278, 280, 282, 283, 291

First Republic, 1, 2, 15, 16, 22, 24, 25, 34, 45, 64, 67, 71, 85, 89, 115, 133, 172, 184, 191, 237, 245, 265, 274, 250, 290
Fischer Verlag, 94
Flesch-Brunningen, Robert Hans, 109
Fliess, Gerhard, 143n
Fliesser, Josef Calasanctius, 177
Fontana, Oskar Maurus, 92, 93
Forty-Eighters, 38
Fränkel, Josef, 151n
France, French, 33, 50, 58-60, 62, 64, 105, 112, 114, 121, 138, 189, 210, 213, 218, 221, 297
Franckenstein, Sir George, 109
Frankl, Viktor, 300
Franklin, Benjamin, 1
Franz Joseph, Kaiser, 19, 20, 58, 67, 123
Fredborg, Arvid, 172, 174, 175
Freies Österreich, 114
Freud, Sigmund, 23
Fricke, Dieter, 143n
Fried, Erich, 104
Friedel, Egen, 104
Friedmann, Desider, 253
Friedrichs, Helmut, 193
Frisé, Adolf, 21n
Frisch, Hans von 135n
Frischauer, Paul, 92, 93, 104
Frischauer, Willi, 109
Frischenschlager, Friedhelm, 236, 240
Fritsch, Gerhard, 42
Froeschl, George, 113
Fuchs, Martin, 143n,
Fullerton, George Stuart, 121
Funktionsjuden, 260
Fürth, Otto von, 161

Fussenegger, Gertrud, 108
Galicia, 123
Gall, Franz, 158n
Gamper, Hans, 214n
Gänserndorf (Niederösterreich), 187, 188
Gay, Peter, 24n
Gedye, G.E.R., 150n
Geehr, Richard, 163
Geeinter Roter Studentenverband, 150
Gehler, Michael, 129n, 132n
Geneva Protocol (1922), 127
George, Stefan, 35, 37
Gerbel, Christian, 181n
German Confederation (Deutcher Bund), 18
German Democratic Republic, 44
German Emergency Society for Sciences (Deutsche Not gemeinschaft der Wissenschaften), 128
German Empire (of 1871-1918), 58, 59, 121, 125, 126, 227
German language, 22-24, 41, 59, 109, 110, 112
German Students Association (Deutsche Studentenschaft), 125, 126, 128-131, 135, 136, 158
German universities, 119, 122
German-Austria (Deutsch-Österreich), German Austrians, 21, 22, 32, 34, 35n, 41, 59, 67, 137, 237, 268, 269
German-Austrian Aid to Science (Deutsch-österreichische Wissenschaftshilfe), 128
Germany, Federal Republic of, 44, 283, 285
Germany, tripartite, 43, 44
Gesamtdeutsch, 144, 289

Gessner, Adrienne, 111
Gestapo (Geheime Staatspolizei), 7, 55, 102, 162, 167, 175, 178, 186, 190, 192, 213, 218, 220, 221, 260
Gilbert, Prentice, 104
Ginzkey, Franz Karl, 95, 96, 108
Glaise-Horstenau, Edmund von, 48, 166
Gleichschaltung, 63, 97, 132, 158, 160
Gleispach, Wenzel, 130, 131
Gloggnitz (Niederösterreich), 32, 33
Gluck, Christoph, 114
Gmünd (Niederösterreich), 192
Goerdeler, Carl Friedrich, 230
Goebbels, Josef, 95, 173
Göhring, Walter, 151n
Goldinger, Walter, 27n, 34, 37, 74n, 75n, 86n, 142n
Gollwitzer, Heinz, 74n
Göring, Hermann, 30, 47, 50, 174, 177, 249
Görz, Oskar, 214n
Graz, 47, 49, 50, 97, 123, 154, 178, 184, 186
Great Britain (United Kingdom), 33, 58-60, 62, 103, 187, 213, 238, 272
Great Gesera, 256
Great Powers, 33, 57, 61, 206, 238, 277
Greater Austria, 38, 43, 45
Green (Alternative) Party, 249
Greinz, Rudolf, 96,
Grieskirchen (Oberösterreich), 179, 180
Grogger, Paula, 95, 96, 108
Grossdeutsch, 3, 238
Grossdeutsche Volkspartei (Greater German Peoples

Party), 64, 65, 68, 74, 77, 83, 131
Grossdeutsches Reich (Gross deutschland, Third Reich, Hitler Germany, Nazi Germany, Greater German Reich), i, 4, 30n, 37, 43, 45, 51, 62, 78, 80, 87, 88, 93, 127, 132, 137, 140, 141, 143, 145-148, 150, 151, 153, 154, 157, 158, 160, 165, 168, 171, 174, 175, 178-183, 187, 190, 191,194-197, 202, 204, 205, 209, 216, 227, 237, 238, 248, 250, 266-268, 273-276, 279, 281-283, 288-290, 292
Grosz, Paul, 12
Gruber, Karl, 211n, 213-218, 278, 298
Gütersloh, Albert Paris, 102, 106
Gypsies, 40n
Haag, John, 7
Habsburg, Otto von, 183, 186, 218
Habsburgs, 58, 61, 66, 87, 138, 194, 241
Hainisch, Michael, 34
Hall, Murray, 113n
Hamburger, Franz, 165
Hammer-Purgstall, Josef, 121
Hammerschlag, Peter, 104
Hammerstein-Equard, Hans Baron von, 47, 93
Handel-Mazetti, Enrica von, 93, 108
Hanisch, Ernst, 32, 170n, 171, 176n, 177n, 180n, 181n, 192n, 241n, 285n
Harlich, Wladimir von, 93, 154
Harmann, Albrecht and Heidi, 205n
Hartmann, Karl Amadeus, 36

Hasiba, Genot, 73n
Haslauer, Wilfried, 249
Haslinger, Josef, 242n, 284n
Hassel, Ulrich von, 29n
Hassinger, Hugo, 144
Häusler, Wolfgang, 26n
Heer, Friedrich, 137n, 168n
Heiber, Helmut, 164n
Heidrich, Charlotte, 74n
Heimatblock, 100
Heimatliteratur, 96
Heimatschutz, 100
Heimwehr, 27, 65, 66, 68, 74, 75, 81, 84, 100, 220
Heine, Werner, 214n
Heinz, Karl Hans, 37n
Heitig, Bruno, 109
Heldenplatz, 11, 31, 237, 250, 267
Heldenplatz (*The Prisoner*), 110
Heller, Celia, 151n
Henz, Rudolf, 102, 106
Herzegovina, 57
Herzl, Theodor, 112
Herzog, Chaim, 303
Hess, Viktor, 160
Heuberger, Helmut, 213n
Hildebrand, Dietrich von, 29, 30n
Hildebrand, Klaus, 27n
Hirnschrott, Karl, 214n
Hirsch, Hans, 144
Hitler Jugend, 181
Hitler, Adolf, 4, 7, 8, 10, 23, 25, 27-30, 32, 34, 38, 39, 40n, 48-50, 53-55, 61-65, 67, 69, 70, 91, 93, 94, 98, 104, 113, 114, 116, 126, 129, 132, 139, 143, 146, 147, 154, 158, 159, 167-169, 176, 177, 179-186, 190-197, 201, 203, 210, 218, 223, 224, 227, 228, 235, 237, 238, 247,

249, 250, 267, 268, 272, 273, 277, 288, 291, 298
attempted assassination (20 July 1944), 8, 29n, 169, 176, 177, 179, 180, 185, 190-194
Hochschule für Welthandel Economics University), 139
Hochschulwache (University police), 155
Hochwälder, Fritz, 105
Hofer, Andreas, 163
Hoffmann, Peter, 191n
Hofmannsthal, Hugo von, 97, 106, 108, 109, 112, 270
Höflechner, Walter, 7
Hohlbaum, Robert, 93, 95, 96
Hollabrunn (Niederösterreich), 181
Holland, 105
Hollywood, 113, 240
Holocaust (Shoah), 239, 247, 249, 250, 257
Holtmann, Everhard, 28n, 85
Holy Land, 255
Holy Roman Empire, 120, 121
Holy See, 227
Holzmann, Ernst, 164n
Holzmann, Hermann, 68n
Holzner, Johann, 209n, 215n, 222n
Hoor, Ernst, 142n
Horak, K., 240n
Horn, Daniel, 150n
Horváth, Ödön von, 105
Hotel Metropole, 52, 53
Hözl, Norbert, 233n
Hradetzky, Anton, 214n
Huber, Anton, 214n
Hudal, Alois, Bishop, 29, 30n
Hugelmann, Karl Gottlieb, 144, 154
Hungary, Hungarians, (Magyars), 19-21, 51, 52, 56-58, 61, 67, 72, 151, 256, 261
Huns, 121
Hunter College, 47
Hupka, Josef, 162
Illegalen, 36, 131, 137
Imperial League of Austrians, 15
Innitzer, Theodor Cardinal, 54, 129, 140, 230, 231, 235
Innsbruck, 8, 22, 49, 50, 123, 154, 209, 212-215, 218, 219, 221, 278
Innsbrucker Nachrichten, 21 22
Institut für Österreichische Geschichtsforschung, 33n
Institut für Zeitgeschichte, Linz, (Institute for Contemporary History), 239
Institut für Zeitgeschichte, Munich, 286
Institut für Zeitgeschichte, Vienna, 286
Institut zur Erforschung der National-sozialistischen Politik, 286
Institute of Technology (Technische Hochschule), Vienna, 126
International Institute for Social History (Amsterdam), 33
International Instituut voor Gechiedenis, 33n
Iron Curtain, 239
"Island of the blessed" (Insel der Seligen), 3, 296
Israel, 204
Issatschenko, Alexander, 47
Italian War of 1859, 58
Italy, Italians, 29, 33, 53-55, 57-60, 62, 67, 72, 74, 80, 212, 221, 238, 288
Izinger, Karl, 156n

Jägerstätter, Franz, 9, 202, 203, 205, 208
Jagschitz, Gerhard, 79n, 83n, 86, 141n, 280n
Jaminskyi, Boris, 139n
Jedlicka, Ludwig, 34, 75n, 79n, 141n, 144n, 190n, 193n, 275n, 286
Jehovah's Witnesses, 220
Jelinek, Gerhard, 280n, 293n
Jelusich, Mirko, 93, 95, 96, 99, 108
Jerusalem, 255
Jewish Community of Vienna (Israelitische Kultusgemeinde), 253, 254, 260, 261
Jews, 12, 16, 21, 24, 36, 40n, 41, 52, 56, 67-68, 80, 81, 85, 86, 88, 94, 95, 97, 100, 103, 114, 123, 124, 126, 127, 129, 130, 132, 136, 140, 141, 143, 149-151, 159, 161, 164, 220, 235, 240, 241, 243, 244, 253-264, 280, 298
John Paul I, Pope, 3
John Paul II, Pope, 203
Johnson, Lonnie, 10
Jordan, Max, 55
July Agreement (Juliabkommen) of 1936, 26n, 29, 61, 63, 85, 141, 142, 146
Jung, Jochen, 39n
Jury, Hugo, 193
Kaiser, Jakob, 230
Kaizl, Josef, 24
Kakania, 20, 21
Kämmerer, Jürgen, 147n
Kaltenbrunner, Ernst, 126, 193
Kampfbund, 95, 97
Kann, Robert, 23n

Karner, Stefan, 170n, 171, 176n, 178n
Kärnten (Carinthia), 47, 67, 140, 170, 171, 186, 276
Kassner, Rudolf, 106
Kastelic, Jakob, 43n
Kater, Michael, 164n
Katholischer Schriftsteller verband, 100
Katzburg, Nathaniel, 151n
Katzenstein, Peter, 168n, 171n
Kelly, Reece, 165n
Kelsen, Hans, 23
Kershaw, Ian, 177n, 189n
Keyserlingk, Robert, 168n
Kindermann, Gottfried Karl, 289n
Kindermann, Heinz, 99
Kirchschläger, Rudolf, 139
Kirchweger, Ernst, 240
Klagenfurt, 182
Klahr, Alfred, 26n
Klar, F. 240n
Klaus, Josef, 230, 231, 258
Kleinwaechter, Friedrich, 22
Klemperer, Klemens von, 31, 64n, 66n
Kluge, Ulrich, 76n
Klusacek, Christine, 169n
Kluwick-Muckenhuber, Christl, 81n
Knöpfelmacher, Wilhelm, 161
Knab, Jakob, 205n
Knight, Robert, 235n, 281n
Knoeringen, Waldemar von, 217n
Knoll, Fritz, 157
Koepke, Wulf, 113
Kokoschka, Oskar, 109
König, Franz Cardinal, 301
Konrad, Helmut, 156n
Körber, Robert, 139
Koref, Ernst, 228
Kornfeld, Paul, 104

Kotschnig, Walter, 138
Kraus, Hans Peter, 109
Kraus, Karl, 227
Kreisky, Bruno, 15, 236, 240, 248, 258
Kreissler, Félix, 168n, 184n-186n, 190n, 266n
Krems (Niederösterreich), 78
Křenek, Ernst, 301
Kretschmayr, Heinrich, 137
Kriegsarchiv, 48
Kristall-Verlag, 117
Kristallnacht, 68, 160
Kruckenkreuz, 156
Kulturgemeinde, National Socialist, 95
Kunschak, Leopold, 68
Labor unions, 2, 73, 81, 82, 84, 89, 196, 231
Lachmeyer, Frederick, 275n
Lager, 1, 156, 238, 245, 265
Lammasch, Heinrich, 23
Landbund für Österreich, 74, 76
Landsmannschaften, 149, 158; Balthia, 149
Landräte, 176
Lang, Fritz, 113
Lang, Hilde Verena, 74, 86n
Larsen, Stein Ugelvik, 171n
Lateran Council (1215), 256
Lausanne Protocol, 130
Le Monde, 296
League of Front Fighters (Frontkämpferbund), 66
League of Independents (Verein der Unabhägigen, VdU), 234
League of Nations, 33, 59
Lederer, Edgar, 161n
Lederer, Karl, 43n
Lederer, Zdenek, 162n
Legitimists, 37, 61, 87, 194, 218, 220

Leibnitz (Steiermark), 249
Leidler, Rudolf, 161
Leitner, Helga, 70n
Lendai, Paul, 242n
Leoben (Steiermark), 136, 154, 159, 178
Leopold VI, Duke of Austria, 255
Lernet-Holenia, Alexander, 106, 107
Leser, Norbert, 290n
Leuschner, Wilhelm, 227, 230
Lichtenberger-Fenz, Brigitte, 25n, 130n, 159n, 160n
Lilienfeld (Niederösterreich), 187, 189
Linz, 50, 148, 154, 177-180, 187, 191, 192
Little Entente, 59, 60-62, 66
Ljubljana, 47, 55
Loewi, Otto, 160
London, 18, 188, 274
Los Angeles, 114
Lothar, Ernst, 92, 105, 110, 111
Low, Alfred, 61n, 64n, 65n
Lowe-Porter, Helen Tracy, 109
Löwenthal, Josef Freiherr von, 34
Ludwig, Emil, 104
Lueger, Karl, 24
Lutz, Heinrich, 21n, 168n
Luža, Radomír, 8, 148n, 163n, 168n, 171, 175n-178n, 183n, 186n, 286
Machatschek, Fritz, 144
Machtergreifung, 65, 153
Mackowitz, R., 214n, 215n
Mader, Ernst, 205
Maderegger, Silvia, 88n, 136n
Maginot Line, 60
Mahler, Gustav, 37
Mair, John, 271n
Maleta, Alfred, 28, 82, 89, 231,

301
Malina, Peter, 285n
Mann, Reinhard, 270n
Mann, Thomas, 109
Marboe, Peter, ii
Marie Antoinette, 110
Marogna-Redwitz, Rudolf Graf von, 190
Mars in Widder, 107
Marxism, Marxists, 27, 28, 145, 136, 149-151
Massiczek, Albert, 152n-155n
Mauterndorf (Salzburg), 249
Mauthausen (Oberösterreich), 301
Mayer, Theodor, 96
Mein Kampf, 62
Meisel, Josef, 173n
Meissl, Sebastian, 281n, 284n
Meldungen aus dem Reich, 169
Melk (Niederösterreich), 192
Mell, Max, 95, 96, 106, 108
Mendelssohn-Bartholdy, Felix, 53
Menghin, Oswald, 144, 148, 157, 159, 163
Merinsky, Judith, 160n, 161n
Merton, Thomas, 206, 207
Metternich--Statesman and Lover, 111
Miklas, Wilhelm, 34, 37, 73, 74n, 85
Milano, 105
Ministerial Council (Ministerrat), 259
Ministry for Foreign Affairs, Austrian, ii, 253
Ministry of Education, Austrian, 163, 285
Mischehen, 260
Mischlinge, 159, 160
Missong, Alfred, 26, 29, 30n
Mistelbach (Niederösterreich), 188

Mitterand, François, 297
Molden, Fritz, 70n, 180n, 183n, 194, 212, 213n, 217n, 222n, 298
Molden, Otto, 214n, 217n
Moldenhauer, Hans and Rosaleen, 35, 37
Molisch, Hans, 128, 149
Mommsen, Hans, 286n
Monarchists, 84, 114, 162, 167, 183, 186, 196
Mongolians, 121
Monicault, Louis de, 16
Moore, Erna, 113n
Moravian Compromise (1905), 24
Morgenthau Plan, 205
Moscow, 196, 272
Moscow Radio, 174, 185
Moscow Declaration (1943), 4, 8, 9, 167, 169, 184, 185, 194, 96, 211, 223-225, 239, 272-275, 278, 281-283, 299
Moser, Jonny, 41n
Mueller, Ralph, 215n
Mühlen, Hermynia zur, 109
Müller, Franz, 31n
Mulley, Klaus-Dieter, 280n, 281n
Munich, 29, 129, 147
  Agreement of 1938, 33
  Putsch of 1923, 139
Musil, Robert, 20, 21, 93, 96, 115
Mussolini, Benito, 27-29, 33, 50, 61, 63, 79, 87, 100, 181, 182, 288
Nabl, Franz, 93, 95
Nadler, Joseph, 99, 144, 148
Napoleon, 113
National Assembly (Nationalversammlung), Austrian, 65
National Committee, Austrian (POEN), 212, 213

National Council (Nationalrat), Austrian, 258
National Socialist German Students League (Nationalsozialistischer Deutscher Studentenbund, NSDStB), 129, 136, 139, 153, 158
National Socialists, Nazis, Nazism, 4, 5, 7, 8, 10, 11, 18, 26, 32, 36, 37, 39, 40n, 41, 42, 47-56, 60, 63, 65, 68, 69, 77-81, 83-89, 91, 92, 95-97, 99-104, 106, 107, 109, 112, 114, 116, 124, 126, 128, 129-132, 136, 141, 142, 145, 147, 150-153, 155, 157-165, 169, 171, 173, 174, 176, 177,179, 181, 184, 186, 187, 190, 192, 193, 195, 196, 199, 202-204, 209-211, 213, 219, 220, 224-227, 229, 231-235, 237-239, 241-243, 245, 248-250, 258, 265-271, 273, 276, 278-286, 288-292, 298-301
National Socialist Shop Cell Organization (Nationalsozialistische Betriebszellenorganisation, NSBO), 156
National Socialist University Instructors League (Nationalsozialistischer Dozentenbund), 159, 164
Neck, Rudolf, 75n, 79n, 83n, 141n, 245n
Neue Freie Presse, 112
Neues Leben, 100 102
Neugebauer, Wolfgang, 80n, 56n, 181n, 241n, 269n, 285
Neunkirchen (Niederösterreich), 182
Neumann, Jacob, 93
Neumann, Robert, 92, 109
Neustädter-Stürmer, Odo, 27
New York, 110, 111, 114, 121
Nicholas V, Pope, 256
Nicholson, Harold, 60n
Niederösterreich (Niederdonau), 11, 27, 170, 176, 179, 182, 188, 190, 191, 193, 280
Nobl, Gábor, 161
Normandy, 188, 192
North America, 26
North, Oliver, 200, 201, 208
Norway, 47
Nothnagel, Hermann, 123
Numerus clausus, 124, 126, 159
Nuremberg Laws, 98
O 5 (Gruppe O5), 213, 214, 218
Oberösterreich (Oberdonau), 170, 176, 179, 188, 192, 193
Oberdonauer Zeitung, 185
Oberkofler, Josef Georg, 96
Oberpullendorf (Burgenland), 192
Occupation, Allied, 2, 3, 9, 239, 284
French, 16
German, 3, 7, 104, 169, 223-228, 231, 235-239, 247, 271, 273, 275, 277, 279, 282, 286
Soviet Union, 280, 281
United States, 281
Office for Foreign Affairs, State Chancellory, 16, 17
Office of Strategic Services (OSS), 212
Orlow, Dietrich, 179n
Ortner, Hermann Heinz, 95, 96, 103

Österreich im Prismen der Idee, Katechismus der Führenden, 109
Österreichische Hochschülerschaft, 142, 155, 300
Österreichische Industrieverwaltung, A.G., 302
Österreichischer Landesverlag, 32
Ostmärkische Sturmscharen, 15, 26n, 131
Ostmark, 16, 32, 160, 174, 177, 179, 185, 187
P.E.N. Club, 92-98, 102, 104, 112
Palestine, 69
Pan-German (Alldeutsch), 227-230, 242
  Pan German (Alldeutsche) Party, 58
Panzenböck, Ernst, 38n
Papen, Franz von, 31n, 100
Paris, 105, 190, 215, 296
Paris Peace Settlement, 57-59, 98, 237, 268
Paritätische Kommission für Preise und Löhne (*see also* Sozialpartnerschaft), 2
Patsch, Sylvia, 105n, 109
Paul, Hertha, 105
Pauley, Bruce, 6, 238n, 269 270n
Pelinka, Anton, 9, 81n, 234n, 239n, 245n, 284
People's Court (Volksgericht), 175, 181
Peoples Party, Austrian (Österreichische Volkspartei, ÖVP), 3, 16, 218, 223, 228, 232-234, 238, 240, 248, 249, 273, 284, 288, 301
Perkonig, Josef, 95, 96
Pernkopf, Eduard, 157
Penter, Hans, 136, 154, 155

Peter, Friedrich, 240, 258
Petersen, Jens, 27n
Petznek, Leopold, 27-28
Peukert, Detlev, 181n
Pfabigan, Alfred, 149n
Pfaundler, Wolfgang, 222n
Pfeiffer, Edda, 43n
Piefke, 270
Plan, 101, 102
Plebiscite, 13 March 1938 (proposed), 11, 30, 49, 50, 63, 101, 104, 155, 268
Plebiscite, 10 April 1938, 31, 34, 40n, 54, 158, 202, 229, 268, 289, 290
Pohl, Walter, 41n
Poland, Poles, 21, 59, 60-62, 67, 122, 151, 210, 211, 261, 266
Popovici, Aurel, 20
Prague, 24, 105, 123, 215
Preminger, Otto, 113
Preusse und Österreicher, 270
Prinz, Friedrich, 23n
Propaganda, 47, 53, 54, 68, 69, 77, 84, 100, 112, 135, 143, 158, 167, 185-187, 193, 220, 227, 234, 241, 267, 269
Proporz, 244
Protestants, 177
Provisional Austrian National Committee (POEN), 212, 213
Prussia, Prussians, 119-121, 123, 125, 126, 183, 226, 270
Przibram, Hans, 162
Purge of June 1934 ("Night of Long Knives"), 29, 146
Putsch of 25 July 1934 (Juliputsch), 29, 61, 63, 66, 83, 140, 146, 244, 288
Quadragesimo anno, 82
Quisling, Vidkun, 278
Racetrack Speech (Trabrennplatz-

Racetrack Speech (*continued*)
  Rede), 79, 82
Raffelstettner Zollordnung (903), 255
Rath, John, 6
Rathkolb, Oliver, 281n, 282n
RAVAG, 106
Reader's Digest, 110
Red Army, 192
Reder, Walter, 236, 240
Redlich, Oswald, 146
Reich, Emil, 164n
Reichs Association of Austrian Printers and Newspaper Workers, 16
Reichs Association of Jewish Legitimists of Austria, 16
Reichs Association of Midwives of Austria, 16
Reichs Commissioner for the Reunion of Austria With the German Reich, 16
Reichs Institute for Mothers' and Infants' Welfare, 16
Reichsbildungsausschuss, 15
Reichsdeutsche, 11, 125
Reichsgaue, 16
Reichsgeschichte, 17
Reichsinstitut für Geschichte des neuen Deutschlands, 164
Reichsorga, 16
Reichsparteileitung, 16
Reichspost, 15
Reichsrat, 20
Reichsschrifttumskammer, 95, 96, 116
Reichsstatthalter, 16
Reichstag, 164
Reichsverband Deutscher Schriftsteller, 95
Reimann, Viktor, 38n, 234
Reither, Josef, 190

Renner, Karl, 21-23, 32-34, 37, 195, 225, 227-229, 233, 235, 242, 259, 274, 289
Republic of Austria, 18, 22, 33, 43, 44, 248, 282, 292, 301
Republicans, 114
Resistance, 197-200, 205, 208, 238
Resistance, Austrian, 8, 42, 43n, 89, 103, 115, 155, 167-172, 175, 178, 183, 184, 186, 194, 197, 205, 209-222, 229, 234, 244, 247, 266, 267, 278, 280, 291, 298
Reut-Nicolussi, Eduard, 214n
Revolution of 1848, 58
Revolutionary Socialists, 218, 241, 242
Rhineland, 59, 63, 174, 186
Riccione, 79
Richard I, King of England, 255
Richter, Elise, 162
Ried (Oberösterreich), 179
Riedelsperger, Max, 225n
Riepl, Hermann, 28n
Rilke, Rainer Maria, 106
Ringel, Erwin, 168n
Ringler, Ralf Roland, 191n
Ritschel, K.H., 242n
Röbbeling, Hermann, 99
Robertson, Esmonde, 29n
Rockefeller Foundation, 122
Röhm, Ernst, 146
Romania, Romanians, 20, 59, 67, 151, 261
Rome, 164
Roosevelt, Franklin Delano, 114, 271
Rosenberg, Alfred, 95, 145, 147
Rosenkranz, Herbert, 41n, 161n
Rot-Weiss-Roth-Buch, 225
Roth, Josef, 30, 105, 115

Index 319

Rudolf IV, Duke of Austria, 142
Rudolf, Crown Prince, 28
Ruhrgebiet, 176
Rumpler, Helmut, 21n, 168n
Russia, Russians, 18, 57, 176,
    182, 183, 187, 257
Ruthenes, 122
Sackenheim, Jörg, 214n
Safrian, Hans, 42n, 241n
St. Charles Church (Karlskirche),
    34
St. Germain, Treaty of, 22, 57,
    268
St. Stephen, Crown of , 19
St. Stephen's Cathedral (Stefans-
    dom), "Mahnwache," 300
Salomon, Ernst von, 162n
Salten, Felix, 92-94, 112
Salzburg, 23, 32n, 50, 103, 171,
    186, 190, 212
Sandgruber, Roman, 280n
St. Pölten (Niederösterreich), 178,
    179, 188, 189
St. Valentin (Oberösterreich), 178
Sassmann, Heinz Hans, 108
Schärf, Adolf, 33, 175, 226-228,
    230, 259, 278
Schaukal, Richard von, 108
Schausberger, Norbert, 267n, 87n
Scheibbs (Niederösterreich), 188
Schlomo the mintmaster, 255
Schmädeke, Jürgen, 27n
Schmidl, Erwin, 30n, 265
Schmidt, Hugo, 106
Schmieder, Ernst, 195n
Schmitz, Richard, 28
Schneeberger, Josef, 214n
Schneller, Martin, 146n
Schnitzler, Arthur, 97, 112
Schoeller, Berndt, 270n
Scholz, Karl Roman, 42, 43
Schönbauer, Leopold, 165

Schönberg, Arnold, 36
Schönbrunn, 22n
Schöner, Josef, 34n
Schöner, Rita, 34n
Schönere Zukunft, 145
Schönerer, Georg von, 58, 98
Schönherr, Karl, 95, 106
Schreyvogel, Ferdinand, 95, 96
Schrödinger, Erwin, 160
Schulmeister, Otto, 38, 39n
Schuschnigg, Kurt von, 11, 15,
    25, 26, 28, 30, 31, 38n, 47-
    50, 52, 56, 63, 65-67,
    75, 80, 82-85, 87, 94, 99-
    101, 104, 131, 136, 141,
    143, 144, 146 149, 154-156,
    220, 238, 254, 265-267, 289
Schutzbund, 78, 85
Schutzstaffel (SS), 52, 136, 152,
    156, 164, 190, 193, 279
Second Republic, 1, 9, 12, 16,
    38-40, 44, 45, 70, 168, 195,
    196, 224, 226, 235, 236,
    239-241, 243, 244, 246, 265,
    268, 271-275, 284, 285
Seewann, Gerhard, 230n
Seidl, Siegfried, 162
Seipel, Ignaz, 24, 37, 38, 45, 64
Seitz, Karl, 128, 190
Sella, Gad Hugo, 220n
Serbs, 57
Seymour, Charles, 60n
Seyss-Inquart, Arthur, 34, 48, 49,
    154, 157, 163, 231
Shuster, Greorge, Doris, 47, 50-
    52, 54, 55
Siberia, 233
Sicherheitsdienst (SD), 169, 179,
    181, 185, 193
Siedler, Richard, 181n
Siegert, Michael, 139n
Siegfried, Klaus-Jörg, 146n

Sigismund, King of Hungary, Holy Roman Emperor, 256
Skalnik, Kurt, 26n, 86n, 147, 272n
Skorzeny, Otto, 182
Skubl, Michael, 47, 155
Slapnicka, Harry, 169n, 170n, 171, 177n, 178n 181n, 183n, 184n, 187n
Slavs, 22, 121, 123, 125, 193, 229
Slovenes, 67, 88, 122, 276
Social Democratic Party, Social Democrats, 25, 26n, 27, 28, 38, 50, 58, 64-66, 68, 69, 80, 81, 85, 88, 100, 125, 128, 130, 131, 141, 151, 155, 156, 195, 221, 225, 227-229, 233, 237, 238, 240, 241, 288, 289
Social Science Research Council, 56
Social Working Group, 82, 88
Socialist Party, Austrian (SPÖ), 3, 223, 225, 228, 229, 231-233, 238, 241-243, 261, 273, 284, 289, 301
Socialist Working Youth, 15
South America, 105, 110
South Tirol, South Tiroleans, 23, 59, 61, 63, 67, 186
Soviet Union, 58, 61, 62, 213, 221, 260, 272, 280, 281
Soyfer, Jura, 104
Sozialpartnerschaft, 2, 243, 297 (Social partnership; *see also* Paritätische Kommission) für Preise und Löhne)
Späth, Ernst, 152, 154, 155, 157
Spalek, John, 106n, 113n
Spann, Gustav, 285
Spann, Othmar, 82, 93, 144-146, 148, 152, 154, 162
Spiel, Hilde, 92, 105, 106
Spitzer, Alexander, 162
Spitzky, Hans, 153
Spunda, Franz, 93
Srbik, Heinrich Ritter von, 38, 99, 144, 146-148, 163, 164
Staatsrat, 253
Stadler, Karl, 168n, 171, 179n-181n, 227n, 269n, 286
Stalingrad, 8, 167, 169, 171, 174, 179, 183, 194
Stanford University, 122
Starhemberg, Ernst Rüdiger, 100
State Treaty, Austrian (1955), 9, 196, 224, 275-277, 281-283, 291
Staudinger, Anton, 26n
Stauffenberg, Klaus Schenk Graf von, 190
Stebich, Max, 116
Steiermark (Styria), 47, 66, 96, 170, 171, 177, 178, 186, 249, 276
Steinacher, Harald, 156
Steinberg, Michael, 143
Steiner, Herbert, 286
Steiner, Kurt, 70n, 269n
Steiner, Ludwig, 214n
Steinert, Marlis, 174n, 179n-181n, 188n
Steininger, Rolf, 31n
Steyr (Oberösterreich), 178
Stiefel, Dieter, 276n, 284n
Stockert-Meynert, Dora, 93
Stockholm, 172, 173
Stourzh, Gerald, 3, 15, 31n, 224n, 225n, 272n, 276n, 282n
Stourzh, Herbert, 29, 30n
Straffner, Sepp, 77
Strauss, Johann, 271

Streicher, Julius, 139n
Strelka, Joseph, 106n, 113n
Strobl, Karl Hans, 93, 96
Stunde Null, 239
Stundner, Franz, 43n
Sturmabteilung (SA, Brownshirts), 36, 52, 136, 152, 155, 262
Sudeten Germans, 22, 32, 33, 59, 157
Sully, Melanie, 9, 296, 297
Swastika (Hakenkreuz), 29, 34, 48, 129, 154, 155
Sweden, Swedes, 47, 105, 172, 242
Switzerland, 17, 19, 23, 26, 36, 37, 44, 94, 105, 212, 213, 216, 237
  German Swiss, 44
Tálos, Emmerich, 80n, 181, 241, 285n, 285n
Taglicht, Israel, Chief Rabbi, 41
Tausendmark-Sperre, 102, 238
Taylor, A.J.P., 60n
Theresienstadt, 162
38 (Thirty-Eight, a film), 115
Thun, Leo Graf von, 119
Tidl, Marie, 151n, 156n
114,115, 121, 203, 206, 212-215, 219, 221, 272, 281, 298
Tirol, 8, 23, 31n, 47, 170, 171, 176, 183, 209-222
Todeschini, Guido, 214n
Torberg, Friedrich, 92, 102, 113-115
Traditionalists, 218, 221
Trieste, 18
Triska, Helmut, 141n
Truk, Jerry, 215n
Tulln (Niederösterreich), 187
Tumler, Franz, 108
Tunisia, 181

Turks, 38, 121, 125, 267
Übersberger, Hans, 131, 154
Uhrig, Robert, 217n
Ukraine, 190
United Nations, 202, 282, 297
United Socialist Party, 15
United States of America, 51, 53, 55, 62, 101, 105, 109-111
University of California, Berkeley, 122
University of Graz, 120, 126, 129-131, 135, 141, 144, 160
University of Innsbruck, 128, 131, 136, 141, 156, 161
University of Linz, 239
University of Minnesota, i, ii
University of Vienna (Rudolfinum), 7, 24, 33n, 38, 121, 124, 128, 129, 131, 135, 137-139, 141, 144, 148-154, 156-162, 165
Unter anderer Sonne, 110
Untermeyer, Jean, 109
"Unterseeboote" ("submarines"), 36, 260
Urbanitsch, Peter, 18n
Urbanitzky, Grete, 92, 93, 98
V-1 (Vergeltungswaffe Eins), 189
Vaterländische Erziehung, 137
Vergangenheitsbewältigung, 5, 250, 251, 259, 298, 303
Verordnungsblatt, 163
Verosta, Stephan, 275n
Vienna, 6, 21, 24, 36, 37-39, 41, 47, 48, 50-52, 54, 55, 67, 68, 92, 97-99, 101, 103-108, 112, 115, 121, 123, 125, 127-129, 136, 140-144, 146, 148-150, 153-155, 158, 162, 164, 167, 170-176, 178-181, 183, 185, 186, 188, 190-194,

Vienna (*continued*)
  209, 211-213, 216, 224, 238,
  241, 248, 250, 253, 255-257,
  260, 261, 267, 278
Vienna, Municipal Council
  (Wiener Stadtrat), 77
Vienna State Opera (Wiener
  Staatsoper), 301
Vienna Stock Exchange (Wiener
  Börse), 302
Viereck, George, 24n
Viertel, Berthold and Salke, 109
Vietnam, 204
Virgil, 36
Völkisch, 24, 108, 139
Volksdeutsche, 124
Volksgemeinschaft, 243
Volksstämme, 24
Vorarlberg, 23
Vormärz, 119
Vranitzky, Franz, 10, 248, 249
Wache, Karl, 149n
Waggerl, Karl Heinrich, 95, 96
Wagner, Georg, 142n, 168n
Wagner, Richard, 271
Wagner-Jauregg, Julius, 148
Waldeck, Heinrich Suso, 95
Waldheim, Kurt, 4, 5, 9, 10, 115,
  168, 201-205, 208, 236, 241,
  244-250, 261-263, 265, 285,
  290-293, 296, 299, 301
Waldinger, Ernst, 105
Waldner, Wolfgang, ii, 6
Wandruszka, Adam, 18n, 74n,
  144n
Washington, D.C., 121
Webern, Anton, 35-37
Webern, Peter, 36
Wehrmacht, 8, 9, 50, 63, 106,
  212, 214, 218, 279, 283
Weissensteiner, Friedrich, 34n,
  74n

Weigel, Hans, 102, 105
Weimar Republic, 60, 130
Weinberger, Lois, 229, 230
Weinert, Willi, 156n, 159n
Weinheber, Josef, 95, 96, 102,
  106, 107
Weinzierl, Erika, 26n, 86n, 155n,
  180n, 234n, 239n, 272n,
  286, 290n
Weinzierl, Ulrich, 105n
Weiss, Ernst, 104
Weizsäcker, Richard von, 283,
  284
Wenter, Josef, 96, 108
Werfel, Franz, 105, 112, 113
Whiteman, Harold, 60n
Whiteside, Andrew, 58n
Wied, Martha, 105, 109
Wien--Bild und Schicksal, 104
Wiener Neustadt (Niederöster-
  reich), 181, 182, 187-189
Wiener Philharmoniker (Vienna
  Philharmonic Orchestra), 172
Wiesenthal, Simon, 258, 300
Wilder, Billy, 113
Wildner, Heinrich, 17
Wilhelm I, Kaiser, 123
Williams, Maurice, 270n, 271n
Wilson, Woodrow, 59
Wiltschegg, Walter, 74n, 148n
Winter, Ernst Karl, 26, 28-30, 37,
  51, 52, 81, 82n, 141
Wirtschaftsstelle reichsdeutscher
  Hochschüler in Österreich, 143
Witek, Hans, 42n, 241n
Witzmann, Erich, 153n
Wolf, Wilhelm, 230
Wolfe, George, 164n
Wolfram, Herwig, 41n
Wöllersdorf (Niederösterreich),
  141
World Jewish Congress, 263

World War I (Great War), 6, 72, 80, 98, 120, 121, 124, 126, 182, 237, 298
World War II, 1, 10, 39, 70, 89, 97, 167, 170, 195, 199, 204, 207, 220, 239, 295, 297-299, 303
Wörthersee (Kärnten), 140
Würgner, Hans, 105n
Würthle, Friedrich, 214n
Württemberg, 186
Yugoslavia, 59, 67, 177, 210, 216, 276
Zaar, Birgitta, 31n
Zeitgeschichte (contemporary history), 4, 285, 286
Zernack, Klaus, 27n
Zernatto, Guido, 99-101
Zessner-Spitzenberg, Hans-Karl, 26, 162
Zilk, Helmut, 248
Zionism, Zionists, 58, 69, 151
Zoitl, Helge, 126n
Znojmo (Znaim), 36
Zöllner, Erich, 17, 18
Zsolnay, Paul, 93, 98, 99
Zürich, 104
Zweig, Stefan, 91, 96, 97, 103-105, 110, 111, 115
Zwölf aus der Steiermark, 96

ARIADNE PRESS
Studies in Austrian Literature, Culture and Thought

*Major Figures of
Modern Austrian Literature*
Edited and Introduced
by Donald G. Daviau

*Major Figures of Turn-of-the-Century
Austrian Literature*
Edited and Introduced
by Donald G. Daviau

*Austrian Writers and the
Anschluss: Understanding the
Past—Overcoming the Past*
Edited and Introduced
by Donald G. Daviau

*Introducing Austria
A Short History*
By Lonnie Johnson

*Coexistent Contradictions
Joseph Roth in Retrospect*
Edited by
Helen Chambers

*The Verbal and Visual Art of
Alfred Kubin*
By Phillip H. Rhein

*Kafka and Language
In the Stream of
Thoughts and Life*
By G. von Natzmer Cooper

*Robert Musil and the Tradition
of the German Novelle*
By Kathleen O'Connor

*Blind Reflections:
Gender in Elias Canetti's
Die Blendung*
By Kristie A. Foell

Conversations with Peter Rosei
By Wilhelm Schwarz

*Austria in the Thirties
Culture and Politics*
Edited by Kenneth Segar
and John Warren

*Stefan Zweig:
An International Bibliography*
By Randolph J. Klawiter

*Austrian Foreign Policy
Yearbook*
Report of the Austrian Federal
Ministry for Foreign Affairs
for the Year 1990

*Quietude and Quest
Protagonists and Antagonists in
the Theater, on and off Stage
As Seen Through the Eyes of
Leon Askin*
Leon Askin and C. Melvin Davidson

*"What People Call Pessimism":
Sigmund Freud, Arthur Schnitzler
and Nineteenth-Century
Controversy at the University
of Vienna Medical School*
By Mark Luprecht

Arthur Schnitzler and Politics
By Adrian Clive Roberts

*Structures of Disintegration
Narrative Strategies in
Elias Canetti's Die Blendung*
By David Darby

*Of Reason and Love
The Life and Work of Marie von
Ebner-Eschenbach*
By Carl Steiner

*Franz Kafka:
A Writers Life*
By Joachim Unseld

ARIADNE PRESS
Translation Series:

February Shadows
By Elisabeth Reichart
Translated by Donna L. Hoffmeister
Afterword by Christa Wolf

Night Over Vienna
By Lili Körber
Translation by Viktoria Hertling
& Kay M. Stone. Commentary by
Viktoria Hertling

The Cool Million
By Erich Wolfgang Skwara
Translated by Harvey I. Dunkle
Preface by Martin Walser
Afterword by Richard Exner

Buried in the Sands of Time
Poetry by Janko Ferk
English/German/Slovenian
English Translation by H. Kuhner

Puntigam or The Art of Forgetting
By Gerald Szyszkowitz
Translated by Adrian Del Caro
Preface by Simon Wiesenthal
Afterword by Jürgen Koppensteiner

Negatives of My Father
By Peter Henisch
Translation and Afterword
by Anne C. Ulmer

On the Other Side
By Gerald Szyszkowitz
Translated by Todd C. Hanlin
Afterword by Jürgen Koppensteiner

The Slackers and Other Plays
By Peter Turrini
Translation and Afterword
by Richard S. Dixon

The Baron and the Fish
By Peter Marginter
Translation and Afterword
by Lowell A. Bangerter

I Want to Speak
The Tragedy and Banality
of Survival in
Terezin and Auschwitz
By Margareta Glas-Larsson
Edited and with a Commentary
by Gerhard Botz
Translated by Lowell A. Bangerter

The Works of Solitude
By György Sebestyén
Translation and Afterword
by Michael Mitchell

Krystyna
By Simon Wiesenthal
Translated by Eva Dukes

Deserter
By Anton Fuchs
Translation and Afterword
by Todd C. Hanlin

From Here to There
By Peter Rosei
Translation and Afterword
by Kathleen Thorpe

The Angel of the West Window
By Gustav Meyrink
Translated by Michael Mitchell

Relationships
An Anthology of Contemporary
Austrian Literature
Selected and with an Introduction
by Adolf Opel

Three Late Plays
By Arthur Schnitzler
Translation and Afterword
G.J. Weinberger

Professor Bernhardi and Other Plays
By Arthur Schnitzler
Translation G.J. Weinberger
Afterword Jeffrey B. Berlin

Translations Series:

The Bengal Tiger
By Jeannie Ebner
Translation and Afterword
by Lowell A. Bangerter

Three Flute Notes
By Jeannie Ebner
Translation and Afterword
by Lowell A. Bangerter

Farewell to Love and Other Misunderstandings
By Herbert Eisenreich
Translation and Afterword
by Renate Latimer

The Sphere of Glass
By Marianne Gruber
Translation and Afterword
by Alexandra Strelka
Preface by Joseph P. Strelka

A Man Too White
By György Sebestén
Translation and Afterword
by Michael Mitchell

The Green Face
By Gustav Meyrink
Translated by Michael Mitchell

The Ariadne Book of Austrian Fantasy The Meyrink Years 1890-1930
Edited and translated
by Michael Mitchell

Walpurgisnacht
By Gustav Meyrink
Translated by Michael Mitchell

On the Wrong Track
By Milo Dor
Translated by Jerry Glenn
and Jennifer Kelley

Night Train
By Friederike Mayröcker
Translation and Afterword
by Beth Bjorklund

Memories With Trees
By Ilse Tielsch
Translation and Afterword
by David Scrase

Return to the Center
By Otto von Habsburg
Translated by Carvel de Bussy

View from a Distance
By Lore Lizbeth Waller

Five Plays
By Gerald Szyszkowitz
Translated by Todd Hanlin, Heidi Hutchinson and Joseph McVeigh

Anthology of Contemporary Austrian Folk Plays
By Veza Canetti, Peter Preses & Ulrich Becher, Felix Mitterer, Gerald Szyszkowitz, Peter Turrini
Translation and Afterword
by Richard Dixon

The Condemned Judge
By Janko Ferk
Translation and Afterword
by Lowell A. Bangerter

Thomas Bernhard and His Grandfather: "Our Grandfathers Are Our Teachers."
By Caroline Markolin
Translated by Petra Hartweg

The Convent School
By Barbara Frischmuth
Translated by
Gerald Chapple and James B. Lawson

The Calm Ocean
By Gerhard Roth
Translated by Helga Schreckenberger
and Jacqueline Vansant

Remembering Gardens
by Kurt Klinger
Translated by Harvey I. Dunkle